About the Author

Bill 'Swampy' Marsh is an award-winning writer/performer of stories, songs and plays. He spent most of his youth in rural south-western New South Wales. Bill was forced to give up any idea he had of a 'career' as a cricketer after a stint at agricultural college was curtailed because of illness, and so began his hobby of writing. After backpacking through three continents and working in the wine industry, his writing hobby blossomed into a career.

His first collection of short stories, *Beckom Pop. 64*, was published in 1988; his second, *Old Yanconian Daze*, in 1995 and his third, *Looking for Dad*, in 1998. During 1999 Bill released *Australia*, a CD of his songs and stories. That was followed in 2002 by *A Drover's Wife*. He has also written soundtrack songs and music for the television documentaries *The Last Mail from Birdsville—The Story of Tom Kruse* and *Source to Sea—The Story of the Murray Riverboats*.

Bill runs writing workshops throughout schools and communities and is employed part-time through the Adelaide Institute of TAFE's Professional Writing Unit. He has won and judged many nationwide short story writing competitions.

Great Australian Droving Stories follows on from his very successful fourth and fifth books, *Great Australian Shearing Stories* (2001) and *Great Flying Doctor Stories* (1999).

Bill performs his stories and songs regularly on radio, television and stage, and his plays have been performed across Australia.

GREAT AUSTRALIAN
DROVING
STORIES

BILL 'SWAMPY' MARSH

ABC
BOOKS

To Margaret, Lea and Nicole Worth
—with love

Special thanks to the Australian Stockman's Hall of Fame, especially to Jim Cuming, Jane Stuart and Jenny Wilson for all their help and advice, and to Fran Davies, a true drover's daughter, for her transcriptions.

Thanks to those who watered and fed me along my travels: the Byrnes, Norris, Langley and Connick families, David and Christine Harris, Stuart Neal and Sharon Guest, Terry Beltrame and Heather Kimber, Lisa Davies (Tourism SA, the Great Australian Cattle Drive), Mum, my sisters—Barb Meredith and Marg Loveday—Bill Rawson, Margo and Mitchel Meredith.

Thanks also to Annika van Pelt and Bonny and to all those who so willingly supplied research material, contacts and information on drovers and droving, especially Jane Stuart, Shirley Norris, Peter 'Snowy' Meale, Jack Goldsmith and George 'Blue' Ellis.

The ABC 'Wave' device is a trademark of the Australian Broadcasting Corporation and is used under licence by HarperCollins*Publishers* Australia.

First published in Australia in 2003 by ABC Books
for the Australian Broadcasting Corporation
Reprinted by HarperCollins*Publishers* Australia Pty Limited
ABN 36 009 913 517
harpercollins.com.au

HarperCollins*Publishers*
Level 13, 201 Elizabeth Street, Sydney, NSW 2000, Australia
Unit D1, 63 Apollo Drive, Rosedale, Auckland 0632, New Zealand
A 53, Sector 57, Noida, UP, India
1 London Bridge Street, London, SE1 9GF, United Kingdom
Bay Adelaide Centre, East Tower, 22 Adelaide Street West, 41st Floor,
    Toronto, Ontario, M5H 4E3
195 Broadway, New York, NY 10007, USA

National Library of Australia Cataloguing-in-Publication data:
Marsh, Bill, 1950–
Great Australian droving stories.
ISBN 978 0 7333 1335 6 (pbk.)
1. Drovers—Australia—Anecdotes.
2. Drovers—Australia—Social life and customs.
I. Australian Broadcasting Corporation.
II. Title.
636.0830994

Typeset in 9.7/15pt Bookman by Midland Typesetters, Maryborough, Victoria
Colour separations by Colorwize, Adelaide
Printed and bound in Australia by McPherson's Printing Group
The papers used by HarperCollins in the manufacture of this book are a natural, recyclable product made from wood grown in sustainable plantation forests. The fibre source and manufacturing processes meet recognised international environmental standards, and carry certification.

Contents

Contributors

Great Australian Droving Stories is based on stories told to
Bill 'Swampy' Marsh by:

Joe Atkinson	George 'Blue' Ellis	John Magor
Gordon Beetham	Azzie Zilla Fazulla	Luke McCall
Geoff Black	Betty Forster	Mary Patricia Mitchell
Francis Booth	Shirley Forster	Frank Partington
George Booth	Les French	Norm Pont
Ivan Boucher	Mick Gallagher	Amy Pulford
Colin Broad	Jack Goldsmith	Ted Roche
Merv Buckley	Frank Gorry	Joe Saunders
Mike Coventry	Rob Greenhill	Bruce and Tess Smith
Jack Cunningham	Wal 'Dusty' Harkness	Emily and Luke Smith
Joe Daley	Reg Hart	Ben Taylor
John Davies	Len Hill	Jim Travers
Arnold Dodd	Sam Lovell	Neil Warne
Judy Dowling		

. . . and many other unsung heroes

The story from Norm Pont was adapted from an interview by David Mulhallen for ABC Radio. The stories 'They Rushed at Well 40' and 'The Canning Stock Route' have been adapted from a work in progress of Len Hill's memoirs. Stories from the late Ben Taylor were adapted from an interview by the late Judith Hosier for the Australian Stockman's Hall of Fame (16.11.90).

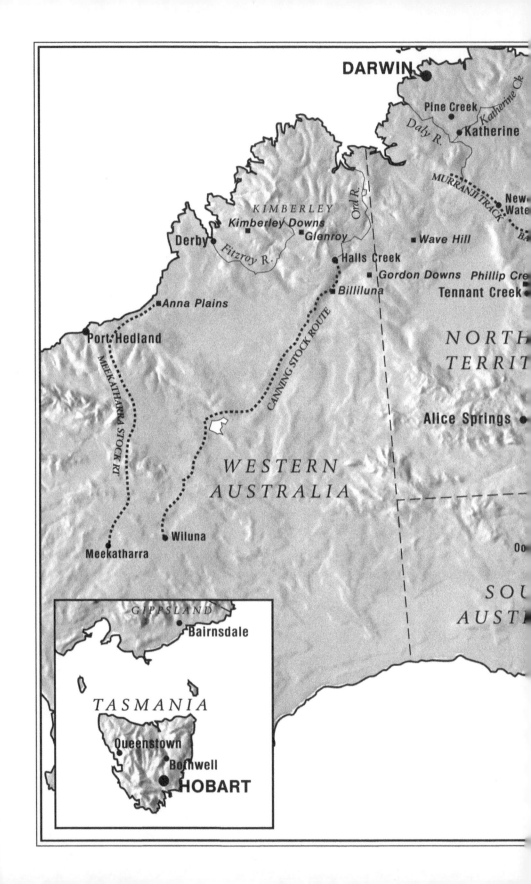

The author, aged seven, preparing for his first droving trip.

Introduction

When I was a young kid, living in the south-western New South Wales township of Beckom (Pop. 64), every so often a drover would pass through town. I was fascinated by these people. What a life, I thought, just wandering along behind a mob of sheep or cattle, day in and day out, sleeping under the stars (The Star Hotel) without a worry in the world. Well, the writing of this book has certainly changed that perception. The drovers were a group of people who lived and worked across some of the most harsh environments in the world and faced almost insurmountable challenges on a daily basis.

It's said that, 'First came the explorers, followed by the surveyors, then the stockmen and drovers.' But of course, Aborigine people were there first, and they also became an integral part of Australia's droving history. Many of the stories I heard from black, white, half-caste and mixed race people were blunt and forthright in their opinions and beliefs. And being middle-class and white myself, there were times when I was working in my comfortable, city-style office that I was tempted to temper a few of these stories to suit those readers who may be concerned about 'political correctness'. But I didn't because it would only distort the reality of those times—and my whole aim is to relate our history through the voices of those who actually lived it.

Also, of the three books I have written so far, concerning the various cultural aspects of Australia, this has been the most difficult. Initially, I found that many of the drovers were extremely private people, which mirrored the often isolated nature of their lifestyle. They weren't as 'jokey' as the shearers I spoke to for *Great Australian Shearing Stories* nor were they as 'eloquent' as many I interviewed for *Great Flying Doctor Stories*. Yet I stuck with it, and things started to turn around when I came into contact with Jim Cuming and Jane Stuart from the Australian Stockman's Hall of Fame.

Then followed one of life's great adventures.

With some help from ABC Books, I set out on a story-collecting trip from Adelaide, through the Riverina to Sydney, then up the coast to Brisbane. Following a meeting with Jim and Jane in Brisbane, I drove out to Longreach where I attended a Drover's Reunion at the Australian Stockman's Hall of Fame. This was a highlight as, over three days, I sat, talked, ate, drank, laughed, mucked about and, on occasion, shed tears with many of the old drovers (and some young ones) while they shared their stories with me.

Then from Longreach I drove down to Birdsville where I met up with my musician mate, David Hansford, and we spent the first ten days on the Great Australian Cattle Drive as 'camp-fire entertainment', singing my songs and relating my stories. For all her help and assistance, I'd like to thank Lisa Davies from the South Australian Tourism Commission. That journey touched many of us.

In all, the droving industry has been a very important part of our cultural and economic history. I came to admire the drovers greatly. And I owe it to all those I interviewed to tell their stories in the same direct and honest manner that they told them to me.

And what a tough life it was. As one of the old drovers said in describing how, as a 13-year-old, he was sent droving in the outback to earn money to help his struggling parents, 'We might've just been kids but we grew up quick and we learnt a hell of a lot.'

A Drover's Wife

I didn't beat about the bush. I met the wife-to-be on the Saturday night and I asked her to marry me on the Sunday night. The only problem she could see about that was that I was still recovering from a tangle with a horse while I was out droving, and she reckoned we should wait until I got off my crutches.

But I just knew that there was something about her. And what's more, I knew she didn't want me for my money because she knew full well that I never had none. So that was in 1950, and it happened out at a place called Coolah, which is about a hundred and twenty or thirty mile north-east of Dubbo, there in central New South Wales.

Anyway, when I finally got off the crutches she still seemed keen on going through with it even though I was having a bit of trouble with the mother-in-law-to-be. I mean, we ended up good mates in the end but at that stage we weren't. Anyhow, I hadn't been home to see my folks in three years so naturally, they hadn't met the wife-to-be so I said to her, 'Do yer want'a meet my parents?'

'Okay,' she said.

Now my parents lived down south, down near the Victorian border, which was a long way away. So for the first stage of the journey we were all day and all night on the train until we got into Sydney at about five in the morning. Then with nothing better to do, when the shops were open, we got a taxi to drop us off up town so that we could have a look around. Anyway, we were walking past a Registry Office when I got this bright idea, see, so I very romantically said to the wife-to-be, 'How's about tying that figure eight knot that yer can't undo with yer teeth, right here and now!'

'Okay,' she said.

But then, when we asked in at the Registry Office they said that one of us had to live in the district. Now, the-wife-soon-to-be, she'd been on a holiday, visiting relatives, in the area about three years beforehand so she give them that address. So that was all right.

The next problem was that we had to have two witnesses and, what's more, they had to have known us for at least six months. That was a bit more difficult because we were in a bit of a rush and I was new to Sydney. Anyway, I was feeling a bit disappointed so we walked outside and three taxis were going past so I whistled one up and, oddly enough, the driver was the very same bloke that'd brought us up town. So I grabbed him and explained the situation and asked him if he wanted to be a witness at our wedding.

'Okay,' he said.

Then I said, 'Thanks, and also can yer dig up a mate to be a second witness and be back up to the Registry Office at about three this arvo.'

'Okay,' he said.

So that was fine. Then we went to buy the ring. Now the only problem there was that I couldn't spend over three quid because that's all the money I had. So in the end we ended up having to go to three or four different jewellery shops before they had any sort of decent ring I could afford.

Then at about three, the taxi driver turned up with one of his mates. And when the feller at the Registry Office asked them how long they'd known us they said, 'Oh, we're old mates.' 'Known each other fer ages,' they said, and that did the trick.

And what's more, they turned out to be pretty nice fellers, too, because they gave us a quid each for a wedding present. That was good money in them days. So then we had a piece of cake and a coffee for a wedding breakfast and at seven o'clock that night we jumped on the train again. Then we spent that night on the train and we got to my parents' place at about nine o'clock the next night.

Then after we got back from visiting my parents I took the wife back out droving with me. At that stage I was working with another chap and his wife—this was with sheep. The chap drove the truck and caravan, his wife did some cooking, and I had the horses and dogs.

But my wife, she turned out to be petrified of horses, just petrified. But she still helped out. She paid her way, all right. She'd get busy and she'd go ahead and help get the yards up and things like that for when I arrived with the sheep.

So that was that, and that's how she became a drover's wife. Then twenty-five years after that, I lost her. She died. But she done a good job to put up with me for that long, I reckon, so you could say that I had a honeymoon that lasted twenty-five years.

A Fine Romance

I left school when I was a young boy about fourteen and I picked up a bit of droving, working for different old drovers. That was around the Forbes area, in central New South Wales, and I also done a bit around other places in New South Wales, like Wagga, there in the south-west. Then about four or five years later I started out with my own plant, and then I come up to Queensland.

Well with me, my father was born in Mount Morgan, near Rock-hampton, and he'd been a bushie. He used to love being in the bush and bushwalking and all that sort of thing. But I remembered his stories from back when I was a young girl and also I just never felt comfortable in the city. I just never fitted. Then about fifteen years ago, after I'd done a cookery course in Brisbane, I got offered a job as a station cook out at a merino stud in western Queensland. So I took the job because I thought it was somewhere to start and it'd give me a good look at the countryside.

So I started cooking there, but I didn't like the manager and I didn't like his wife. Then I met Bruce in town one night and he invited me to come out camp-cooking for him. So I guess that things between us just went from there.

At that time, I was mustering feral cattle on a property near a town called Wyandra, which is halfway between Charleville and Cunnamulla. There was me and several ringers. It was pretty dry then. So anyhow, me and Tess met. Then three brothers I knew, from up around Augathella, they put a mob of five thousand merino sheep together—that's a good manageable mob—and they trucked them part-way down in two prime movers. Those were some of the first three-trailered prime movers. They had four decks on the first two trailers, then one double-decker. That was in 1988, when you had to have a special permit. So we left all our horses

The trucking of livestock heralded the ending of droving.

and stuff at Wyandra and we went up with a couple of motorbikes just to take the mob over.

Well, we actually only had one motorbike because we blew the other one up. That's motorbikes for you. So we walked them back down, just the two of us. We had the caravan and the truck. I was the driver and I was also the cook.

But a lot of the time, when we're out on the road, we share the cooking because I'm not a bad camp-oven cook, even if I do say so myself, even though the caravan's all decked out with a stove and things. Anyway, we headed south on the Cunnamulla to Bourke road, heading down towards Barringun, which is just over the border into New South Wales. But before we got there we shore them at Owangowan Station on the Queensland–New South Wales border.

What happened was, the owners hired their shed out so we could get the sheep shorn and we got a two weeks' breather while they were shearing. Well we thought that we'd get a breather anyway, but we let them go on the reserve while they were being shorn, then, boy, we had some fun, I can tell you.

See, we were following the Warrego River down because that's where the feed was. But by the time we got to Owangowan there was only waterholes along the river so the sheep split up. There was four of us by then because we were rotating the sheep to the shearing shed and back. But then they had rain up where the Warrego starts and when the water came down, well, a lot of sheep got stuck in behind the channels so we had to go in and bring them onto the higher country. It was over belly deep in places and we had to swim a good few out. But we eventually done it.

Then at the end of shearing, we got a big five inch wash of storm which flooded us in. We couldn't get in or out. So we were well and truly stuck and we'd just about run out of food. We didn't have any bread and we only had enough flour to make a few dampers. So we ended up living on tinned braised steak and onions with rice. That really tested my cooking skills, trying to be creative with tinned braised steak and onions, I can tell you. Then finally, after a week or so, the owner of Owangowan got in with some fresh vegetables and meat and bread. And boy, was I glad to see him.

I mean, we couldn't even get out to get a killer because the caravan was on one bit of a high sand-banky area and the sheep were over on another sandy area, and there was a big, flooded claypan between us.

We couldn't even walk across it because our feet'd sink right up to our knees. It was all soupy. So we couldn't even get over to kill one of the sheep for food.

Then when we finally got out we headed along the Widgeegoara Creek, on to the Cunnamulla to Bollon road. Then just before we got to Bollon the owners turned around and they decided to truck them home again because it'd rained up north so there was enough feed for them now, back on their home property.

And that trip was four and a half months. But the relationship from camp cook to wife just happened. We worked together for about six months and things just developed into a closer relationship. Then in late February '89 the stock and station agents approached us about walking a mob of sheep to a property at Charleville. And boy, it was forty-five degrees in the shade and we had four thousand sheep, straight off their mothers.

I mean, it was an uphill battle right from the start. Being straight off their mothers they didn't know how to walk, they didn't know how to water properly, plus, they had pink-eye. Pink-eye's like conjunctivitis. It's contagious. All that's got to happen is for just one of the infected sheep to rub its head against another one and the germs get across.

It's caused by too much dust and grass seeds, and they get pussy and scabby eyes and it sends them blind.

So the pink-eye was raging through them. Anyhow we set out and it wasn't too bad for the first couple of days, then they started going blind.

Then to make matters worse, I'd been away visiting friends that Christmas, down the coast, and I'd picked up gastroenteritis. So I was absolutely, horribly sick on this trip, working and trying to keep fluids down because it was so hot.

So we struggled on until mid March when we ended up behind floodwaters and we couldn't continue on the stock route because there was too much water. So then we had to divert out and walk them around through private country. But they ended up being diseased condemned and, naturally, the property owners didn't want pink-eyed sheep going through their country so the sheep's owners ended up trucking them out from there, back to their property near Charleville.

So that was the end of the job and I was still sick and so I ended up going to the doctor in Cunnamulla and he said, 'You haven't got gastroenteritis, you're pregnant.'

And I said, 'You're joking.'

'No I'm not,' he said. 'You've got a little drover on the way.'

A Town like Alice

Well old feller, I haven't got much to tell. First, I was born around a place called Inverell, which is west of the New England area, in north-eastern New South Wales. Then I left there when I was about fourteen and I went up into the Gulf Country and worked around cattle stations there until I ended up at a place called Dalgonally, south of Burketown. Burketown's right up there in the Gulf of Carpentaria.

Anyhow, in those days you could pick up old buck-jumpers, here, there and everywhere. So while I was working at Dalgonally, me and another young feller by the name of Jackie Watt, we were picking up horses for a droving plant. Then in '39, Jackie and me, we put our first droving plant together.

So then we eventually wound up down at a place called Margaret Vale. An old bloke called McInerny owned it. It's part of Donors Hill, now. Anyway, we took five hundred head of fats (cattle in good condition) down from Margaret Vale into Kajabbi, there in north-western Queensland. In those days Kajabbi was one of the big trucking centres for all them Gulf stations. It's all closed up now, but back then it was very, very big; both Kajabbi and Gilliat, on the Julia Creek side.

But a funny thing; at Kajabbi you had to get the cattle sprayed for buffalo fly before they could be trucked. Now as far as this spraying business went, see, there was a telephone line going from Cloncurry up to Normanton and the authorities reckoned that anything from the west of the telephone line had this buffalo fly and anything from the east was bloody okay. So all the cattle coming from over Lawn Hill way, and from over in the Northern Territory and all over the peninsula there, well, when they went into Kajabbi they had to be sprayed. Then all the others, you could take them to Julia Creek or down that way. So all them cattle, well, it was only

'Well, old feller, I haven't got much to tell.'

a bloody telephone line that divided them. I mean, by the way them authorities carried on about it, you'd have reckoned that the buffalo fly knew the difference, aye, between one side of this bloody telephone line and the other side. Intelligent buffalo fly, aye.

So then when we finished with that last mob, Jackie and me, well, we sold the plant and we went and joined the army and we were away until '46. Now I don't know what happened to Jackie Watt after that. He disappeared and I went back into the Gulf and I was running the stock camp, away up in the foot of the peninsula, for a feller called Jack Bell. Of course, there was all blacks up in them camps back then. They were all through that area. There wasn't too many of us white fellers up there, I can tell you. Not in them days.

Anyhow, the Chaplains, they owned some big properties up around the Gulf and also down around Cloncurry. So they bought this 1250 head of mixed cattle and I took them with a station plant to Fort Constantine, outside Cloncurry.

But see, I was always on the lookout for horses with the idea of starting me own packhorse plant. And when I got to Fort Constantine they had plenty of old buck-jumpers they didn't ride. Because see, a lot of the good men had gone to the bloody war, so during that time they just couldn't get good ringers to ride them. That's why these horses were just let go to waste. Good solid horses they were, too. So I bought a mob of around thirty off them, for about a pound a head.

So then I started off with that mob then, and I went droving with a bloke called 'Ringer' Edwards—Jimmy Edwards was his real name. But you might've read about Ringer. He was the instigator of the film *A Town like Alice*. See, Ringer was the storyteller to old Neville Shute. How that come about was that, at one time, Ringer was managing a place called Glenore Station, up around Normanton, for the Quilpys. Anyhow, old Neville Shute, well, he come out to stay at Glenore for some reason or another and Ringer sat down and he told him the whole story. The whole lot. Then this Neville Shute, well, he went back and he wrote it all up in a book and then they used it in the film.

So there's something for you, aye.

A Word of Warning

A word of warning. Look, I know some of these drovers that you'll be talking to, I know them well, so just be a bit careful because, let's face it, they're going to try and lay the bull on. You'll get inundated with stories about rushing cattle and roping brumbies out of trees and riding them next day, and they'll be on about just how smart they are, horse-tailing and the like.

Take for instance, 'When I got to the Armstrong River it was in flood and the only way I could get the cattle across was to swim them. So there I was battling against the raging current and I was getting a bit tired and that's when this log came floating by so I grabbed onto it and blow me down if it didn't turned out to be a 40-foot crocodile!' That sort of rubbish. Or, 'One day we had a massive cattle rush. The whole lot of them went. So there I was, riding flat out. Then when I finally got up the front to try and turn them around, blow me down if there wasn't a wallaby sitting up there on the lead bullock.'

Now, those bullshit type of stories were okay once because everyone knew that it was bullshit. But nowadays there's people that think it's true. And that's why I say that that sort of stuff should be clearly labelled 'tall stories'.

Then there'll be others saying, 'I did this and I did that and I did something else.' Well, to be honest, skites give me a pain in the arse too, I'm sorry to say. And anyway, you'd think that if some of these blokes had been any good in the first place then someone else would've been talking or writing about them long before they started blowing their own horns. I mean, all you've got to do is to read the books that these blokes write. Some of the things they reckoned they did, well, if you did that sort of stuff with a good boss drover you'd get your arse kicked pretty quick-smart, I can tell you.

Tell it as it is, I say, because, you can take it from me, you'll get inundated with crap, all right. Just take them horse whisperers. As a friend of mine says, 'Nowadays they're jumping out from under every bush and toilet.' What a load of rubbish. There's nothing special there. Because, to be honest, thousands of drovers and stockmen—black, white, bridled and with pink spots—had that sort of insight into animals, and that's because they liked them. That's the thing, liking them.

No one can teach someone to love animals, you know. That's got to come from within. I mean, there's a lot of instruction-type books about 'Natural Horsemanship' and 'Australian Horsemanship', and all that. But if a kid starts off working with a couple of rough pricks well, naturally, he's going to learn bad habits. I firmly believe that every young feller should work for, and with, good drovers and stockmen because then the good habits will rub off on him.

But even then, you can teach a bloke the proper ways but you can't make him love it, can you? It's like sport. If a kid's got all the talent in the world but he doesn't like the game, well, he's not going to succeed at it, is he? So it's that love and instinct for animals. It's like when you go to someone's place and within two minutes the cat's sitting on your lap. That's because he knows you like him. And dogs; there's that old saying about how you might be able to fool the parents but you can't fool the dog or the kids. They know if someone's a mongrel bastard or not, aye.

So, just tell it as it is, I say. Because the thing about droving is that, when it's done properly, there's not too many stories to tell. Just as long as you watch your lead and you do the right thing, then the cattle will, generally, conform. Of course there'll be times when they're hard to handle. Take a dry storm, for instance. When that happens the cattle get all tense and move around, trying to get to the smell of the rain, especially when it's been a dry day and they're thirsty and there's rain falling in the distance. They get a bit on their toes then and you can hear their horns clashing. But mostly, droving's pretty monotonous in many ways, so I think that a lot of these stories are just made up because some of these blokes have to find a way of occupying their time and imaginations.

But I was no different from a great number of kids back in those days. I just got my swag and my saddle and I headed off. Thousands of kids did that; going to the big stations out around Longreach or Windora. Some went to Bedourie: all over Australia.

I went up into the Gulf Country first. I was about fourteen. I'm sixty-nine now, going on seventy. I don't mind saying my age. Then after three years, I went across to Camooweal to work on another station and that's when I started thinking that I'd like to go droving. So I just asked a boss drover for a job and I ended up riding over to the Kimberleys and helping bring cattle back into Queensland, to the fattening depot or to a railhead. Then on another trip we went out to Gordon Downs, in north-western Western Australia.

But what I liked about droving was that it was nice and enjoyable and satisfying just to be riding around on a horse and reciting poetry or singing on night watch, even though I couldn't sing for shit. And I liked looking after cattle. I must have, aye. I did it for fifty years. And I liked knowing that they were full and they had somewhere to camp at night.

I just liked animals, all animals, though I've never worked sheep. But that's just the way it was. But I did like goats. There were goats in my little home town. I loved goat's milk. Of course, the old billies used to piss all over themselves but when you grow up with them you even get to like that smell too. Most Queensland fellers like goats. And as the Victorians say, 'If it hadn't been fer rabbits 'n' blackberries we'd-a starved to death.' Rabbits were called 'underground mutton', you know. But no, I've got a soft spot for goats, and I like mules and donkeys too. I don't mind camels either.

But the life out in the droving camps just suited my personality. I was a bachelor and I've been a bachelor all my life. When blokes got married they either went to the mines or worked with the council or on the railway, somewhere where they were closer to home, with a job that had superannuation. Droving just wasn't compatible with the married way of life, not unless your wife was the cook on the station or whatever.

So you'd go droving this year. Then, say, you finished up in October and they weren't going to start again until the following

'Most Queensland fellers like goats.'

March, well, then they can't afford to keep you on over the slack times, not unless they owned a property. So you might go out on a station for another year or two and then you'd go back droving. Then the next year you might reckon on going over to the Gulf and getting a job with a drover and taking a mob down into the Channel Country. It depended on how you were thinking at the time. Though, as a rule, you could pick up work pretty easy.

But being a drover meant something once. It means nothing now. I mean, it's not like they go out into the Kimberleys like they used to and bring cattle back in. It's changed a lot, now. Now it's real modern with road trains or moving them with a couple of motorbikes and three or four horses and a truck or whatever. And these days they hardly watch the cattle of a night-time because they put up electric fences. And I guess all that's okay, just as long as they look after the cattle and the horses. That's the main thing, looking after your animals.

Then when I got to sixty-five I had a hip replacement and I got crippled up so I couldn't do it any more. I had hoped to be riding horses until I was ninety. But let's face it, I was lucky to get to sixty-five.

So that's about it for me, mate. That's about as much as I can tell you. But just watch out for them skites and bull artists, they'll lead you on good and proper.

Amy

They had me on the television, you know. All over Australia. It was *Big Country*, and they called the show 'Amy', after me, and that was all about the droving and things I done through me life. Though here in Tasmania, we call it shepherding more than droving. Droving's more on-the-road-work, while we took our stock up into the high country of the summertime and we stayed there for about six months, looking after them.

So I done the shepherding for most of me life. And though I was learnt to ride a pony, right back when I was four, I'm not a very good scholar. I didn't start school until I was about nine. That was at The Shannon. And even then I used to dodge it so I could go with Dad. I used to go everywhere Dad went, and Dad did the shepherding. So I guess, I just cottoned on from him.

But back in about 1946 we came to live on a place named The Ripple, which is south of the Great Lake, in central Tasmania. At that stage it belonged to Colin Campbell from Bothwell. He was the man who Dad was employed by. So then we started taking the sheep and cattle up into the high country for the summertime because there was a lot of good feed up there, native grass and tussocks and things like that. So they was kept in very good nick. And we'd take them from run to run and we'd keep an eye on them. Then in about March, we always wigged them—took the wool from around their eyes. And we also drenched them, down their neck with a drenching gun, for worms and stuff like that. Then at about the end of April, we'd bring them back down to the low country.

See, how it worked was that, in about November–December, they'd bring all their stock together in at the accommodation paddock, at a place called Tea Tree Creek, on the Bothwell road. If it was the sheep, all up for the summer, you'd probably have about ten thousand or so. Then the next morning we'd ride our horses down

Leaving for the high country.

to Tea Tree Creek and we'd head the mob up into the high country, to what was called The Banks, which was out near The China Walls, way. With the sheep, it'd take us about five days to get there.

But to start with there was mainly just Dad and me and me sister, Margaret. And the hut we stayed in was nothing flash. But it was shelter, and it did the job. It was made of split board timber, with a tin roof. The floor was boarded, roughly made, and at one end we had this big open fireplace where we did all our cooking and things. That was made out of rocks, and there was a tin chimney going from the top of the rocks, up out the roof.

To have a wash we had to boil the water in a kerosene tin, then we'd pour the water into an old tin dish and we'd wash out of that. But oh, there was cracks in the doors and the windows and when it was snowing it'd blow straight in through. And you'd get up of the morning time and you'd look out, and there was nothing to see, you know, just two or three feet of snow, all over the paddocks.

Then as our day went, we'd get up early and we'd have toast and fat (dripping) with a bit of salt on it. The horses weren't hobbled. They was kept in paddocks. So just before daylight, we'd go around and check the rabbit traps. The rabbits was the first thing we done. Then you'd ride your stock, checking them. That'd take three or four hours. Then we'd come back for lunch. And we made a lot of stews in the big pot, over the fireplace; mainly rabbit stews. For a change we'd stew up black jays, the birds—black jays are very nice eating—or we might have mutton chops. In those days you didn't have lamb, you had real mutton. Then in the afternoon we'd go off, setting the rabbit traps, and at night we'd go around with the spotlight and take the rabbits out of the traps.

But oh, the rabbits were up there in their thousands. So they became a bit of a sideline. We'd catch them with those steel rabbit traps, and we had a corner in the paddock where we skun and cleaned them. Then we'd pack them into boxes and we'd take them by horseback down to meet the bus as it come through from Launceston and they'd take them straight to a butcher in Queenstown. We'd get paid a shilling a rabbit, sometimes two shillings, which wasn't too bad.

But we was always busy because we also had to keep a real good eye on things. See, the sheep were fat and they'd lay down in the snow and they'd roll over in the ditches and the dips in the ground and they'd get stuck and they wouldn't be able to get back on their feet again. So if we didn't roll them back over, they'd die. So we lost a few there. And I remember once with the cattle and we had this big fall of snow and it covered a lot of the calves up as they was being born, and it smothered them, and they died too. That happened several times, really. So the snow did get quite bad at times. One stage, we never saw the ground for twenty-eight days because it was covered with snow.

Another time we was out picking up rabbits and we got a big batch of snow, and one of me brothers—that was young Graham— he got so cold he couldn't walk. So we had to put him up on the draughthorse to get him back to the hut as quick as we could and even then he was nearly freezed by the time we got back, so we revived him on brandy.

Then when I was about seventeen or eighteen I went out on me own. That was at Split Rock, for Ken Campbell. There was just me doing the shepherding. That was it. I done the whole job on me own. But like they say, 'Self-praise, no recommendation.' Anyhow, I reckoned I was just as capable as me brother and me father. They couldn't be any better than what I was so, that was it. And I done a good job. So I worked for Ken Campbell for a while then I went to another job at the Skittle Balls, over on the Marlborough Highway, on the way to Queenstown, and I was shepherding there for John Fowler.

But I had plenty of dogs so, when I went up in the high country, I took the dogs. I had about four or five good sheepdogs, and because I was still doing the rabbits I also took anything from twelve to twenty hunting dogs, spaniels and hounds and staghounds, sheep-dog cross, and all those kinds. They was great for hunting rabbits. And I fed them on kangaroo or rabbits, or whatever we had. And I'd still ride the stock of a morning. Then after lunchtime I'd get the hunting dogs and go digging out rabbit burrows. And a chap by the name of Lenny Whatland used to come and pick up the rabbits and take them back to Hobart.

Then around 1986, I was crippled in the car accident. So that was the end of the shepherding then. It was too cold in the high country to stay up there with no circulation to my body. But I missed it. I certainly did. Because, you know, when I was staying up in the high country, living in the hut, looking after the stock and doing the rabbits, I never got bored. I can't make out these people who say they're bored. And even though I was up there all by myself, I never got lonely. You never get lonely up in the high country.

Bastard, Liar and Thief

I'm ninety-two, though I haven't quite made it yet because my birthday's in a couple of weeks time. So that makes me being born in 1910, the year Comedy King won the Melbourne Cup, and I still live by myself in Branxholme, in south-western Victoria, just south of Hamilton. And they must've reckoned that I've lived there for so long that they went and they named the street I live in after me. So how's about that.

But when I was a youngster, see, I wasn't too keen on school. I used to run away all the time. When I run away the first time I talked an old schoolmate, Bob Patterson, into running away with me, see. So Bob and me, we run away to a place and, oh there was a good garden there, so we had a big feed of loquats and then we went swimming. Then the next day, when we went back to school, we got a big hiding. We always got hidings. Oh yeah, that Mr Gunning, he used to belt everyone for anything, the girls and all, he did.

But Bob Patterson only stood that one hiding. He reckoned that it hurt him too much so then I had to talk another bloke into running away with me, Jack Annett. Then I had two hidings, see. But Jack Annett went on to be five times tougher than Bob Patterson because Jack stood five hidings before he quit running away with me, while Bob only stood the one. But I was pretty cunning, see. One time when I run away I turned up the next morning with me arm in a sling. Then another time when the old feller give me a whack I fell over backwards, pretending I was out to it. That put the wind up him.

So then Mr Gunning left school. And oh, I felt sorry for him because he was dying of cancer, see. Then a new teacher took over. His name was Mr Dunstan. And this Mr Dunstan, gee I liked him. I got on that well with him that I started to get a bit of confidence, doing better and not running away so much.

Anyway, there was this Roy McKellar that I sat with whenever I was at school, and this Roy, gee he was good at arithmetic. He might go a whole three months without making a mistake. So I'd say, 'Stuff it Roy, show me how yer do that.' And he'd show me how to do things what puzzled me and then I'd copy him, see.

'Thanks for that Roy,' I'd say.

But even then I still didn't last long at school. I just didn't like it. Bugger it, I thought, so I left. Then soon after, this Mr Dunstan came over to my place and he did something special. See, I had an answer book—it was the same one I copied in when Roy McKellar showed me how to do the arithmetic, and Mr Dunstan had found it.

'I went through the records,' he said, 'and you had one hundred per cent right in arithmetic.' Then he said, 'I've been head teacher in a lot of different places and I've never heard of such a thing.'

But I didn't say anything about Roy McKellar, see. I was cunning.

'Anyhow, Joe,' he said, 'what I'm going to do is to give you your Merit Certificate without you sitting for it.'

Then he asked me back, especially, for the last three days of school, and I went. But I didn't tell him how I got all my arithmetic right. So I got my Merit Certificate in a crooked sort of way I guess you could say. And I'm only saying this now because I'm pretty sure that it's too late for them to come and take it off me because I'm ninety-two in a couple of weeks time, so it was a long time ago. But anyhow, I reckoned I must've had a bit of talent back then, aye, even if I was a dunce.

So I left school then. I was about thirteen and I went full-time horse breaking with me father, see. And I also rode as a jockey around local places, and I won a few, too. And I also did some buck-jumping and working as a pick-up man at the rodeo. I picked up champion riders like Ray Herman and Jimmy Maguire and Bonny Young and Chiller Seaney and all them fellers. That all helped me too. It made me even tougher.

Running away from school, working at the rodeo and playing football, all made me tough. Because I played football for years, right up until I was fifty-two, I did. Then one year I took a season off and I only come back when Branxholme was short of players.

So we ended up with three generations of my family, all playing together. There was me, there was my son, Alex, and then there was my grandson, Allan. Allan, he went on and he played over a hundred games for Collingwood.

But on one of the days when we all played together, that Barry Gavin was there. Barry used to play with the Imperials at Hamilton then he went on and he was the physio for Hawthorn. For thirty years he done the physio. Well Barry come over and he talked all about how he patched up Dermie (Dermott Brereton) in the grand final and sent him back out onto the field again after he broke his ribs. And Big Dipper (Robert DiPierdomenico), he got put into hospital but Barry got him out when they were short of players.

And this Barry Gavin, well, he seen me playing footy that day and he said, 'Now that's what you call buck-jumping toughness.' That's what Barry said. See, I was fifty-two back then and I was still playing football, and I'm almost ninety-two now, and he'd heard all the stories about how I got the hidings when I run away from school and he also remembered me from my rodeo days. 'That's buck-jumping toughness,' he said.

Anyway, after I left school I started horse breaking with me father and I also did the buck-jumping and the jockeying for a bit of extra money. But then, in about 1930, when the Depression was starting there wasn't too much to be made out of the horse breaking so I went droving and I took some of the owner's sheep around the roads for feed. All I had was a long shaft jinker and blankets and that—that's a horse breaking jinker, a cart. Dad'd have a horse that he'd taught to lead and I'd put it on and take it with me. But I'd just go off by meself, meself and three dogs.

I always had dogs. Out at the station I'd have half a dozen or so dogs, and they was well trained, and no young ones. And I could drive two mobs of sheep at once without getting them boxed in the paddock. These dogs'd keep them separated. See, I had two teams of dogs and I'd ride between the two mobs on the horse. And I'm quite proud that these dogs'd not only bring the sheep into the yards, to me, but they'd also take them away from me, as well. See, very few dogs'll take them away from you. They all want to bring them to you.

So I could have afternoon tea at the shearing shed and, as long as the gates were open, the dogs'd take the shorn ones away into the second paddock. So you could say that I was pretty good with dogs because I wasn't any good at anything else, especially not at school. You've got to be good at something, aye.

But I was never a full-time drover like them fellers up in Queensland or over in Western Australia and that. I only done the droving for feed in the Depression, and I only done it in the summer. Because I was talking to a feller just the other day who was full-time cattle droving, taking them over into New South Wales. Well, I've never been a whole year droving like that bloke. I done more like station droving.

See, I started working for the Whiting family on Bassett Station in about 1939 and I've been there for fifty-two years, now. And because I live in Branxholme I still drive the car out to work each day even though I'm nearly ninety-two, though I'm not quite there, yet. I've still got another couple of weeks to go. But they give me what's called a half-a-licence. That's where you're not allowed to

Setting out on a droving trip with cart and dogs c. 1930.

drive on the highway but you can still drive around the scrub and around the town to get your mail and do a bit of shopping.

So I've worked for three generations of the Whiting family. And now, even the young feller's started to give me orders. He's fifteen. So you could say that I've worked for near on four generations. And I move the mobs for shearing. That's station droving. See, Bassett Station's four thousand acres, which is pretty big for Victoria. So I bring the sheep in and I do the drafting and whatever and then I take the shorn ones away, and I've been doing that for fifty-two years.

But one story about droving: back in the Depression when I was walking sheep for feed, see, there was all these crossroads around the place. Like at one crossroad you can either go to Hamilton or to Digby. There's lots of others about that area, as well. But they all had signs on them, see, and when I was walking the sheep I used to fill in time by looking at these signs. So one day I saw that half a dozen sheep drovers had put their names up on these signs, at the crossroads, advertising themselves. Like, one'd say something like, 'Tom Barker, sheep drover, Hamilton'.

Anyway, I was only sixteen or seventeen so I thought I'd put me own name up there as well, to do a bit of advertising for meself. So that's what I done. I wrote a sign that read, 'Joe Atkinson, horse breaker, drover', and I put it up at the crossroad.

'That's all right,' I said to meself. 'It looks good.'

Then when I come back a few weeks later someone had added the words 'bastard, liar and thief' to the sign. So it now read, 'Joe Atkinson, horse breaker, drover, bastard, liar and thief'.

I mean they only done it for fun, see. Well, at least I think they did. I don't think they meant any harm. But after that I reckoned that it didn't pay to advertise, aye, especially when you're a young drover.

Bluesy, the Black Boys and Me

I first went droving, I don't know, I guess I was about three or four, or something like that. That was with my father. Then I went to school down in Sydney and after I come back, that's when I went droving properly. So I was about sixteen or seventeen or around that age, when I really started droving. And to begin with, that was mostly up in central northern New South Wales, around the Bourke area, and into the lower areas of Queensland.

But I worked mostly with cattle because I don't like sheep too much. See, I prefer the cattle because, while they haven't got too many brains, at least they've got more brains than what sheep have. But still, every three or four years I always went back and did about three months' sheep work, and that's because I reckon it makes a better cattleman of you. It learns you a lot more patience. And if you've got that patience you can do anything with cattle. One man can handle 1000 head of cattle if he's got the patience and he works out wide like a sheepdog.

But also, with the sheep, you couldn't go as far. They're much slower. Sheep only go about 5 or 6 mile a day, while cattle can go twice as far, sometimes less, all depending on how the feed is; the feed and the water.

The water's also very important. One time on the Birdsville Track, in north-eastern South Australia, we went close on four and a half days without water for the cattle. That was in about '62 when we were taking 1200 head of Brunchilly weaner steers from Marree up to Clifton Hills Station. Brunchilly Station's in the central north of the Northern Territory, out of Tennant Creek. So they trained them down south and we got them off the train at Marree then we took them out to Clifton Hills Station. I forget who owned Clifton Hills back then but I do remember it was about 30,000 square miles of country. Mind you, there was only about

5000 head of cattle on it, plus a hell of a lot of sand and gibbers, except for the Goyder's Lagoon in season.

And along the Birdsville Track in them days it was 30 mile between the bores. So it depended on how they were bloody feeling and how they were walking as to how far you took them in the day. See, you normally water your cattle and horses early in the morning. Then you walk them during the day and, if you're lucky, you get to water again that afternoon, and you camp there for the night. But if you don't get to water, like what happened on the Birdsville Track, you still have to water your horses. So you may have to take the horses 10, 12, 14 mile to the nearest water then back to the camp again. Then the next day you have to go a dry day with the cattle and you, hopefully, get to water the following day at dinnertime. So that Birdsville Track trip was a pretty tough one because, as I said, they went close on four and a half days without water.

But the toughest trip was when we took a mob of cattle from a station south of Halls Creek, in the north of Western Australia, right across the desert to a place over the border into the Northern Territory. They were just opening that desert country up then.

Surveying new country.

Anyhow, at that time, I was head stockman at the Western Australian property so I handed the mob over at first light to the boss drover at a set of yards about 30 mile from the main station. I won't mention the boss drover's name, nor the property names, because too many people still know the chap and I wouldn't like to run him down. Also, he's a bloody good bloke. But anyhow, this boss drover had a crew of Alice Springs black boys with him. So we handed them over, then me and my boys did a bit of cleaning up, ready to shift camp, see. So the next morning, just as we was about to move off, a big mob of cattle come in to water.

'That's them same mob we bin' give 'im longa drover,' one of my black boys said.

And it bloody was, too. They'd somehow got away from the drover that night and they'd come back. What's more, they were just about perishing. So anyway, we stuck them on water and we held them there until about three o'clock in the afternoon. Then, instead of following the same track as the drover, we cut straight across bush to where he'd camped the night before.

So we travelled all night with these cattle. Then about nine o'clock the next morning we came upon the drover who, by that stage, was only just starting to look for his missing cattle. And this's a whole bloody day and a night after they'd gone. But as it turned out, he'd had trouble with his blackfellas. For one reason or another they'd kicked up a stink and they'd pulled out and that left him there to try and look after things by himself, which was impossible, so the mob just took off.

Anyway, the drover said to me, 'Bugger this,' he said, and he packed up his gear and he went back to Alice Springs, picking up his blackfellas along the way. So me and my boys, we took over these cattle and we walked them over the border into the Northern Territory, to their new destination, and we stayed there track riding them.

Now, you may not know the term 'track riding'. Track riding's when you ride in a wide sweep around your cattle and keep turning them back on to the water and feed so that they can't return to where they came from. By doing that you're getting them

accustomed to the feed and the water in their new environment—
you're breaking them in to the new type of country they're in.

So anyhow there was just me, five black boys and there was a
blue dog of mine, Bluesy. She was a blue cattle dog. A bitch, she
was. But it took us about six months to break these cattle in and
stop them from trying to bugger off back home. And we also had
to stop them from following the storms, because if they did that,
they'd wander too far away and they'd perish before they got back.

Anyhow, after a few months stuck out in the middle of bloody
nowhere, track riding these cattle, day after day, with five black
boys and a dog, you begin to wonder about your sanity. So that's
what I started doing and, as the days went by, it got worse and
worse until, finally, I woke up one morning and I said to me dog,
'Good morning, Bluesy.'

And the dog looked over at me and she said, 'Good morning,
mate.'

When that happened I didn't know who was going the maddest,
the bloody dog or me. 'Christ almighty,' I said to myself, 'this's
going a bit too far.' So I reached over for my gun to put a bullet into
her. But by the time I turned around again she'd taken off. So then
I started thinking that perhaps she'd started to read minds as well
as talk.

Anyhow, that's my story. But they were good times, those days.

Booties

In '42 we delivered out of Lake Nash, which is just over the Queensland border into the Northern Territory, and we came in through to Brewarrina, in central northern New South Wales. Now, although we were delivering cattle we came across a lot of fellers droving sheep. And these sheep drovers, all they had was just a little old sulky or something and a couple or two horses and half a dozen dogs or so, and maybe they didn't even have any other people helping them out.

Now the sheep drover did it a lot different than the cattle drover. What the sheep drover did was that he'd pack up of a morning and he'd go on ahead in his sulky and he'd set up camp down along the stock route. Then the dogs'd come along later, bringing the sheep along the fence, all on their own. Oh, those sheepdogs, they were bloody marvellous things, you know.

But the biggest mob of sheep I ever seen on a droving trip, a feller called Lenny Cant had them, and when we saw him he was taking them between Boulia and Winton. And Lenny had nineteen dogs and twenty men working with him. And I tell you what, there were so many bloody sheep that, for as far as you could see, it looked like the whole earth was moving. That's how many sheep he had. Upwards of 25,000, I'd say.

But what got me was that Lenny's dogs, the whole nineteen of them, they all wore these little booties to protect their foot pads from the big galvanised burr and the goathead burr that was all through that area.

Box Hold and Beyond

I went bush when I was about eleven. That was out at Nundoora Station—Box Hold they called it—which is up between Broken Hill and Tibooburra, there in the north-western corner of New South Wales. So, like many young fellers, I worked out on a station before I started droving.

How it all came about was that we were living in south Broken Hill and times were tough. This's in about the late '30s or early '40s when I was still in sixth class. Now why I say that I was '*still* in sixth class' was because I'd been stuck in sixth class for three years. But see, I couldn't learn any more and Dad and Mum never had the money to send us to Marist Brothers.

So anyhow, one day, I was giving a bloke a hand to put up a fowl house and this other feller came around and he asked me if I wanted a job out on a station. Now I won't say this feller's real name, I'll just call him Tom. But this Tom was the manager of Box Hold, where he was running about 30,000 head of cattle. And see, I always wanted to go out and work in the bush. Even when I was a real little kid, you know, I had this fancy, like you do. So after this Tom asked me to go bush, I went and saw Dad.

'Where to?' Dad said.

'Well,' I said, 'I met a feller today who's the manager at Box Hold Station.'

Now, Dad knew where Box Hold was because he'd been a bushie all his life.

'Well, bring the bloke down here 'n' let me meet him.'

So I did. 'Dad,' I said, 'this's Mr So-and-so.'

And Dad said straight off to this Tom feller, 'Look, I've heard about you,' he said, see, because he'd heard about how Tom was very tough, especially on the black boys. He'd belt the Christ out of them. Oh, he was a cruel bloody man, you know. He was even cruel on me but I won't go into that because it still gets to me, even after all these years. But I didn't know nothing about it at that time, like. So then Dad said to this Tom, 'I've heard a lot about you and about how yer belt the boys up 'n' all that sorta crap 'n' tie 'em up to trees 'n' so forth. So if yer ever touch my boy, I'll come right up there 'n' I'll kill yer, I will.'

And he would've too. Dad was a touch over 6 foot 2, 18 stone, and he'd been in the bush most of his life. And what's more, he'd been in a scrap or two so he knew how to use himself.

Then when that was all settled, Dad said to me, 'Yeah, okay, son,' he said, 'yer can go up bush.'

So the next day I left Broken Hill with a straw hat, a pair of shorts and me sandals. That's all I had, and I headed up to this cattle station. Then when I got there, Tom put me up for a few months out in the stock camp where I done the cowboy job with about ten or twelve other blokes. All men, they were. So I was up there for about three years and in between times I used to help drove cattle down to Cockburn, on the South Australia–New South Wales border, where they'd truck them down to Adelaide.

Then after that I went droving up to Bulloo Downs. That was a Kidman-Reid place. They had about three million acres up there, just near the border, this side of Thargomindah, in the south-west of Queensland. And then I went to Naryilco, where I drove cattle for Dick Nunn across to Bourke, over what they called the Cut Line, which was one of the main droving routes up that way. There's bores all along the way where the stock can camp. Good bores, most times, too.

See, with the Cut Line you went down through Milparinka, which is a little town, about 25 mile this side of Tibooburra. It had a population of about four or five back then. It used to be a gold-mining place. I know that because me dad used to drive the Cobb & Co. coach up there from Broken Hill. So you come down past Milparinka then head east, over to Wanaaring, then on until you got to Bourke where Tankred Brothers had the meatworks.

So we took about six mobs over to Tankred's with old Dick Nunn. Dick finished up managing the biggest cattle station in the

Cobb & Co. coach.

world, a place called Anna Creek, up in north-eastern South Australia. A great bloke was old Dick, and a great bloke to work for. He was very slow in his manner and his speech, but you could always understand what he said.

Then I also worked for Kidman. Now they reckon that old Sir Sidney was a lousy bastard to work for but I worked for him quite a bit and he was all right to me. Just as long as you ate the tucker, he never said too much. See, he didn't like waste. Like, if you were a smoker and you were sitting by the fire and you used a match, well, he'd sack you on the spot because you were supposed to use a stick from the fire to light your smoke, not the match. Or if the cook was pealing the spuds for the tucker and he was peeling them too thick, that was no bloody good neither, you know.

Then there was his son-in-law, Kidman-Reid. He used to come out more often than Sir Sidney. And then there was . . . what was his name . . . he used to come out too. I don't know if he was an uncle to Sir Sid or what, I'm not sure, but he had St Vitas-dance something bloody awful, you know. One time we were droving cattle from Box Hold down to Cockburn and he came out to meet us. Our boss drover was a feller called George Stanford, and George said that we were going to kill a beast for our tucker.

Now, I was with a bloke called Turner, Frank Turner, and we were working the tail of the mob. So I give this uncle or whoever, this old 32/20 Winchester rifle, and this rifle had no stock. You might remember, it was the type John Wayne used to use in his films. But there was no stock in the bloody thing and you just had the two pieces of iron and you'd have to put this stock into it and screw it down.

So this uncle feller, he gets off the horse and he grabs a lump of mulga to balance on, and he's shaking all over, just like that. Anyhow, he rams it onto the ground and sorts out the rifle, then he gets back on the horse and he leads up through the mob, looking for a good one to kill. And there's this Frank Turner and me. And I said to Frank, 'Look at this bastard.' And fair dinkum he was like this with his legs and arms going everywhere, shaking, and he had this rifle, trying to point it at a beast.

'We'd better stay low,' I said to Turner, 'just in case the shakes get the best of him 'n' he misses completely.'

Then *bang*—and he hit that beast fair and square, and down it went. I was surprised. Now I never thought that he'd be able to do that twice in a row because he shook all over so much. But he did. That's right, it was old Walter Kidman. Jesus Christ, I tell you, he never missed, shakes and all.

Then there was another character. This was at Bulloo Downs and, I tell you, there were some wild bastards out there, real wild. We had an old boss drover called Whatty Johnson. Whatty was as mad a bastard as you'd ever see. How on earth he got away with the things he did beats me. But he was a good cattleman. He could ride like a stick-fast-flea. Anyhow, we were between droving trips and this old Whatty was a married bloke, and I remember we were having a cup of tea one night down at his place and his kid was crying. It was only a little baby. So he said to his missus, 'Fer Christ's sakes shut that bloody thing up, will yer.' But no matter what she did, she couldn't shut this kid up, so Whatty said, 'Give him 'ere, then.'

So his missus hands over this little baby and Whatty, he grabs a bottle of raw brandy that was sitting on the cupboard and he got a couple of teaspoons of the stuff into the little kid. And that baby didn't wake up until about nine or ten the next morning. That's true. That's a true story. Raw bloody brandy.

Then we had another drover bloke called Bill Till. Bill'd be about sixty now, I suppose. He was a good old cattleman. He'd ride nice and steady. Now the thing about Bill was that, like all good boss drovers, he never used a whip. He always had one with him, mind you, just in case, but he was never keen on using it. But there was also this other feller with us at the time, a bloke called Briggs. Briggsie, we called him, and oh, he was a two-bob lair, the type who'd get you killed, you know. But he could ride a bit. He was about twenty.

Anyhow, this Briggsie, he was as mad as a cut snake. He'd get back about three or four hundred yards and he'd gallop flat out straight into the mob, then he'd jump onto one of the cattle and he'd jam his spurs into it and yahoo and carry on. He got thrown a lot of times too, he did.

But this Briggsie and old Bill had a big blue when we were out droving between Salt Lake and Cockburn, one time. I forget right now what it was all over. But anyhow, this blue got real bad and they got their stockwhips out and there they were, on horseback, belting the living Christ out of each other. Their shorts were all cut to ribbons and everything. Blood and all. And old Tom, the manager feller I told you about, well, he sacked this young Briggsie. It was the best thing he ever done. He just wrote Briggsie's cheque out and told him to get on the next mail truck.

So there was some real characters out there. And from all those experienced, good and bad, I started writing songs about the bush and the people in the bush—the drovers, the ringers, the real bush people, not like the ones you get these days. So that's how I wrote *Trumby*, for Slim Dusty. Oh, I've wrote other songs for him as well but that was the best one, by far.

But now, while you've got me going—I'm all worked up—I've gotta say this; back to this feller I've called Tom, my first boss.

See, the thing was that his wife thought the bloody world of him, she did. But she never knew what he was like. She never ever knew just how cruel that bastard was, and I never told her because she was such a beautiful lady. She'd be about eighty or more now.

Granted, he was a rough bugger, and tough, I'll give him that. All he used for a swag was a blanket, and he had an eight by ten camp sheet. That's all he had, summer and winter. And in winter the rest of us'd be wrapped up in leather coats, gloves and bloody coarse underwear, everything, and still your feet'd be shaking in the stirrup irons. It was that bloody cold. And there he'd be, sitting there, with just his gabardine riding strides on, no bloody singlet, he never wore underpants, the shirt opened at the neck, sleeves rolled up, and it's bloody freezing. And I said to him one time, I said, 'Don't yer feel the bloody cold?'

'It's all up in 'ere,' he said, pointing at his brain. 'If yer not cold, yer not cold. Youse blokes're all wrapped up in everything. Why don't yer try it sometime.'

'No bloody fear,' I said. 'It's too cold fer me.'

But to give you some idea just how cruel he was; when I first went up from Broken Hill, he put me into the camp, there on the creek, out at a place called Yantera, an out-station with just a few huts and a beautiful big set of drafting yards. Anyhow, we had 1000 head of cattle that we were getting ready to take on a droving trip out past Salt Lake, which is up this side of Tibooburra, and this Tom, he said to me, 'See that little bay mare over there, Joe.'

'Yeah.'

'Well,' he said, 'saddle her up.' That's all he said, 'Saddle her up.'

So I saddled her up. And there's these two or three blokes who'd already mounted their horses, ready to go, and they said, 'Christ, are yer ridin' her, Joe?'

Now, like I said, I was new there so I could hardly ride to save meself. So I said, 'Yeah, I'm riding her.'

'Jeez, yer bloody game, aren't yer?' they said.

'Why's that?' I asked them.

'Well, that bloody mare's killed three men already,' they said.

'Yeah,' I said. 'Well, I'm not gettin' on the bloody thing, then.'

So I started to walk away, see. I just couldn't believe it that Tom'd get me on a horse that'd already killed three men, especially after Dad'd had a go at him about not doing anything cruel to me. So there I was, still in the yard, when Tom comes up and he says, 'Are yer gonna get on that mare or not?'

'No, I'm not,' I told him.

'Why?' he said. Mind you, this bloke could use a stockwhip. He could carve his name on the flank of a bull, no worries, you know.

And I said, 'I don't wanta get killed.'

Then he said, 'Get on.'

'No,' I said.

Then I seen him go for his whip. So I scooted for the rails. But I only get halfway through and me bloody belt gets caught. So I'm stuck there. And this Tom, well, he just stood back on his horse and he tattooed my arse with his bloody stockwhip. Fair dinkum. Christ, I couldn't ride for days. I had welts on me arse that big. And Christ it hurt bad. For three days I couldn't ride.

Then another time we were bringing in three or four drafting horses—Bill, Patch and Taz. They were all sisters, mares, like. Oh, you could put them in harness. You could pack them. You could do anything on them, they were that quiet. And one of them, this Bill, she had a little foal, a lovely little black thing it was. So we're having breakfast and I said, 'Mr So-and-so,' I said to this Tom. 'Bill's just had a foal.'

'Don't worry about it,' he said. 'I'll fix 'er up.'

Then after we finished breakfast he goes over to this little foal. And he wore these bloody spring-sided leggings with a pouch in them where he carried his pocket knife. We all did. So he walked up to this little foal and he put his hand up under her neck, just like that, and he stretched it back, just like that. Then he got his knife out and he cut its throat.

Oh Jesus, I thought, what a wicked man. So I said to him, 'You're cruel.'

And he said, 'Do you want the same treatment, young feller?'

'Oh no,' I said, 'yer too big for me. I'm only a kid.' Like I was still only eleven, going on twelve, by then.

So then we got on our horses and we're just about to ride out when I hear this sound like a bleating. And the dirty bastard, he hadn't even cut the throat properly.

Then there was another time when we were cutting out five hundred head of cattle at a place called Kidman's Selection, and Tom was riding a horse called Jardine. He was a beautiful draft horse; not the heavy draughthorse like you might be thinking. These were special horses for drafting cattle, a cutting horse. We didn't use quarter horses or nothing. Anyway, these were as good as any bloody quarter horse, I reckon.

So anyway, Tom was pushing this Jardine something terrible, chopping and changing, going this way and that. And this poor bloody horse was getting so tired that he missed a beast. So Tom gets the end of his whip and he flogged that poor bastard of a horse until the blood was racing out of his flanks. God, he was a cruel bastard, he was.

But this Tom feller didn't go droving with us, thank Christ. I mean, he'd come out and organise things to get us under way, and that. But in them days the managers were working managers. They didn't sit on their arses like they do today, with a computer. Anyway the bush's stuffed as far as I'm concerned. It's all done with the turn of a bloody key now, you know, motorbikes and choppers and all that. And all they do is frighten the cattle, get them all tense. Then they throw them onto a truck and truck them for about ten or twelve hours until they get to the meatworks. Then they kill them as hot meat.

And believe me, there's nothing worse than hot meat. I mean, cattle can smell blood as well as fear, you know. There's no doubting that because when we were droving we'd kill a beast a week, maybe two, depending on how many men there were. But you'd ride around and you'd pick one out of the mob, nice and easy. And it'd just stand there, the poor bastard, and you'd be on your horse with a rifle and it'd probably say 'moo' or something, and look up at you. Then *bang*, it'd go straight down, just like that, and that was your tucker. No stress, nothing. None of this galloping around and crap.

But I did enjoy the droving. You get to see a lot. And it was good to get away from Tom, too. But what I told you is only the half of it because if my old man would've found out all what he done to me, he would've killed the bastard. And what he done to them poor black boys, I tell you, I pity them boys, I do. But the bastard's dead now, anyway, and so's me dad.

Still, I'd appreciate it very much if you changed his real name because, like I said, his wife was a beautiful, beautiful woman and she didn't know how cruel that bastard was, and it might hurt her if she found out. And I wouldn't like that to happen.

Broken

I left school when I was about twelve or thirteen, when I got a job out at a place called Ned's Corner Station, up there in the top corner of Victoria, New South Wales and South Australia. That was in about 1939. So I got this job with a drover, but what I didn't count on was that I'd have to work seven days a week for two and sixpence per week. And not only that, I also had to get up and do a two or two and a half-hour watch every night of the week and live on damper and corned beef then, for a change, we'd have corned beef and damper.

But anyhow, I stayed there for a good long while and over that time I had a few tangles, mainly with horses. Like, four or five years ago I had some special infra-red ray tests on my lungs and they told me that I've had twenty-two broken ribs. Some might be just cracks, I don't know. So you could say that I've not only broken a few horses in, but also a few horses have broken me in, too.

There was one time, back when I was packhorse droving, when a horse kicked my ribs in and I ended up with a big red-blue patch you could cook an egg on. But anyhow, I kept on working, then ten days later, when it was time to come home, I couldn't get up on the horse so I had to walk all the way back. That one hurt so bad that, after a while, I went to a doctor and he said that one rib was sitting on top of another and the underneath one was all split. Apparently it'd tried to knit but it kept breaking off and it'd gone into a big abscess. See, bones have to knit straight. They can't knit crooked.

Then I've got a few bumps on my foot. See, just there. That happened in '49 or '50 when I broke the bones right across the top, there. It was a Saturday morning, and it'd started to rain, and a couple of mad bullocks had come down from out of the Blue Mountains, so I said, 'I'll just go up and grab these two bullocks.'

So I flew up a narrow ridge through wire grass, this high, and the horse went straight into a rabbit warren. He didn't even see the thing. Anyhow I managed to get clear but when I saw that the horse was trying to get back up, I got back in the saddle. So I got back up but then the horse scrambled in the wet and he slid right down the side of the hill.

Now, I don't know exactly what happened but I heard the bones break and I felt my foot crack. I think that the tail of my boot must've hooked against a stone or something and it brought my foot back around like that, twisting it right up, and *snap.* Then when I looked down, I saw these two bones sticking out of my boot, so I cut the boot off. A good pair of boots, too, they were.

The horse was all right, though. He was better off than me. He was just covered in mud from sliding down the side of the mountain. But then he couldn't get back up to where I was because it was too slippery and there was a fence in his way so I ended up having to crawl for eight hours until I got to help. And I tell you, I was getting a bit worried there for a while because it was still pouring with rain and the gullies were getting fuller

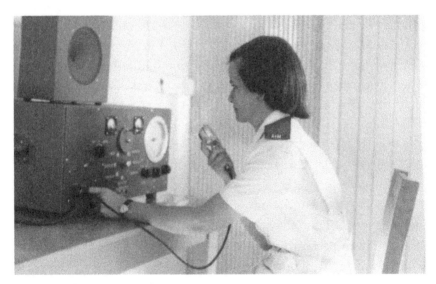

The Royal Flying Doctor Service keeping in contact via transceiver.

and fuller and the water was flowing faster and faster. Anyhow, I eventually made it back.

But a couple of the bones just wouldn't knit so they had to re-break them again. But because it was so hard to get the bones dead straight, for them to set, they had to keep on re-breaking them. In the end I think the foot had to be broken seven or eight times until, eventually, they set. And then they had to scrape out all the bone chips.

Then there was the droving trip when we hadn't been on the road too long. Anyway, I'd drawn two horses to ride and one of them was pretty flighty, and I knew that if this feller got his head right down, he'd do me, so I had to keep his head on his chest. I mean, he was a good horse but he just never wanted to go to work in the morning.

Anyway, one morning, just after daylight, the bugger threw me and broke my arm. And he done a proper job of it too, because it was all bent around the wrong way. Now this happened somewhere before we got down to Barringun Gate, on the Queensland–New South Wales border. The area was all new to me but, luckily, the boss knew his way.

So they tucked the arm up there, like that, and they put it in a sling, then the boss and me jumped on our horses and off we went for help. Now I reckon we rode for about 20 or 30 mile before we come to a dogger's camp. Doggers are blokes who go out setting dingo traps. So we got fresh horses there, then we done another 20 mile until we came across a mustering camp. So we got fresh horses there again and then we rode another 20 mile to the homestead. I forget the name of the place now, but the Flying Doctor was only an hour or so away and when he come he took me in to the butcher's table.

See, at the homestead there was one of those huge big tables for laying a bullock on to butcher it. The top end was made of wood so that they could cut the beast with knives then the other end was steel so that you could slide half a bullock around. I mean, it was a pretty solid table, bolted down to the floor and all. And it had to be, because you didn't want it to tip over when you dumped a bullock on it.

The Flying Doctor arriving at Lake Nash Station.

But anyhow, running at an angle from the table, to just down the legs, there were these iron stays. Now as I said, my arm was pretty badly broken and, for it to have any chance to set, first they had to straighten it out. So they just put my broken arm through one of these stays and the doctor got his feet against the table and he yanked like hell on the arm until he got it back into position. Boy, it hurt. I reckon my eyes shot off in different directions, all at the same time.

'There you go,' the doctor said. 'That didn't hurt much, did it?'

Like bloody hell. I mean, it was my arm that was broke, not bloody his.

Anyhow, after the bloke pulled my arm back together, he plastered it up and I went out and I sat in the sun to let it dry off a bit. Then at about five o'clock that night, after I'd had a cup of tea and a bite to eat, the boss and me, we set out again and we relayed horses all the way back until we got to our camp at daylight, just in time for me to start work again. Anyhow, with my broken arm all plastered up, I went and picked out a nice quiet horse this time.

But I tell you, that night, I was never so pleased to see a dinner camp in my life. Then one of the other blokes, a ringer mate of mine, a blackfella, he said, 'Don't worry Dusty, I'll do yer watch tonight. She'll be all right.'

'Beaut,' I said, and I didn't even wait to have dinner. I just went and curled up in my swag and I slept for hours.

Then about six weeks later I was supposed to go to a doctor to get the plaster cut off. But I didn't bother about that. I just got a pair of tin snips and I cut the bugger off, myself.

Broken In

Droving's been my life. I started ringing when I was nine year old, and I took delivery of my first mob of cattle just before my seventeenth birthday. And there was nothing bloody romantic about it. It's just what happened. So I don't know why it is, but a lot of these buggers you hear telling stories these days, they're not bloody drovers and never have been.

See, the drover's nothing more than a contractor, pure and simple. You signed a contract and, in that contract, it stated that you could travel the cattle no more that 56 mile per week. Then they had all these blanked-out spaces where they put in whatever the hell they wanted to put in. So that was 8 mile a day, and you had to handle them in a 'workman-like manner'. So you were bound by all that.

Now the drover did the job for a fixed, or a percentage, price. 'If he don't deliver, he don't get paid.' So once you counted the bullocks or cows over, from then on, they were yours and you got paid two and sixpence per head, per 100 mile. That was up until '49. It changed in '50. Now that mightn't sound much for just the one beast but if you've got, say, 1500 head, that's where the money mounts up.

Then because, more times than not, we drovers didn't have any money, every 100 mile we were paid a percentage into our banking account. From that payment you bought your rations at an outpost station or a little shop, way out in the middle of nowhere.

Now, like the captain on a ship, there's only one drover. If somebody comes up to the mob and says, 'Where's the drover?' he'd be looking for the drover, the drover-in-charge. They never said boss drover, that only come in later in books. So you might say, 'Oh, that's me.' Or you might say, 'Oh, the bastard's up there, asleep under a tree.' You might even tell him exactly where he is. But it was always the drover or the drover-in-charge, and that was it.

And the drover supplied everything, the horses, the saddles, the bridles, the horseshoes and shoeing gear, and enough packs for each man. These were leather packs, bags, that hung from a hook on the saddle. You supplied everything bar swags, whips and spurs. The whips and spurs were personal. If the ringer thought he needed them, I didn't mind unless I saw someone using them excessively, then I'd give them a chat.

Then there's the cook. It takes no telling what he is but his job is to keep everybody fed and happy. He writes out the ration order and then you check it in case he mightn't have got enough stuff or, if you were a mean so-and-so, you might cut it back. That

doesn't always occur but it sometimes happens. And the cook's in charge of the tucker pack, which is the pack that the cooked food's kept in, like the cooked meat, the bread and all that he's using day by day.

A beast's generally allowed to be killed every ten days for rations, though we killed more or less to suit ourselves. I mean, it was well known how you rarely killed anything you were moving yourself because they muscled up with the walking. They got a bit hard. But say, for argument's sake, if you were droving for Vesteys and you couldn't pick up a fat one that'd been lost from a previous trip, then you'd be pretty bloody weak. And every night the cook'd lay the meat out so it'd cool, even if it's salted. Now, although on a few occasions I've finished just a few days before Christmas, predominantly droving's done through the winter when you can keep meat. So that's the cook.

Then there's the horsetailer. A very, very important person is the horsetailer because without the horses, I mean, you're on foot. His job is to look after the horses' every needs. And I tell you, a lot of them were touchy, more touchy than the cook sometimes. Like, if he'd picked a nice patch of grass for his horses and the cattle go near it, oh, he'll go stark raving mad. Oh yes, some of them were very, very touchy.

Then there's the ringers—the white stockmen. They're called ringers because they ride around the cattle. They 'ring' the cattle. They didn't have a contract so there's nothing to hold them. Sometimes you'd wake up in the morning and they were gone. They might even leave without collecting their wages. Oh yes, I've had that done too. God only knows why, maybe they're temperamental or just pure swine.

There was one time when I'd delivered into Dajarra, south of Mount Isa, in north-western Queensland. I was putting things together to head back for another mob and these two ringers were slow getting out of bed. Now I could tell there was something going on, see, so I said, 'What's wrong with you pair 'a buggers?'

'Oh,' they said, 'Johnny Darcy's payin' a pound a week more than you.'

So I said, 'Then what're yer doin' sittin' round my fire? Git over 'n' git it.'

And that was it. They packed their swags up and away they went, and those blokes sat on their arses for six weeks and they never got work. But anyway, that was just a minor little hiccup that come along.

So then you had your Aboriginals. Though they did the ringers' job they were called 'boys'. They might be fifteen or fifty but you still called them boys. So that was them.

Then after you picked up the cattle or whatever, what you were going on was a droving 'trip'. There's none of this 'drive' business. If you want to drive, get in a motor car or join the CWA (Country Womens' Association) and go on a lamington drive. And you went along a stock route, not a root. It's rubbish how they're putting everything in Yankee-fied. I mean, I've heard these Yanks saying that you should never use this word or that word, well, they can all get stuffed. Those are the words we use, and that's it. And it's always a 'track', never a trail. If someone said, 'Where's Georgie Booth's mob?' you'd say, 'Oh, he's up the track.' or 'He's down the track.' Mind you, he might be two or three hundred mile away but it'd still be up or down the track.

Then if you came along to somebody and said, 'Where were you last year?' he might say, 'I did a trip with Georgie Booth. We went inside to Collarenebri.' There's another short-hand term, 'inside'. If you were in the Territory and you did a trip into New South Wales, that's inside.

So after you've taken charge of your cattle, you do a day's stage and your packs or wagonette go ahead and the cook sets up camp. Now at night you feed the cattle on to camp, nice and easy. There's none of this hillbilly business of racing them up with yells and screams. Then after they're on camp it's customary for the drover to change to his night horse and do the 'dog watch' from six till seven when the cattle are settling down. The rest of the night watch is made up with two or two and a half-hour shifts, beginning with the horsetailer and depending on how many men you have. The drover then does the last watch from two till four in the morning then he wakes up the horsetailer and the cook. The tailer gets the horses ready while the cook sorts the food out. Of course everyone had to be up and have a wash before breakfast. I was pretty strict on that.

So by piccaninny daylight, you'd be on your way again. And when you take them off camp in the morning, you feed them off. Once again, there's none of this 'yippee-yi-yoh' like you see in the pictures. You feed them off, nice and steady. Then when they're full they'll lift their heads and come together, and they'll walk until there's water. That's if there's water. Now if there's water, they'll have a drink and that might be your dinner camp. Then after dinner camp, they might walk out a bit or they might start feeding, and you feed them right up until you put them on the round camp at night.

Now if you don't get to water, you still have to take the horses for water. See, being cud chewers cattle can last where horses will dehydrate. If horses go without water for more than a couple of days they go funny and they'll just wander off and leave you on foot. People have perished that way.

I've been four and a half days without water, and that's a fair while. One time I brought some cattle down to Cloncurry, there in north-western Queensland. The powers-that-be had an imaginary tick line there. We used to joke that the railway line was it because the ticks couldn't crawl over the tracks. 'They can't catch hold,' we'd say, just to annoy the authorities.

So you dipped your cattle at Cloncurry and you stayed on a reserve there for anything up to a week; whatever they told you. Then after you dipped the second time, you had to go. It didn't matter what the hell. But the thing was, when you force the cattle through the dip yard they're getting knocked about and you chivvy shit out of them. Then all they want to do is get away from that bloody yard as fast as they can. So even in a lot of places where there's water right beside the dip, they won't drink it.

Then while you're on a trip both the horses and the cattle get broken in. There's a word you'll have to look after—broken in. It doesn't mean you flog them until they don't know any better. It's training them. Take the horses, for instance. When you've got a

team of horses—and that depends on how many cattle you have—
you've got to break them in to stand on camp. Then after a few
days or a week they know when they're going to stop, and the
horsetailer's able to walk among them and hobble them or catch
fresh horses or whatever. Once they're broken in, one man can
handle a lot of horses.

It's the same with cattle. After a while, as soon as they see or
smell the camp they'll poke up and they'll pick their spot to drop
down. I mean, there'll always be one or two who'll want to wander
away from the rest. But several of my horses were broken from
green to do nothing but night work, and they'd walk up and give
the beast a tap with their foot. Then if it didn't move, he'd give it
a nip and the beast'd jump up and go back into the mob. You
wouldn't have to do anything. You just sat there and the horse did
it all.

But oh, I've had cattle that were so broken in they'd come right
down and lay beside the fire at night. You could even smell their
hair singeing, they were that close. And even when the other cattle
would splash, or even rush, well, these ones, they'd just stay there
and they'd stretch their neck out along the ground as much as
to say, 'Oh shit, not again.' And they wouldn't move. That's what I
mean by being broken in.

Bush Blacks

Back around 1900 the Western Australian government put a line across through the top of the Kimberleys to try and stop the spread of tick fever. That meant that only those from further down south could use the stock routes into the metropolitan markets while the Kimberley cattle now had to be taken across to coastal places like Derby and that, then boated down from there.

But from my reckoning, a lot of those Kimberley cattle were tick clean to begin with, and now they had to walk through infested tick country on their way across to the coast. So I don't know the logic in all that. Then there was the trouble of loading them onto the boats and some dying on the way down with redwater fever. So I reckon that's why they decided to see if they could put in a stock route down through the clean country, through the desert.

Anyhow, Canning done the first survey and, according to reports, how he went about finding where the water was, was that they'd go out and take a few bush blacks then give them a feed and tie them up till they showed them where the next blackfella soak was. And they done that all the way down the track. So really, the Canning Stock Route only went from blackfella's soak to black-fella's soak, right from Wiluna, in the central west, all the way up till they got to Lake Gregory, at Billiluna, up in the north-east.

Now these blackfella soaks, they'd probably just started out like a kangaroo digging then, each year, when the blacks were passing through on walkabout, they'd dig a few more inches out as they followed the water down. So after 1000 years or so the soak might end up being 10 feet deep, you know. But oh, there's plenty of water under the sand, out there. You've just got to know where to look.

So after Canning done that first survey, they went back a couple of years later with a big team of camels and drays, loaded with gear and timber, to put in the wells. But the drays were no good because there was a lot of areas with nothing but spinifex, sandhills and low scrub. So they left the drays and they just used the camels to carry their timber, then if they came across a patch of desert oak they'd use that.

But the first drovers who took cattle down the Canning were Thompson and Shoesmith. They went down a couple or so years after with another feller, Fred Teroni. So they started off around Halls Creek, but by the time they got down to Billiluna this Fred Teroni had gone blind with sandy blight and he had to come back. So Thompson and Shoesmith and their mob, they went on till they got down to Well 37, and they also got sandy blight, and that's where the bush blacks attacked them and ransacked everything and let the bullocks go.

Anyhow, a month or so later there was another feller, Tom Cole. I knew Tom afterwards. He died at the Rock Hole Station just outside of Halls Creek. He's buried there at the moment. But when Tom went down he came to Well 38, which is a big rock hole, and there were some stray cattle and a few horses watering there. And one of the horses was a favourite mare of either Thompson or Shoesmith and she still had some of her riding gear on. Then thinking that something might be wrong, Tom left his cattle and plant there and a couple of them went on and they found Thompson and Shoesmith and all his team, dead around the Well 37. So they buried them there and they picked up the strays that hadn't gone off into the desert and perished. Then when Tom got to Wiluna he reported it all.

So it was pretty wild country back in them times, with the bush blacks and all. And things hadn't changed much by the time I went on my first trip with George Lannigan in the early 1930s, because we took plenty of labour just in case. Like, we always had two horsetailers and two camel boys so that they could watch each other. One of them couldn't go out on his own. Well they wouldn't go on their own, anyway. It just wasn't safe.

Like, we had a couple of bullocks that was starting to annoy the mob so we cut them out and left them behind. Then when we went back in the morning the blacks'd come in and there was only the hide and the feet laying on the ground.

Then you'd come in to one of the wells and they'd be there. And when they saw you they'd take off. Sometimes they even left their spears or their firesticks behind. Oh, they were always trying to get water out of the wells, but because they didn't have camels or horses to pull the water out, sometimes they'd try to wind it up themselves and they'd get so far and they'd stop to have a blow and the handle'd fly back and crack their skull. Then other times they'd throw a big old tree down the well and they'd try to climb down that, to get water. So every now and then you'd find one down the well, you know, mostly dead.

But you never camped at the water. It wasn't policy. Quite a lot of drovers made the mistake of camping at a well, and there's still a lot of people buried out there, you know. You kept your distance. You'd go in and you'd get your water and you'd water the cattle then you'd go back out and camp a distance away, to let them come into the trough.

'It was pretty wild country back in them times, with the bush blacks and all.'

But you'd see them roaming about in groups. Sometimes there'd be thirty or forty, sometimes there might only be half a dozen. And quite often you'd see their smokes, out over the sandhills, a mile or so away. So it never felt like you was on your own. But you'd just go from day to day and, if you did the right thing, you were usually all right, you know.

One time I remember, we were going down and a couple of young bush black kids come in and mated up with our black camel boys, and they wanted to stay with us. That was okay by me. So they come along and they helped the camel boys out, right up till they sighted Wiluna, then they shot through in the night.

So we delivered into Wiluna and we stopped there for about three weeks to give the horses a bit of a blow and to allow the blokes to grog up. Then going back, we got about a 120 mile out and these two kids met up with us again, and they stayed with us then, like, as part of the plant. But when we got up to Well 25 or 26 we came across a mob of bush blacks, sitting on the sandhills. So we filled our canteens and things and we shot through a mile or two to let them come in and have a drink. Then in the morning, one of the camel boys come around and he said, 'Them bush blacks, they pinched them kids last night and took 'em bush. Maybe gonna kill 'em.'

Anyhow, I tried to get my blacks to go after them because I thought they might've been able to make sign language or talk with this mob, to find out what was going on. But not on your life. There was no hope in the world of getting our fellas to go off into the desert after these kids.

'Well,' I said, 'I might have a go at pickin' 'em up, meself,' I said.

So I got a riding camel for me and I put a horse canteen on one side and a pack saddle on the other, with a bit of tucker in it. Then I got the best leader of the pack camels and I put a pack on him and two canteens. Then I followed the blacks' tracks out across the desert, going from one little blackfella soak to another little blackfella soak.

Then on the fourth or fifth day, I saw some smoke. So I come to a sandhill and, away in the distance there was this mob of blackfellas sitting at a soak in a hollow and, oh, probably a couple of hundred yards away the two kids were sitting under a tree. So I sat in the sandhill trying to work out how the hell I was going to get these kids away, you know, that's if they even wanted to come, anyway.

Anyhow, the sandhills sort of went in a half circle. So I worked me way around till I got the kids between me and the soak. Now I'd also taken along some camel bells because an old bloke'd once told me how he'd given the blacks a real start by ringing a bell, you know. So I come riding over the hill with these camel bells rattling, and I fired a couple of shots in the air, and the bush blacks all scattered. And when the kids saw me they raced straight over so I just plonked the lead camel down on the ground and they clambered onto it and we took off.

Now a camel will trot all day but, once you break him into a canter, you'll blow him out. So we trotted at about fifteen or eighteen mile an hour, from about half past three in the afternoon to about nine or ten the following morning, with these two kids bouncing around, hanging onto the pack at the back.

Anyhow, we eventually got out on the stock route, about 160 mile from where I'd left my mob. Then when we got back, all our blacks come out and, oh gee, they were excited to see these two kids. And they stayed with us then. They went up to Billiluna and they stayed there for a while. Then one of them died not long after. I don't know if he got killed or something. But I think that the other one's still around, up there somewhere.

Bush Smart

I turned eighty-one last week. It was pretty quiet. These days I know more dead people than live ones. That's the way it's getting. And I reckon that a few of those people might've thought that some of the things I done in life were funny. But that was the thing, see. That's what you do. If you pretend to be dumb, and these people are no good, then when they try to put one over you, you catch them. You've got them. And then you can take them for a ride. So that's how I lived, because I mightn't have had the best of educations but I was bush smart.

See, you learn a lot in the bush. You learn to watch, you learn to listen and you don't miss a thing. I had eyes like a fox. The darker it was the more I could see. If you go out a lot at night-time, especially when you're young, you get used to the blenky light. An Aborigine trained me all that, years ago, out there on Martin's Well, about three or four hundred mile north of Adelaide. And with the listening, when we went kangaroo shooting, he'd say, 'Listen. Listen, boss. Here comes one.' And you'd listen and you'd hear the bloody roo coming from up to a mile away— thump . . . thump—thumping the ground. You try it, in the dry country. You put your ear to the ground and you can hear a man walking. You can. You can hear your enemy coming. See, that's the lurks of the bush, that's the smartness, and that's what I carried through life.

But oh, I've been droving and mucking around in the bush all me life. We started from nothing and we done everything and anything to get a quid. And I learned pretty quick that when you first get a mob of sheep together you always picked out your leaders, your markers, then you picked your centre sheep, then your tail-enders. And by doing that, I knew every sheep in the mob so I could tell if any was missing. It's like if you're watching 1000 people, everyone's different. If you're watching sheep or stock, all your lifetime, you get to know that there's a different look in every one of them.

Also you need a good dog. I had a dog called Sandy. He was a red dog. I bought him for five shillings when I was crutching one time. He was the best lead dog I ever had. As soon as I pulled up the cyclone fencing (the sheep break) he'd go forward with the lead sheep. And he'd keep working backwards and forwards. Then when I give him a whistle he'd stand straight up on his hind legs and he'd wait for me to tell him what to do next. You bet. Anytime I give him a whistle he'd stand up on his hind legs and he'd hold them. So I'd tell him what to do and he'd keep moving them ahead, feeding them, whatever you wanted. Oh he was a marvellous dog, Sandy.

Then I had another dog; that was when we were taking a mob of 1250 sheep on the road for feed and we went down through Williamstown, just north-east of Adelaide. A little blue heeler, it was. This was when the drought year was on. Another joker was with me, a returned soldier lad. We used to go under the names of Joe and George. And this George, he was friends with me before he went to the war. Then when he come back he was beggared, so George was droving with me. And all we had was an old spring dray, a two-wheeler and we'd prop it up against the fence post of a night-time with the chain that was on the old mare. And that's all we had—that, and an old push bike that we did all the scouting on.

At any rate, we went down towards Adelaide, you see, and this little dog, he used to go into the vineyards and he'd do the side run, up and down, up and down. And you'd give him a whistle, 'Hey Blue, git 'em out.' And he'd get them out of the vineyards, and the fruit yards, too. Oh he was a champion dog, he was. And I also had a black and tan one who used to stay with me and the tucker cart at the back of the mob. Nothing'd go past him.

When we got around Paracombe, we'd shut the sheep up of a night-time in the orchards and you'd lay awake listening to all these chewing sounds. Then in the morning you'd see that they'd been eating these dried plums that were on the ground. They spat the seeds out and all, they did. And also, we used to go down to the packing shed, down the Paracombe road there, where they threw out all the apples they didn't want, and the sheep'd eat them, too. Oh, they'd fight for them. So the sheep used to live on fruit. And we'd go down the Torrens River and we'd water them down there. The Torrens was running at the time. This's away back in '44 or whatever.

But the amount of people we got to know was unreal. Old Mick Moody used to have the pub there at Houghton. And we fed right down to where old Mr McEwen had the jam factory. And we'd take a tin with us and we'd get our jam for fourpence ha'penny a tin. Like, a shilling was a shilling in them times and a quid was a quid. That's when wages was only a pound a week.

Any rate, we fed right down the Main North Road, around the Old Spot hotel. And George, this joker that was with me, he'd go ahead while all the tail-enders followed me on the tucker cart. Anyhow, he'd go into the hotel and he'd yelled out, 'When yer coming past Joe, I bought yer a schooner!' So when I went past I'd go in and have the schooner.

Then we'd water our sheep just up the road a bit, there at Scammel's. Scammel was the manager of Fauldings. Then I fed the Main North Road right down to Symons' Chicken Hatchery. That was right on the corner, there. This's fifty-odd years ago, now. Then we fed back to where Elizabeth is. Back then you could buy any amount of land for twelve pound an acre. Then we went back towards Golden Grove. Golden Grove was only paddocks full of artichokes then. Now it's a city. So we fed back until, eventually, the season broke around Manoora. So I left George there with the sheep and I went shearing then, because it was about September.

Any rate, this was the first time that George'd ever managed the mob by his-self. But we had them pretty well trained by then anyway, so all he had to do was go ahead and the sheep'd follow him. Then later on, when he was around Farrell Flat, I went back to him. And this's what I mean about being bush smart and knowing your sheep.

I had a look over the mob and I said to George, 'Yer've lost five sheep.'

And he said, 'I don't think I have.'

'Yes you have,' I said. 'For starters yer've lost that good woolly wether.'

Like, one'd had about eighteen months' wool on him and, in the mornings, he'd always come up and drink the water out of the bowl that you washed your face in, and one thing and another. And he'd eat pieces of apple or bread, or anything, out of your hand. Anyrate, he was gone and I knew that another four had gone with him.

Now, a funny thing that I was going to tell you about. See, that was in September. Then later on, me brother, Harold, and meself, we went down to this place crutching. So we were at this place, you see, and I said to Harold, 'Don't crutch that sheep.'

'Why's that?' he asked.

And I said, 'He's one of those five sheep we lost, there a while back,' I said.

At any rate, the joker we were working for, he come up and he said, 'Why haven't youse blokes crutched that sheep?'

'Well,' I said, 'he might have your brand on him but I don't reckon he's yours,' I said.

'How can yer tell?' he said.

'I can tell by the look in his eyes,' I told him.

'Bull,' this joker said.

Then I said, 'I tell yer what. You bring me an apple and a bowl of water,' I said, 'and if that sheep'll eat the apple out of me hand and drink out of the bowl, well, he's mine.'

Then the joker went real shy on it. 'Well,' he said, 'if yer think he's yours, yer'd better take him.'

So I caught him, see, and I got that one back. But the joker had the other four. I'm bloody certain he did because those five sheep wouldn't have gone off separately. They would've stayed together. I know. So at anyrate, life's only what you make it, aye. You meet a lot of people, and you meet a lot of bloody rogues, too, aye.

Bush Tucker

In my experience, if your team was made up from blacks and whites then you'd have trouble all along the bloody road because the blackfellas and the whitefellers, they'd be arguing and they'd be fighting and you'd be forever having to go and settle things up. So I thought, 'This's no good in my bloody book.' And that's when I decided to go for the black boys. Because if you had an all black team then you've got a real team of men. And even though they were Myalls—they weren't educated or nothing—they were still a good mob of boys and they were always very good with the cattle.

And also, I only ever used a packhorse plant right up until halfway through my last droving trip. And that was out of the Gulf Country, in north-western Queensland, taking 1500 head of Kidman-Angliss bullocks from Vanrook Station down to Julia Creek, where they were going to be put on a train and trucked to market.

So this last trip was in 1954, and we headed off, me and the black boys. At that stage I still only had packs. Then we get halfway down and we get seven inches of rain on us. Seven inches. So then we're stuck for three weeks at a place called Canobie Station.

Anyway, as I said, I only used packs because if you've got a truck or a wagonette, well, you've got to have one man doing that job, all the time. But with the packs it doesn't matter if someone pulls out or they get sick or they leave you, because you can still poke along. You just put the extra packs on a horse in the plant.

See, as far as the plant went, I used to work on about forty head of horses for 1500 head of cattle, sometimes more. Then if you still got into strife you could always pick a few up along the track. Someone might say, 'Oh, I've got a bloody buck-jumping bastard. You can have it if yer'd like to ride it away.'

'Yeah, okay,' you'd say, because you knew that after a week with the cattle they'd be a real good horse.

Anyhow we're on this droving trip, it's rained and we're stuck for these three weeks. Then when we finally get going again, a bloke comes along with a 30 hundredweight Ford truck and he wants to sell it.

'I'll buy it,' I said.

So I did. And we're camped on a big, flat sort of a creek. It was running water about knee deep. So we watered the cattle and we drove the truck across the creek. Now, to all intents and purposes, it looked like being a real easy trip from there on in so we pulled all the packs off the horses and we put them on the back of this truck. Anyway, none of the black boys could drive but there was a white bloke there who wanted a job so I said, 'Okay, you can drive the truck.' So then me and the boys started off again with the bullocks.

'I'll catch up with yer soon,' this whitefeller said. 'I'll just back this truck into the creek a bit and I'll fill these containers up with this beautiful water.'

'Okay,' I said, 'see yer.'

Anyhow we get about 3 mile down the track and along comes this feller, the truck driver, but he's riding a horse, and he says, 'Oh that truck, she's bogged.'

'Well,' I said, 'I can't give yer a hand. I'm busy moving bullocks. Yer'll have to go back 'n' sort it out yerself.'

So he went back and he went up to a nearby property to get some help. The only trouble was that everyone was away, so he had to wait until they got back. In the meanwhile, of course, me and the boys, we're without our swags and by gee, around June it gets very cold up in that basalt country. But we're not only freezing without our swags, we're also hungry because our food's also back on the truck. So I said to one of the boys, 'We've got no food so yer'll have to go out 'n' find some bush tucker for us to eat.'

Anyway, off he goes and when he comes back he's got these three goannas hanging over his saddle. So that's what we ate. It tastes like fish. And it's pretty good tucker, especially if you're

Goannas are pretty good tucker . . . especially if you're hungry.

hungry. But I used to just cut the tail off and I'd only eat that. And the boys used to rib me because, see, they were used to living on that sort of thing in their wild state. 'By jeez, you know, Jack,' they'd say, 'them's good this other part.'

'Well,' I'd say, 'you just go ahead 'n' eat all that other part 'n' I'll stick with the tail. That's good enough for me.'

Anyhow we were a couple of days eating nothing but goanna when along comes a bloke driving a little old utility around, out in the middle of nowhere. So I said, 'Have yer got any tucker?'

'Not really,' he said. 'All I got's half a bag of onions, here in the back.'

'That'll do,' I said.

So then at night, I'd be chewing on a tail of a goanna with one hand and in the other I'd be munching away on a bloody raw onion. Then when we finally get to Julia Creek, the railway line's been washed away, so there's no train. So then we had to walk them all the way up beyond Charters Towers to Wando Vale. So we were sixteen weeks on the road with that mob. Then just as we were counting them over to the boss the whitefeller turned up with the bloody truck.

Close Shave

Those camels are randy buggers. Oh, they can cause some real trouble, I tell you, especially when they come into camp looking for horses to ride. Oh yes, they'd go for anything, camels would.

One time I was out on a droving trip. We were just this side of the Diamantina. I was the horsetailer and I had the horses a few miles out, at the base of a sandhill. Anyhow, there I was in camp—the cook was getting the tucker ready and I was shoeing a night horse— when I heard a disturbance out among the horses. I just thought that some brumby bucks had got in with them so I grabbed the .44 hand gun and I jumped on this night horse, barebacked, and out I went to shoot them.

Now as it turned out, it wasn't brumby bucks at all. It was these bull camels, and they were in there trying to mount the horses. So I decided to chase them and put them down. And for the life of me, I don't know how these American cowboys can ride a horse and shoot straight at the same time, like they do in the films. It's got me beat because, when it come to taking aim, there I was going up one way while the horse was going down the other and the camel was going either-which-way; so much so that I nearly shot the bloody horse that I was on. So I gave that idea away pretty quick and I went back to camp and got the .303 rifle, and then I eventually got a couple of them.

But talk about close shaves. Are you religious? Well, I'm not. But another time I was stuck with some bad cattle. I tell you, they were the worst mob I've ever been with. So we were out on this droving trip, right, and they were getting very toey. This was at night. And you know when you get the feeling that something terrible's going to happen. That's exactly how I felt. I could just sense it.

Anyhow, I said to my mate, Bronco Simms, I said, 'Bronco, I think these bastards are going to jump.'

The horsetailer getting the horses ready for another day's droving.

And at that very moment, they jumped, and off they went.

So I, up and on the night horse and headed off to hit the lead then try and turn them around. We were in a lane, about 8 mile wide by 12 mile. So I hit the lead. Then I thought, 'There's a bloody fence out here somewhere.' Then the next thing—*bang*—I hit the fence with the horse and down I went.

Remember, this's all at night so it's dark. But anyhow, I managed to get back in the saddle but by then all the bullocks were coming past me so I ended up in the bloody middle of them. And being in the middle of them meant that there was absolutely nothing I could do, so me and the horse, we just had to go with them.

Now, if you can imagine being stuck in among a thousand or so rampaging bullocks, and it's dark, well, it's a frightening thing. But that's where I was, so I had to stick with them. And I remember at one stage looking down and seeing sparks coming off the bullock's horns as they clashed against the stirrups of my horse. Then the horse got horned. So I just hung on for dear life because, if that horse would've went down, it would've been the end of me. I'd have been trampled to death.

And that was the only time in my life that I prayed. The only time. And somehow that horse managed to keep on its feet.

Crack!

There was a drover I met once. I was around eight years old at the time and we had a farm out at a place called Corbie Hill, which is near Leeton, in the Murrumbidgee Irrigation Area of New South Wales. Anyhow I used to walk home from Leeton Primary School, which was roughly a mile and a half away. Then I reckon I had about another quarter of a mile of dirt track leading from the road up to our front gate before I walked across a paddock to our house. A full car-sized gate it was.

So I got to the front gate this particular day, it was in about 1950 or '51, in the middle of summer, stinking hot, you know, and this drover was droving a mob of sheep. I don't actually know where he was taking them but he was heading up Corbie Hill Road in the same direction that I was going. So there this bloke was, just pushing these sheep along on his horse like, nice and gentle. There was quite a mob of them.

Then I went to open the gate and there, right in the middle of the gateway, was this huge brown snake. Now there's two types of brown snake around that area; there's the common brown snake which is dangerous in its own right, then there's the king brown, and that's the one that'll have a real go at you. People have been killed by them. And I was pretty sure that this one was a king brown.

Anyway I ran straight back to the edge of the road and bellowed out to this drover, 'Hoy! Hoy!' and he came racing up on his horse.

'What's up, sonny?' he asked.

Now we used to call the hill on the property Stony Hill because it was so stony. We just used to grow the occasional crop of oats on it because there wasn't too much else you could do with it. So anyway, I called up to this drover bloke, 'Snake. Snake,' and I pointed over to where it was.

'All right sonny,' he said, 'you just stay here.'

Then he rode across to this snake. As I said, it was a fair-sized king brown. And like I said, it was a stony paddock.

Now I don't know if you've ever seen a snake move but when they get wound up they can really travel, you know. So off went this snake and the drover took off after it, on his horse. And I can still picture it now. There's this horse, picking its way through the rocky ground, and this drover was on its back, with the reins in one hand and a stockwhip in the other.

And oh, it was beautiful to watch, really. Brilliant horsemanship. Anyway, when he got close enough to the snake, that drover let go with the whip and *Crack!* and the snake's head flew off in the air. It just come right off, just like that. Crack! Done.

Then he spun the horse around and rode back and said, 'Do yer wanta ride back down to the house, sonny?'

'No,' I said, 'I'll be all right now, thanks.'

'Okay, then,' he said, 'I'll get back to me sheep.'

And hell, that was about fifty year ago, and I can still remember it to this day; that horse dancing between the rocks and the drover with his whip. *Crack!* and that snake's head flying right off into the air.

Watch out for snakes!

Dingo

See, I don't know what gets a mob of cattle to jump, like. Maybe they're just spooky or maybe they're dreaming. I mean, the quails could've upset them through the day and when they lay there at night-time they dream that the birds are coming. And it mightn't only be the quails because when we was droving down the Georgina another bloody thing that used to kick them bullocks away was them little budgerigars that nested in them low-set gidgee trees, about so high. And then there's the kite hawks. During the day they fly down into the cattle trying to get at the little birds.

See, when you're droving, it's like follow-the-leader. First the cattle come along and disturb the ground which upsets the little birds—the quail, the budgerigars, the finches and all that—then the kite hawks come in to kill the little birds for tucker. So yes, those kite hawks, they follow you all the time, looking for a bit of dinner, and they might even find a lizard or a snake if they're lucky.

It's the same with the old dingo, he trots along, away in the background, looking for his bit of dinner, too. Like, when you kill a beast for your tucker, you generally lay it out on a bloody windbreak or the bushes, about a quarter of a mile upwind from where you've camped your bloody cattle. Then for that first night you just bring in, say, the rib bones or whatever. So then in the night, the little old dingo might trot up and grab a bit of that fresh meat from off the bushes before you load it up in your packs, or 'chest bruisers' as we called them, the next morning.

Now by saying the 'little' dingo, I mean some of them are fair brutes of dogs, like. We shoot quite a few to keep them away from our calves. And these days I've got a big four-wheel motorbike that I poke about on, and when you can lay the hindquarters of a dingo over one side of the bike and his head hangs down over the other side, well, he's a fair lump of young yumpy, aye.

Dingoes often trot along behind the drover looking for their bit of tucker, too.

And I also hang a few on the netting fence just to show the Good Samaritan neighbours that I got him. And I hang them by the bloody shank, from the top wire of the fence, and his head touches the ground. I mean, that's a good 6 foot. And they're only the young dogs because the old fellers are too cunning.

But there's been some mean dingoes, I tell you. One time, when we were droving over near the Northern Territory–Queensland border, Dad used to make me and the brother, Dave, go out to do the horsetailing together so that one feller could watch the other feller's back, in case the dingoes went for him. Oh yes, they'd go for you. That was around 1950, down along the Georgina. I mean, they called them dingoes but they were just too big, you know. I still reckon that the domestic dog was well bred into them, even back then, because they were huge crossbred-looking things.

And, also at that time there was a tale going around about how some dingoes had put a blackfella up a tree, there at Urandangi. So they must've been pretty bad, aye. Apparently this old blackfella was walking along and these big dogs, they went after him so he shot up the nearest tree and he sat up there all bloody night until they finally left him alone.

Then when he got back to the camp his mates said, 'Where you been?' Because the thing was, when he went missing, his mates just thought that he'd gone off chasing a bit of that sweet stuff. You know what I mean by 'sweet stuff', don't you—a woman. But then he told them how the dingoes had put him up a tree.

So that was his story. And a lot of people believed him, me included, because I knew them dogs out there were real bad. And even now, you get them big fellers trotting along behind you. And I reckon, all you'd have to do is fall over and injure yourself and they'd be into you like a shot. Oh yes, they'd be more than keen to give you a helping hand into the next part of the world, I can tell you. So they're a big bloody dog, the old dingo, aye.

Dishonesty Never Pays

I was born and bred into droving. It was through the whole family, the grandparents and all. Our grandfather almost made it to a hundred but he died when he was ninety-nine and seven months, and he spent a lot of time droving up there in the ranges around Mount Jimbour and all them places in the south-east of Queensland. So before I was twelve or thirteen I was with Dad, helping him take cattle down to the sales in Ipswich. Sometimes we even went down to Brisbane. There was a meatworks and saleyards there, too.

Then I also learnt whip-cracking and how to break in horses and I got into the rodeo game. I remember the first time I ever rode at a rodeo was at Brookfield, on me thirteenth birthday. And I tell you, that mongrel of a buck-jumper came out of them gates and he lined up a hurdle out there in the ring and he went straight over the top of it. But I stuck to him, and I rode him out, over the hurdle and all. I did me ten seconds, all right. But then we had a couple of uncles who had a droving plant, so I thought, 'Oh well, I might as well go droving, too.'

And we'd go all over the place; all over Queensland and that. We were never out of work. Like, we also did mustering for shearing and so forth because droving doesn't go all the year around. But we'd go to the sales and different fellers there would buy stock and they'd wanted them delivered out to their property. See, even if it was only a dozen or so, here and there, you could end up with a couple of hundred head. And if we didn't do the smaller ones, we knew that we wouldn't get the bigger jobs. That's how it worked.

Then we also worked for the bigger companies like Vesteys and Wincom Carson and Goldsborough Mort. That was later on when I was based out in central Queensland, at a little place called Geera, about 11 mile this side of Barcaldine. So they might have a mob over at one place and they'd ask you to come out and take them somewhere else. I mean, just to get out to where the mob was, it might take two or three days. And then you had to be careful because sometimes there was a bit of a catch because you mightn't be paid until you actually got to where you picked the mob up. There was none of this being paid for all the travelling out there.

Then of course, in those days us drovers were only packhorse drovers. There was no motorbikes or anything; no road trains. And at times, back in the '50s, the stock were so poor that you could only walk them a few miles a day. So sometimes we could be a month on the road just to take them a hundred mile because the only way they'd pick up a bit of condition was to walk them for a couple of days then let them feed out for a couple of days. And you'd be flat out getting the equal of five to six dollars a day, plus your keep. You always had your keep, of course, and that helped.

But like I said, there's seasons to droving so in the off-season you had to find something else to do, and that's how I started travelling with Stan Gill's sideshow. What happened there was that Stan had a famous buck-jumper, a horse called Red River, and they used to give a prize of eight quid to anyone who could ride him for ten seconds. Anyway, they were at the Lowood Show one year. Lowood's up on the Brisbane Valley line, up Esk way and that, Yarraman, and them places. So I decided to have a go on this Red River and Stan said, 'Well, if yer can ride him yer got a job.' So I did. I rode him, and that's when I started working for the Gills.

And I had a great time riding around the rodeo tent and the sideshows. I actually liked it so much that I stayed with Stan for the couple of years, right up until he got shot at Gayndah. See, Stan had another buck-jumper, The Gyra Ghost. A good horse he was, too. But Stan wouldn't let anyone ride this Gyra Ghost that had any sting in them, and there was this bloke who had lots of sting in him so Stan wouldn't let him ride the horse.

'No,' he said. 'Yer can't ride him.'

Anyways this bloke got in a huff. So away he went. Then when he come back he had a gun and Stan was standing out the front of the tent and this feller up and shot Stan, just like that. But they

Breaking in a horse.

were great people, the Gills. I mean, I liked travelling with them because, like the droving, you were in a different place every couple of nights. See, it's that freedom.

Then I got married when I was twenty-three, and not even that stopped me droving because I'd go out and get the wild cattle that ran off the ranges. They weren't used of being handled so we couldn't leave them out in the paddock of a night. You had to hold them in the dip yards.

So anyhow, this mob, the wild cattle, we brought them through from Mantuan Downs and we got within 10 mile of Alpha and the boys reckoned that, by that stage, they'd settled down enough to be left out for the last night and not put in the yards. So that's what we did. We left them out. Then at about three o'clock in the morning they rushed. And you should've heard them. You could hear trees and fencing wire breaking for miles.

But we never lost a beast. The next morning we went back to where we'd been the day before and there they were, all standing out along the road. The only trouble was that they'd picked up a few extras from out of the paddocks that they'd rushed through, so we had to muster them out. But we had them all marked. We knew whose was whose. See, each time we went through a boundary we'd check them in and then we'd check them out again, just to make sure we hadn't picked up any spare cattle.

We were pretty sharp about that. I mean, some drovers used to pick up a few along the way, duff them, like. But we didn't. And that's why I say, dishonesty never pays, not in the long run, anyway. I don't care what you do, droving or whatnot, you have to be honest because, if you didn't, you'll finish up in big trouble.

See, cattleduffing was still pretty frequent in them days. Like one time we were coming through from Springsure and this bloke came up saying how he wanted a job. Anyway, I looked him up and down and he seemed like a bit of a ring-in to me. 'We'll have to be a bit careful here,' I said to meself. Anyhow, he was with us for a couple of days, then on the third day some coppers met us up the road and lo and behold, this feller turned out to be one of the bloody police squad. What they were doing, see, was checking if we were picking up any spares on the way through; duffing, like. Oh, they did a lot of that checking. Up on the Carnarvon Ranges, anywhere, you could rest assured that a stock inspector or one of the police'd meet you somewhere along the road.

So then I did the droving up until about '72 or '73, until I had to give it up. I would've only been around forty or so by then, so I was still young. But see, I had this brain tumour and I couldn't sit in the saddle any more. Actually I was flat out sitting in the car. So I had one thirteen-hour operation in the theatre to cut the tumour out, and over the years I've spent quite a lot of other times back in the hospital, as well. But I guess it could've been worse. You look around and there's always someone worse off than yourself, aye.

But I never give up. That's why I got back into this whip cracking. I'd done it when I was a kid and once you get the hang of it you never get out of it. So now I go to a lot of shows. I've even won some ribbons. I won the sash at the Australian Stockman's Hall of Fame, back in 1996. So that was pretty good, aye.

But droving was a great life, especially if you were a non-drinker. It'd suit you then. Also you're not tied up to a boss or anything. And you covered a lot of country because you wouldn't have to stay in the one place. But it's like anything else, aye, if you love it, it's a great life. I mean, even after thirty years, I just can't keep away from the saleyards. They still attract me.

First Day Out

In 1932 there was a partial drought all over Queensland, particularly up there around the Winton–Longreach area, and that's the year my father took up with Albert Clarke. Albert was a Charleville drover, and this all took place on a droving trip out from Dalgonally Station, which is up on the Flinders River, north of Julia Creek, in north-western Queensland.

Anyhow, there was four of us to start with. There was Albert, who was the boss drover, and my Dad, who was the horsetailer. Then there was the cook, Billy Moore, and there was me. I was only seventeen at that time. Now because of the drought, my father and I, along with Billy Moore, we took the horses up from Charleville a couple of months early so that they'd have a chance to freshen up before we used them on this particular droving trip. Then for those couple of months, Dad and me worked on Dalgonally, mustering the cattle. I forget what Billy Moore, the cook, done during that meantime but, just when we were about to start this droving trip, Albert came up and he joined us.

So we set out and we followed the Gilliat Creek—or Gilliat River as they called it—south, down to near the township of Gilliat. Gilliat's only a railway siding, with a pub and a couple of houses. It's about ten mile or so out from Julia Creek. And that's where Albert Clarke brought in this extra stockman, just to give us a hand.

Now I can't remember how this bloke got out from Julia Creek, but he turned up at the camp one morning, ready to work. So off we went. Then later on, as we were rounding the cattle up at camp, this new feller, he was riding one side of the cattle and I was riding the other side. It was near on dark; the night of the same day this new stockman had come out to help us.

So we were just about to bed the cattle down when, the next thing, they scattered. Just like that, these cattle scattered. 'Good

The next thing, the cattle scattered.

heavens,' I thought. Now I was still on my horse so I started off riding around the mob to see what had happened. Then halfway around, my father came out to meet me. 'Don't you go around there,' he said.

'Why?' I asked.

Now I don't know exactly what happened but, all I can think of was, this new feller's horse'd tripped or something and apparently it'd fallen over on top of him, and it broke the feller's neck.

Anyhow Tommy Scanlon, who owned the pub in at Gilliat, he come down in his car. Then the next thing, the police came out from Julia Creek and they took the body away.

So we got this feller out earlier that day and by night-time he was dead, and I never even got to know his name. But that Tommy Scanlon, later on of course, he went over and he got the Argent Hotel in Mount Isa.

First Past the Post

I've worked in droving camps and stations with a lot of Aborigines, or Murries as they're called up in the Gulf, and I've got a great respect for them. I even claim to be the only white person since the landing of the First Fleet that's named my two sons after the tribal name of an Aboriginal—Tahmal Meenyarrawal. Tahmal, meaning the 'ringtail possum' and Meenyarrawal, meaning 'his tracks go back'.

That all came about in between droving seasons when I was working up in north-western Queensland, out of a place called Glenora. This's just after the wet season. Anyway, one night one of the whitefellers, a feller by the name of Chalkley, hit the grog pretty heavy and he started mixing brake fluid with essence of lemon. Now, taking into account that brake fluid's got about 30 per cent alcohol and you add the alcohol from the lemon essence to that, then you can imagine what sort of mess he ended up making of himself.

So the next morning when we were getting ready to go out on the run, one of the packhorses knocked this Chalkley feller over. By that stage he's still half drunk and there's a big blue. So anyway he chucks in the towel and he resigns. Then because it's Thursday—the day the rail motor comes down from Croydon to Normanton—the head stockman says, 'Goldie,' (that's what they called me, see, because my name's Goldsmith) 'Goldie,' he said, 'go 'n' run Chalkley down to the siding.'

By this stage, Chalkley's saddling up a night horse to ride down to the siding. Anyhow, it's smoko and everyone's gone up to the kitchen, so I go and gets a Land Rover to take him down to the siding.

'Don't be a blackfella, Chalk,' I said to him. 'I'll run yer down to the siding,' I said, then I grabbed his port and I threw it in the back of the Land Rover.

Aborigine with tribal markings.

Anyhow, he had a rifle laying on his swag and he eyed me and he said, 'Put that back or I'll drill yer.'

Now I only thought he was joking. But he wasn't. He up with the rifle, and he pulls the trigger and near blows the heel right off me riding boot. So I dive around behind the horse and I'm singing out to him, 'Hey, come on Chalk, don't be silly.' And I'm also thinking that they must've heard the gun shot from up the kitchen and they'd be down in a flash. But they didn't; either didn't or they'd all gone into hiding.

Anyhow, all the blacks were out under the tree having their smoko too, and there's a Murri there called Lightning, and this Lightning, he sees all this and he says to this other Murri, Tahmal Meenyarrawal (his English name was Adrian), 'Adrian,' Lightning said, 'that man Chalkman bin' tryin' to shoot Johnny.'

Anyway, I take a look from under the horse's neck and this Chalkley, he has another go at me and the bullet goes through the stockmen's quarters, just behind me. So now I'm starting to think how I can get to me own gun, an old Winchester lever action .32, which was just behind the door of the stockmen's quarters.

Now where the meat house was, from there to where I was would've been a good chain or a chain and a half. Anyhow, I look up and I see Tahmal Meenyarrawal creeping up on this Chalkley. He was only about eighteen at the time and he had his tribal scars. This was back in the days when they were still doing that. Now, I dare not look at the big Murri because it'd give him away and Chalkley would've turned around and shot him.

But just then, from under the horse I see the shadow of Chalkley and his rifle coming at me. So I jumped. And just as he was about to shoot me, Tahmal Meenyarrawal grabbed Chalkley with his big arms and, as he does, the gun goes off and the bullet misses me by a whisker.

Then of course, now that it's safe, all the whitefellers come running out of the kitchen.

Anyhow, later on I tried to get Tahmal Meenyarrawal a bravery award. But I left the run too late because it was when Bjelke-Petersen was the Premier of Queensland and he didn't have a very good reputation with the Murries. So he missed out. Then he died not so long ago.

But something fantastic. See, back in the early '80s I lived in Cairns and Tahmal Meenyarrawal came all the way from the Kowanyama, away over there on the other side of Cape York Peninsula; he came over just for both my sons' twenty-first birthdays. And I can tell you, he was so proud that a whitefeller'd named his sons after him, especially it being his tribal name.

But there's lots of stories like that up there. Nowadays, those things are lost in history. I mean, the Kalala blacks were still spearing the whites right up until 1948. On Rutland Plains Station, down at the horse yard there's two graves and it's got 'So-and-so and so-and-so, speared by blacks—1949.' So it was as late as that.

Bush grave.

But it worked both ways. Take that copper, Bowman, up in Rutland Plains. Back around 1910 he used to go out with the station owner and shoot the blacks for sport. Oh, and he used to play up with the gins something terrible, as well. Anyway, there was a young Aboriginal kid named Splinter and he made a special spear just to get Bowman. The first 2 foot was made out of a heavy red wood and the other 6 foot was white wood. And he'd sing over this spear like the blackfellas do over special things.

Then Splinter set a trap. When he saw Bowman coming along on his horse he got this pretty young gin, about fourteen, to beckon him. So Bowman sees her and he thinks this gin's a pretty good thing so he trots over with the intention of riding her. But the young gin just keeps a bit in front of him, leading him along like, deeper into the tall grass. So Bowman gets off his horse and he follows her and Splinter's waiting in the grass. Then when he gave a bird call, the gin dropped down and Splinter jumps up out of the grass and he threw the spear and it went right through Bowman's forehead and it come out about 8 inches the other side. And that's true. Bowman's grave's still there. I've got a photo of it.

So there's lots of those untold stories, and they're stories that should be told.

But with the droving, there's one incident I'll never forget. See, back in the early '50s there were still a few bush Murries roaming around. I say a few because the missionaries used to send out other Murries to coax them in, especially on the Mungana Stock Route. But anyhow, I had this pocket watch, one with Roman figures on it; not numbers but Roman figures.

So we're taking bullocks from the Gulf down to Julia Creek this time, and one of the Murries I had droving with me—he'd been working out on one of the wings—he come around and he said, 'Johnny, him big Murri up a tree like him goanna.'

I'm at the tail, see, so I go over and there's this bush Murri. He must've seen the bullocks coming and he scarped it up the tree to wait until they passed by. Now I could see that he hadn't had much contact with whites. He had no shirt on and bit of a pair of trousers. His tribal scars were prominent, across his chest and down his arms. He had a sugar bag, his spear and his woomera, and he also had his firestick for when he wanted to light a fire.

So I says, 'Where you bin go bunjie (friend)?'

'Bin so-and-so, down that-a-way.' It was to a place not far from Julia Creek, a couple of hundred mile away.

Anyway, this fella spoke very poor English but I thought I might be able to use him, so I said, 'You bin tell 'em when other Murri he come along with yarraman (horse), you bin tell him boss says you come along with him.'

'Yeah, right-o boss.'

Then one of the Murries got him and give him a shirt and we saddled one of the packhorses for him, and when we get him up to camp that night, one of the other Murries makes up a bit of a swag for him. Then I got him to wash his hands and we give him a feed.

So I kept him for a couple of days, then I said, 'Now look here bunjie.' What was his name, now? I think it was something like . . . yes, that's right, it was Strike-a-light. So I said, 'Strike-a-light, you bin watchin' them other Murries riding around them minya (cattle). Now you ride around night-time 'n' watch them minya too.'

'Yeah, right-o boss,' he says.

So I got him to ride around with some of the Murries so he'd get the hang of it. Then when I thought he was ready, I decided to give him a go.

Now at midnight, bullocks always stand up and wander off to have a bit of a pick and a crap. You can just about put the clock to it. So I made sure that, just after midnight, I had them all settled down again and then I go to this Strike-a-light.

'Right-o Strike-a-light,' I said. 'Now you bin do 'em watch now like 'em migalo (white man).'

'Yeah boss. Yeah boss.'

So I took out me watch, the one with the Roman figures on it, and I tied a bit of string on it and I tied it around his shirt. Now it was obvious that he'd never seen a watch before so I explained what I wanted him to do.

'You bin watchin' here,' I say, and he looks at the watch. 'See, there's a little man 'n' a big man (the hour and minute hands). The little man he bin goin' across that first post (one o'clock). Then he bin' goin' across to second post (two o'clock). Now the big man, he bin' goin' right around 'n' around, all same along'a boundary rider. So when him come up 'n' meet the little man at the second post, you bin come 'n' wake me up.'

'Yeah boss. Yeah boss.'

Then to make it clearer, I wound the watch around again. Then I made him repeat it a couple of times just to make sure he's got the hang of it.

'Yeah boss, him bin right boss.'

Anyhow, there's these two dingoes that trot into camp but I don't worry about them, I just go and lay down and I listen to this Strike-a-light sing. And oh, I tell you, there's nothing more wonderful than to hear the Murries sing in their own lingo as they go around the bullocks. It's really something.

So I get to sleep and I vaguely remember the horsetailer getting up. He's the first one up, see, so it would've been well past 2 a.m. But I'm sort of having a good sleep. Then when I hear the cook start stirring the fire, I wake up in a bit of a panic and I look around for this Murri. 'Oh,' I think, 'the bugger's cleared out on me.'

But then I see him, he's on his horse, around the other side of the mob.

'Hey, Strike-a-light!' I call out.

'Yeah, boss.'

'You bin come here.'

So he comes around.

'Where's bin watch?' I ask.

'Here, boss,' he says and he gets off the horse and I get the watch and I put it to me ear and it's still ticking away, beautiful.

'Why you for no bin come 'n' wake me up, Strike-a-light?'

'Well, boss,' he says. 'I bin watchin' that little man boss, watchin' him go past that first post, so I put him in me pocket and I sing him songs around minya 'n' I bin lookin' watch again boss, 'n' he bin comin' round 'n' that big man him bin goin' round the boundary. So I put him back in me pocket 'n' I ride 'em round minya again, singin' 'em songs 'n' I bin watchin' him again 'n' that little fella he bin comin' up real close that second post 'n' that big man he bin comin' right up too so I put him back in pocket 'n' I bin ridin' round minya 'n' I bin singin' 'em songs 'n', when I look again boss, that little man him bin gone right past that post, chasin' that big man. So I bin tryin' to catch him next time. But I keep missin' him, boss. I miss him past the post, every time.'

First Trip

Back in '57 I was working on Dotswood Station, which is up in north-eastern Queensland, north-west of Townsville. In those days Dotswood was around 1260 square mile, covering the area between Keel Bottom Creek and the Star River. Facing west was the Burdekin River. At the top end there's the Three River's Hotel, the pub that Slim Dusty sung about. On the eastern side you've got the Harveys Range, the high country where the Black Hawk helicopters went down a few years ago.

At that stage, Dotswood was owned by William Angliss and was part of a big chain of stations, along the main stock route coming in from the north. Quilps, the part of Dotswood where I was, was the bullock camp for the company. Wando Vale and all those bullocks came in through Dotswood. The Gulf bullocks came down through there as well. They all walked down to the Star River.

From Dotswood the bullocks went down to the Queensland Meat Exports at Ross River, near Townsville. So on my very first droving trip we left Dotswood with around five hundred Brahmans and, on our second night, we camped the bullocks in a wire yard. I was doing the cooking and the horsetailing, so part of my job was to get up before dawn, catch the horses, unhobble them, put the hobbles around their necks, bring them back to camp then hobble them again so the guys could easily catch them when we were going to head out.

But never having been droving before, when I brought the horses back in, I made the mistake of bringing them in on the wrong side of the camp fire. Now by the wrong side, I mean that I took the horses in between the fire and the wire yard where the bullocks were. And of course, all these great shadows got thrown up and they spooked the bullocks. So they jumped up and tried to rush

Many young fellers start out working on station properties before going droving.

and you could hear their horns rattling and the wires singing as they hit the fence. Now luckily, those ones didn't break through, but I'd learned my lesson and we never had any dramas after that.

So then we walked out to the top of Harveys Range. And I remember there were bits of corroded copper sticking out of the rocks where it'd eroded away. They were all green, just like horseshoe nails, almost like a copper wire. And where we camped that night was really thick with possums and they were forever trying to get at our food. So to make it harder for them, we built a tent-like frame and from the crossbar we hung the pack bags and also the bread, on a bit of rope. And I remember eating around the camp fire that night with all these possums sitting around in a ring, watching our every move. And later in the night you'd hear fellers swearing and going on with the possums scurrying in, trying to get to the food.

Then the next day we went down the Harveys Range. Bullocks had been going through there for quite a few years and in doing so they'd made track-like grooves down the range, which had deepened through erosion. In some places they were almost as deep as a bullock, so when it got damp, the cattle just sat on their butts and slid down in these grooves.

The horses did the same. You'd get your horse on its rump and it'd slide down the gradient. And when we were going down, I remember looking over my shoulder and seeing all these bullocks coming down right behind me and I was hoping they wouldn't roll because, if they did, they might've well brought the lot of us down.

Then from the bottom of Harveys Range we crossed Ross River, up where Rasmussen is today. From then on it was nearly all Chiney apple trees. Chiney apples came out during the goldfields days. They were a little yellow apple that grew very bitter. When they dried they looked like a checker. And we also had a dickens of a job getting the bullocks through that area because of the Townsville lucerne. Once they got on that, they didn't want to move.

But we finally delivered them to the Queensland Meat Exports. It's gone now. Where we dropped the bullocks off is now Annandale, one of the top suburbs, right across from where the army is now. And all the streets have names of the stations, where all the cattle came from. And where we slept—a tin shed that'd only hold about four or five guys—now there's all these flash houses. And the fellers'd go into town and come back out drunk and sleep there the night, then head up north again the next day.

And on the way back, because we only had the horses and the packhorses, we left after lunch and we reached the foot of the Harveys Range. And there was a big fig tree, and I remember camping in the swag and listening to these strange coughing noises. And it was those big kangaroo rats jumping around among us, checking for food, and they'd cough as they jumped. They were a fair size too, about half a metre or so.

So I reckon there'd been so many drovers going through that way that both the possums and these kangaroo rats hung about because they thought there'd be some pretty fair pickings, you know. And that was in about '56 or '57 when droving was twenty pound a week and keep, and a ringer got about fifteen pound per week and keep. Some of the better guys might've got a bit more.

Fix the Fence

Our property was settled in something like 1915; around Blighty, down near the Victorian border, between Deniliquin and Finley. Anyhow, by the '50s, when I was still a young feller and money was pretty scarce, well, the fences on the farm weren't up to scratch, and as they fell over we'd just go along and stick in a few steel posts to prop them back up. But the road fence was the real big problem. Now, I don't know if you know or not but some of these bastards of crossbred sheep are real little buggers at getting through fences, even good ones. And that's what I had, crossbreds, so I was forever getting the dog to go out and get these sheep off the road and bring them back into the paddock.

Now as an aside and in conjunction with this story, one day I wanted to take some sheep over to the brother's place to agist them. He lived down the road a bit. But as soon as me dog saw the sheep out on the road, he was out like a shot and he rounded them up and he put them back into the paddock. Now he was a pretty intelligent dog, as you might imagine, so I sort of talked to him in the way that didn't hurt his feelings and that he thought he'd done a real good job, because that's what he normally done—go and get the escaped sheep off the road and put them back in the paddock. And he did that job very good.

Then I went on and explained to him how, on this particular occasion, things were different because I was taking the sheep to me brother's place. So we got it all sorted out, and he seemed fine with that. So then I took the sheep back out of the paddock again and back out onto the road and, like in a flash, the dog was off and he rounded them up again, and he put them back in the paddock.

Anyway, I went through the whole process again; talking to me dog, explaining the situation until he seemed to understand. So

'Well, the fences on the farm weren't up to scratch.'

then I got the sheep back out onto the road, and lo and behold, the dog's out there again, and he's done the same thing.

Now, by that stage I'd come to realise that there was nothing I could do or explain to me dog that'd make him do otherwise. In his own mind, getting the sheep off the road and back into the paddock was his job, and he was going to stick to it by hook or by crook.

'This's no good,' I said to the dog. 'This's no good at all.'

So in the end, I tied him up and I got the sheep out the gate and down the road a bit before I went back and untied him. And it was only when he saw that the sheep were meant to be out on the road, heading down to me brother's place, that it all twigged in his brain. So he was satisfied to give me a hand after that.

But getting back to the story; see, because of the poor state of the fences I was forever getting sheep off the road, well, me dog was, anyway. Then one morning, the neighbour rang and told me that he'd seen some of me sheep out on the road.

'Oh yeah,' I said. 'What's new. I'll get the dog onto it straight away.'

'Yeah,' he said, 'when I was going into town I noticed them out on the road. But then, when I was coming back home,' he said,

'I passed a drover with a big mob'a merinos and I swear he had a few of your crossbreds in with them.'

Now these crossbreds stick out because merino sheep have got a darker sort of wool than the crossbreds. The merino wool; I don't know if it's because of the grease or not, but the wool really collects the dust, while the crossbred's wool stays whiter.

'Anyway,' the neighbour said, 'I reckon that the drover might'a nicked a few of yer sheep.'

'Oh well,' I thought, 'bugger that.'

So I got me dog and we jumped into the ute and off we went.

Anyhow, it'd rained a few days beforehand so we could track where the drover's sheep'd been paddling their way up the road, and it looked like they were heading along the highway into Finley. Now out our way there's all these crossroads and side roads that go off to the various farms, and it come to the stage where these sheep tracks disappeared off the main road.

'Oh well,' I said, 'he must've taken them down that side road, there.'

So we tracked them down there for about half a mile until we come to the next crossroad where he'd turned off again. So we followed them down there for half a mile only to find that he'd turned off again.

'This's funny,' I said to the dog.

So we continued on tracking this drover and he kept on turning down all these little side roads until, as it turned out, he'd nearly brung them right back around to my place. Now by this stage, it was near on bloody dark so we followed them down another side road and that's where we found him. There was just him, a horse and a few dogs and I reckon he might've had six or seven hundred head of sheep, and in among them were a few of mine.

'Hey,' I said to this drover, 'yer've got some of me sheep.'

And he said, 'Well, blowed if I've see'd 'em.'

So I said, 'Look, it's easy.' Then I explained about the different colour of the wool between the merino types and the crossbreds.

'Well, if I never,' he said.

Anyhow, there was at least fifteen of mine in there. So the dog got them out and I tied their legs and put them in the back of the ute, to get them home.

But I just couldn't believe how this drover would come along and take my sheep. Then I started to wonder just how many of everyone else's sheep he'd also picked up along the way. And then it twigged. See, down this particular road where we found him, it was very lonely, and what I reckon was that he'd fence the sheep off. Then when it got dark, his wife or whoever would come along with a trailer and pick up all the sheep he'd nicked along the way and take them back to his own place. I mean, it was a nice little earner, nicking sheep. I really should've gone to the police and got the bugger locked up or something.

Anyhow, after that experience I went and fixed up the road fence. And a funny thing, as an aside to and in conjunction with that, I used to do a stocktake of the sheep. Like, I'd work out from one year to the next, just how many sheep I started with, how many I'd bought and how many were born, then I'd subtract from that how many I'd sold and how many had died. And the figures always used to come out all wrong. But after I fixed up the road fence, I never lost any more sheep. Not a one. So that's some of these drovers for you. They're scoundrels.

Follow the Leader

With the stolen generation . . . well, for me it was a positive thing you know, because without that I would've grown up in an Aborigine camp and I would've stayed there. I wouldn't have had the opportunity of being a head stockman or going droving, or doing what I'm doing today.

But everybody had it different. Some of the other kids had it much harder. I never really had it that hard. I had it hard in a different way. I missed my mother and all that, yeah. That was hard. But it's the mothers; I feel very, very sorry for all those mothers that had their children taken away, far more than I feel sorry for myself. Yes, I think the poor old mother suffered more than the kids did. I'm sure of that.

But a lot of them kids that were taken away, well, they didn't have the . . . I don't know what you'd say. We all had the same teaching but some of us just wanted to go further, I suppose. It's the same with everybody in life. It doesn't matter whatever you are, if you've got the drive and you really want to do things, then you do them. But you've gotta want to. That's important. And also, I think I was very lucky that I had good people around me, all the time. They taught me stuff and I took it all in; people like the Blythe family that took me away from the Aborigine camp.

See, there was three Blythe brothers: Gordon, Keith and Doug. Keith was the owner of Glenroy Station and he was the one that took me away, up to the homestead, you know, and he give me the job as head stockman. So I must've done something right for him, aye. He's passed away now but he must've seen I had some potential. And it was a big job too because I was head stockman of everybody, both black and white. The whole lot. I was in charge of the thing; second to the manager, who was like an overseer. And at seventeen years of age, yeah, that was a big order.

So I was at Glenroy from 1950 to 1955, then from there I went to Kimberley Downs Station, again as head stockman. Kimberley Downs is also in the north of Western Australia. And there's a story about when we took a mob of bullocks to Derby, over on the coast. Now I was never the boss drover on these trips. That was more of a whitefellers job. I was just one of the party. But it was all pack-horse. There was no motor vehicles involved. We carted everything.

Anyhow, it was my first droving trip from Kimberley Downs and what happened was that the station plant went with us for two or three days, to help settle the bullocks down. Then after the bullocks had settled, the drover then took them over.

So it was only the second night out and the cattle were pretty fresh, still unsettled. But I was on the watch, me and another bloke, and we had a rush and the cattle rushed straight at me. And to make it more frightening it was bright moonlight so I could see them coming at me. So I took off and I rode flat out, trying to get away from them. But they must've thought I was the lead beast so it was like follow the leader. And I ended up in a big breakaway— a gully coming into the river—and once I was in there, there was no way out. So these cattle, they just kept going with me along this breakaway, and the faster I went, the faster they went.

Then when I finally got out and up on the flat, they followed me up there too. But now, because I was on a wider area, I turned off and let them go past me. Then once they'd gone past, I wheeled out around them and blocked them up. And that was the most terrifying thing that's ever happened to me while I was out droving. By gee, I was frightened.

But also on that same trip, another thing happened that was sort of funny. See, it was also my first experience of going into tidal mudflats and I didn't know at the time but you get a very high tide in Derby: almost 40-foot tides. And when that happens the water flows out onto this huge tidal mudflat. It might only be six or eight inches deep but it goes right out, very wide.

Anyhow, on the day we arrived with these cattle the tide was very high, right up against the bank, so we had to walk them across this mudflat for about a mile. But the thing that put the

'Look out for the crocodiles, they'll eat yer.'

wind up me was that, as we were about to go over the tidal flat, the other Aborigines were saying to me, 'Look out for the crocodiles, they'll eat yer. Look out for the crocodiles, they'll eat yer.'

And being my first time into Derby, I didn't know that they was only pulling my leg. So I was pretty nervy, aye. So then, while we were going across, my eyes were sticking out, looking here, looking there and looking everywhere, for all these crocodiles. And there was a lot of logs floating around too, moving with the tide, and the more I looked at them moving, the more they was moving around like I imagined a crocodile would move. So yeah, that put the wind up me a real fair bit, too.

Go Away Back

I'll tell you just how good them border collies are. I'd been away out the back country at a place called Coombie Station. Coombie's out the other side of the Lachlan River, there in south-western New South Wales. From Griffith you go to Hillston then you go out behind Roto and, if you're lucky, you'll find Coombie Station.

Anyhow out that way they moved a hell of a lot of sheep around the place. But the manager bloke at Coombie had a border collie. And that dog was held in such high regard by the manager that, when it wasn't working, it'd ride around, not in the back of the Land Rover ute, like you'd expect, but right up there in the front, sitting beside the bloke himself.

I remember one time when it was pouring down with rain and a bloke said to this manager, 'Can yer give me a ride?'

'Yeah,' said the manager, 'hop in the back.'

Well you should've seen the look on that bloke's face. 'Hang on a tick,' he said. 'How's about I hop in the front out'a the rain and the dog gets in the back.'

'Not on yer life,' said the manager bloke. 'That dog rides up front with me.'

So there, that's how highly he thought of his dog. Anyhow a few days later I was working some sheep and the same manager bloke arrived with his border collie and he said, 'I'll take a few of these wethers up to the house fer killers.'

'That's fine by me,' I said.

Then he said, 'Look, I want to see you up at the house, about some business. Jump in the Land Rover and the dog'll take care of the sheep.'

So we drove back about six mile to the house and we were sitting around on the verandah talking business and I happened to say, 'How long'll the dog be?'

'Oh, yer don't have to worry about that dog,' he said. 'It's coming.'

Well, it wasn't that long before the border collie appeared with these wethers. And I don't think the bloke had spoken one word to the dog. He didn't need to. It just knew what it was supposed to do. So anyway, when the dog got nearer the house, the manager bloke, he just walked over to the gate and he opened it. And that dog wandered up with those sheep and took them right through the gate and up to the yard. Like, you wouldn't find two dogs in Australia who could do that.

Oh, them border collies, they're amazing.

Then I had another experience with a border collie. It was a while after when I went out droving with a bloke. Then there was also an old feller. I forget who he was, just now. Oh that's right, he was me father-in-law! Blimey, how could I forget that! Anyhow, me father-in-law had a border collie that he wasn't using and when they haven't got any work they get bored and go a bit ratty, which was what this particular dog had done. He was still only a pup like, about eighteen months. Anyhow the father-in-law said to me, 'Look, this dog's never done no work so take it with yer and see if yer can get a bit'a brains into it.'

Anyhow off we went droving a mob of wethers; the drover bloke, the dog and me. And I just forget where we were, but this night the bloke who was droving with me, well, he woke up and all the wethers had taken off. So he woke me up.

'All the fuckin' sheep've gone!' he said.

So anyhow, I let the father-in-law's border collie go, like. And as you do, I said to the dog, 'Go away back.' And that dog, like I said he hadn't had any training but he was off like a shot, off into the dark. 'Well, here's a go,' I said to meself. 'This's gonna be interesting.'

This's all around midnight, like, and the dog'd taken off. So I saddled up me horse and I hopped onto it and I trotted and I trotted. Then just on daylight I caught up with the dog and he was bringing the mob of wethers back. And like I said, that border collie pup hadn't had any training whatsoever.

'Well,' I said to meself, 'if I never.'

So at that point, I wanted to see just how good this dog of me father-in-law's was, so I went up the back of the mob and checked their tracks. And that dog'd got them in so tight that he'd kept them right on the track, right along the stock route fence line, like. And what's more, he'd got the whole lot of them; the whole bloody lot. Oh, I tell you he was just a born, natural worker. No doubt about it. So then I just sat back on the horse and I took it easy and that dog . . . well, he brought that mob of sheep right back to camp.

Like I said, them border collies, they're unreal.

Harry Tilberoo

My husband looked more after the stock while I looked after the staff and that. So when it come to hiring the ringers, he'd say, 'Oh, can you go into town and find a feller?'

So then I'd go in and go to the different companies and that, and I'd ask if they knew anyone who was looking for droving work. Then if they did, I'd go and see the feller. And if he said 'Yes', well then, I'd lay it on the line and I'd say, 'I'll expect no more or no less of you than what I can do.'

But mostly, I preferred to employ the younger ones, around seventeen and that, because they were the better workers. For some reason they were more willing to learn, while the older ones, say between twenty and thirty, even though half of them had never been out droving, they seemed to be the know-it-alls, and their attitude was, 'Well, if you can bloody well do it, so can I.' Meaning they thought it'd be easy, just because I was a woman.

'Well okay,' I'd say. 'Fair enough. I'll give you a fortnight's try.' Then I'd say, 'But even before the fortnight's up, if it looks like you can't handle the job, then you'll be sent back.'

And that's just how we did it. And we got some good ones and we got some bad ones, too. Some of the bad ones were them that went into town and got drunk and they wouldn't come back out again. And when that happened, it was nothing for the husband and me to have to spend a few nights sharing the watch until I could organise someone else to come out and help us.

But the main thing I learned was that, when you're a woman, working with men, you've got to become one of the guys. So back then I used to swear. By jeez, I did. Because, if the men started loudmouthing and that, the only thing they understood was for you to loudmouth—swear—back at them. That's the only way they understood you were fair dinkum. But there was one thing I really

Droving plant and truck.

stuck to; no one was ever to swear around the children. I really stuck to that.

But you had to be their equal, if not better. Because you do get the smart alecks and some of them would want to pick a fight with you. I guess they thought that I was gonna back down. But I wasn't gonna back down to no one. So when they shaped up at me I'd say, 'You'd better take the first punch feller, but don't miss, because I won't miss when it's my turn to have a go at you.'

So yes, I did have the smarty ones that came out droving with us. But though I might be a woman I can still pack a punch. Too right I can. And what's more, I knew where to hit too . . . Bang, right on the chin and down they'd go. Oh I've decked a few of these ringer blokes. By jeez I have. And I tell you, after they got up, they apologised for what they done. But a few of the real smarty ones, they'd say, 'Well, I've apologised to you so now you've gotta apologise back to me.'

And I'd say, 'No, I won't. You were the smarty one.'

So you had to mix it with them and you'd never let them overstep the line. And that way, they did respect you. So yes, we did get some bad ones, but we got some good ones too; people like Harry Tilberoo.

Harry would've been up from thirty or forty, so he was a lot older than the people I normally employed. He was a dark chap, very dark. He wasn't an Australian Aboriginal or that, because, as it turned out, he come from one of the islands, though I don't know which one it was.

Anyway, we were out droving one time and we came across Harry, carrying his swag along the road, and he offered to work for us, just for his keep. And I said, 'No, we don't do it that way, Harry.' But I said, 'We've got a young feller leaving in a week because he's gotta go back home.' Then I said, 'We'll put you on and if it works out, you've got the job and we'll pay you proper.'

And I found Harry to be more of a gentleman than what I found the white ones to be. Yes I did. And Harry stayed with us for three trips, he did. And he always addressed me as 'boss lady'. And sometimes it'd start to get to me, so I'd say, 'Harry, there's no need to call me "boss lady". My name's Shirley. Just call me Shirley.'

'Yes, boss lady,' he'd say.

So it was always 'boss lady'. And he was a very good worker, and he got on really well with the kids, too. Oh, he'd spoil them rotten, he would. He'd make things out of wood for them and that.

Then one trip we were with cattle, and I got up to do the night watch and when I got to the bottom of the caravan steps I fell over a body. And jeez, didn't I let go with a string of oaths. But it turned out to be old Harry. At first I thought he might've been dead or something. But anyhow he jumped up. 'Sorry, boss lady. Sorry,' he said. 'I didn't mean to frighten yer.'

And I said, 'Harry, what the hell are yer doin' here?'

'Oh,' he said, 'two bad apples yer got workin' 'ere, boss lady. They was gonna gang rape yer tonight while boss man was out.'

By 'bad apples', Harry was talking about these two white guys that we'd just employed.

So I said, 'Truly?'

'Yes, boss lady,' Harry said. 'But they was gonna have to get past Harry first, boss lady.'

So at breakfast that morning I sacked these two fellers, the ones that was going to rape me. And I said to them, 'You're very lucky fellers,' I said, 'because I always sleep with a .22 automatic right at my head.' And I said, 'Youse would'a been dead boys if you'd have tried to do anything to me.' Mind you, more likely I would've just shown them the gun and ordered them out because the children were also sleeping in the caravan.

Then these guys, after I sacked them, they cooked up a story about Harry and they went to the police. But then they didn't even have the guts to come back out again with the police. The police came out by themselves and they started going on with all these accusations about how Harry was bad news around my children, and that the kids weren't getting proper schooling and that. So then, young Lorna Sappy, she used to teach my kids. Lorna was a half-caste. Her mother was dark and her father was white. Anyhow, Lorna said to the police, 'Excuse me,' she said.

And they said, 'Who're you?'

'My name's Lorna Sappy,' she said, 'and I teach these kids their schooling.'

Then the police asked to see their school work so Lorna went and brought it out and she showed them. But by this stage I smelled a rat, so I said to the policeman, 'I bet that one of the fellers what complained to you was a feller who wears a black hat with studs in the band.'

'Yes he was,' the policeman said.

So then I explained that, if it wasn't for Harry, those two fellers would've gang raped me. But as it turned out, Harry'd apparently gotten himself in a bit of strife back over on the island from where he come from, and they were going to take him away anyway. So then I told the police what a good man he was and how, if they let him stay with us, I was prepared to take full responsibility for him and that.

But they just said, 'Sorry, we've gotta take him.'

So they took him away. They took poor old Harry away. And oh, he was so upset about that. And I felt very sorry about it too, you know, because I found him to be a really decent person, and he was respected by both my children and my husband. But no, they just took him away and apparently they sent him back to the island from where he'd come from. But oh, it was sad. That was a very, very, sad day, that was.

Itchy Feet

The droving trips down along the Snowy River, then down to the Murray and into Victoria, they were the ones, like. Gee, they were rough. It was all packhorse, and in them early days there was no roads or anything. I mean, back in the Depression they actually started to put a road in from both the Jindabyne side and the Victorian side, but they only come in about 6 mile each side and they stopped for some reason. Then they never went right through until, well, way on into the '50s or the '60s. That's the road they call the Barry Way. Tom Barry's father, he was on the Jindabyne council; he might've even been the mayor or what, I'm not sure, but they called it the Barry Way, after him.

Anyway we'd set off out of Adaminaby, and it was about 250 mile down to Bairnsdale. There'd be just two of us with a mob of four or five hundred. Then through the real rough country we'd get a bloke who lived out that way, you know, and he'd help us for three or five days, then we'd go on with them. But we'd give ourselves about twenty-four or twenty-five days, and that gave us a couple of days up our sleeve, you know, in case of floods or snow or whatever. Then if we got to Bairnsdale a day or so before the sale, we always had a paddock to put the cattle into.

But it was such tough going down that way because, along the Snowy, the mountains was so steep that you had to string the cattle along in ones or twos when they had to walk along the edge of the river. That's why we only took four hundred or so. It was too dangerous otherwise. Just to show you, after one of our earlier trips, it was written up in the Bairnsdale newspaper how we were the first drovers to arrive there with every beast we'd started out with. I couldn't believe it, but that's what was in the newspaper, anyhow.

But what made a hell of a difference was that our mobs was seasoned cattle. See, most of them had come from up north so they'd

Droving down the Snowy Way.

already been broken in to travel. That made them much stronger than fresh cattle. Because by taking fresh cattle, all the drovers before us, oh, they'd either lost stock or some had been crippled and had to be put down or they got sore-footed or something like that. Too right, I've seen it happen.

But even taking all that into account, the weather used to get real rough too, at times. Once we had twenty-two wet days and two lots of snow along that twenty-four or twenty-five day trip. And we had one camp, on the other side of Jindabyne, where we was camped in a reserve that had this old dance hall in it. They had a lot of them dance halls back then, in different places. And things got so bad outside that we used up our extra days just to camp in the hall.

Then later on, when we come out into the higher ground into Victoria, we couldn't stop at the dance hall there because we'd already lost our time. And I can tell you, it's not very nice when you're stuck in snow or it's belting down with rain and you're running out from under your tarpaulin to pack your horse of a morning. Oh, the conditions were terrible.

And people used to say, 'Why the hell do you go droving down through that country? It's such rough, tough going.'

'Oh well,' I'd say, 'it's me living and it's a part of what I love doing.' And that's what makes all the difference, doesn't it?

So I done quite a few of them trips. Then I got married in about '47 or '48 and I still did a bit of droving, but that was more taking the cattle and sheep up into the mountains and staying there with them for the summer then bringing them back. Those mobs all belonged to different fellers, like, and we just looked after them. We used to stay in an old homestead up there at the head of the Murrumbidgee River.

So we did that for a few summers, then we got a bit of land of our own and we sort of got away from the full-time droving then. But I couldn't settle down, not for the life of me, so I got a forestry lease just under the Burrinjuck Dam and I used to go out there. It was a fortnight going out and a fortnight coming back and that's what kept me sane. But I was like that all through life. And it was because of all this droving business. It got in the blood and if I was ever in one place for too long, I'd get itchy feet.

Just like Dad

My name's Emily. I'm twelve now but when I first started riding horses I think I was about one; I might've been two maybe, when I really started riding all by myself. But I can still faintly remember bits of when there was a drought here in Queensland and there was no feed on the common at Wyandra so we took the sheep and the cattle and the horses down into New South Wales, to feed them down there.

I'm Luke and I was about two years old when I started riding all by myself. Emily and me, we've both got our own horses.

But as for school, you get distance education papers until Year Seven, and with pre-school you get these big plastic boxes, with puzzles and things in them. So you can have fun with them, and we used to do sessions in the morning on HF radios but now they've sent us a phone with a headset and it's got a button on it. That's what we've got now, but you need a phone plug, one that goes into a wall, so you can only use it when you're at home base.

Then when we're out on a droving trip we only do our papers, that's all, and you have to post them back in. From Year One to Year Six your papers are sent over two weeks. Like you have an English lesson that has two sessions in it per day and your maths paper's the same. But when you get to Year Seven your papers go over three weeks and you've got three sessions each day on subjects like science and English and grammar and spelling and handwriting and all that stuff. Oh, and we also do art. So there's a lot more work and also, in Year Seven, some sessions go for thirty minutes and some go for sixty minutes. It all depends.

When we're droving Mum tries to work with us from about eight-thirty to about twelve because I've only got two sessions. I'm in Grade Five and I'm ten. Mum teaches us separately whenever she can. That's if she's not busy, out working with Dad.

But I'd prefer it that way because I love living out of town. Going into town makes me freak. There's too many people. And Luke doesn't like town either. He's the same as Dad. He'd prefer to be out on the road or to be at home near Wyandra. Wyandra's where we stay when we're not droving. It's about 100 ks from Charleville and 100 ks from Cunnamulla. But we're not there just now. Where we are at the moment, it's about 20 ks into Surat.

Yeah, and from the front gate, it's 100 ks up to Roma.

But some of my best memories about droving are when we went down into New South Wales and we followed the snowdrifts around. There was a drought up in Queensland, so down around the snow melts was where all the good food was. We started just at the end of the snowfall, in the first week of September.

Luke was only about two, or two and a half then, and it was pretty cold in the morning. But even their summers down in New South Wales are pretty cold. I think we started at a place called

Showing dad how to do it.

Forbes and then we went towards Cowra. We had just under 4000 head of sheep. Then we crossed the Lachlan River and we went up to Canowindra, then over to near Blayney. We were on the road for about four months with those ones and we finished up around Christmas. I used to ride around on my horse, old Chise, but we had to put him down in 1999 because he ended up with a cataract over one eye and it started to go cancerous.

And I remember when we were walking some sheep in Queens-land and my horse bucked and I fell off onto some rocks and I hit my knee and my leg was all swollen for a couple of weeks. And even now, every time I ride real far, my kneecap starts to hurt.

Then after he fell off, Dad just tightened the saddle up and then Mum went off at us because the sheep were going back to where they'd came from and Luke's horse trotted off after Mum. But the problem was, where the bit comes together in the middle of the horse's mouth, it was pinching her tongue and so that's what made her buck Luke off.

It wasn't real pleasant. Then after I fell off, Dad caught her and just tightened the saddle up and I kept riding her. But she was still mucking up halfway through the day so Mum said she'd ride her for a while, just to sort her out. Anyhow, Mum pulled on the reins and that's when the bit broke in the horse's mouth. It broke right off. And it was a fairly new one, too. Then after we put a new bit in, she was fine after that.

Then the next day we went up over Katherine Creek crossing and there was some rocky hills and there was a lot of slate rock and the sheep decided to go up into the hills and it was a bit hard to ride the horses up through there because the slate was so slippery. So in the end, we ended up walking up to bring the sheep back out onto the road.

But I'd much prefer to live the way we live than be like the town kids because you don't have to do schoolwork all day. When you've finished your sessions you can just go and do whatever you want to do. You don't have to sit there until three o'clock. So we've got a lot more freedom and stuff. And we see a lot more of Australia, too. I can remember one time in New South Wales, with the sheep, where it was really, really hilly and we had our little green ute—an old Toyota, '61 model—and it was fun how we went up and down the hills.

And I can remember one Christmas we spent droving down in New South Wales and they had all these little pine trees planted out along the road. Dad said they were supposed to be windbreaks but he cut one down, and he told us not to tell anyone. Then we had one of those little white sand buckets, so we filled it with dirt and we put the pine tree in it and we sat it in the caravan and that was our Christmas tree. It was fun, that was.

Dad told us that because they'd planted them too close together, there were too many trees there to make a proper windbreak, anyway.

Then for Christmas we got a toy trailer with some plastic cows and horses and we went around the caravan, driving Dad nuts with them.

We were living in a 20-foot caravan so it was pretty cramped. Then another Christmas we got a pushbike each. Mine was pink and it all came in parts. Luke's was already put together. And because we were on the reserve we went into the Stock Route Manager's house for Christmas day. That was fun because, up in Queensland it's usually 36 degrees at Christmas time and down there it was like, ten degrees outside and there was a lot of low, foggy cloud and lots of misty rain, and I said, 'Oh this's just like an English Christmas.'

But I don't think I'll ever live in a town. I wouldn't like to, anyway. I'd like to stay out here and I'm thinking of going cooking up in the Northern Territory for a while, up in the stock camps, there. That'll be cool.

And I don't want to go anywhere near a town. I want to take after Dad.

He wants to take over the business.

Yeah, I just want to be like Dad.

Let the Red Bull Go

Talk about droving trips. One time we were leaving the big runs (big station properties) up in the Gulf Country, heading to Julia Creek. Now the big runs are wide open spaces, thousands of square miles. And with them being that large the cattle don't come across too many fences. But then, as you work your way down the stock route towards Julia Creek, you start coming into the smaller cocky places, and that's where there's lots of fences.

Now the drover's worst enemy is the little sheep cockies and, the law of the land is that, when you pass through these places you've got to give these fellers notice. So more often than not they'll come down to the boundary gate and see you through, just to make sure you stick to the stock route and you don't let your bullocks loose into their property, where the feed's better. Oh, these little cocky blokes, they're a wake-up to all that. Then after they've seen you through their property they'll get on their peddle wirelesses and make sure their cocky mate next door knows you're coming, and he'll also come down and meet you at his gate. So they don't trust you, these fellers. Not one iota.

Anyhow, by this particular stage of the trip we'd been on the road for about four or five weeks. It was near the end of the season and the stock route had been burnt out (eaten out) real bad. So for three days the bullocks hadn't had a decent feed and we were trying to push them a bit to get an extra couple of miles a day out of them.

Then just as we were about to come into these cocky places, the boss drover got word that his father had died so he went back to Normanton and left me in charge. Anyhow, I had four Aborigines with me—Murries we called them. So I came to the first fence at one of these small properties and, noticing that the cocky wasn't there to keep an eye on me, I let the bullocks wander into his place so they could get a decent belly full of feed.

Then that night, after they'd had a good feed, I camped them in the corner and just watched them from the fire. Now that's strictly a no-no because you should never camp bullocks on a fence line or in a corner. As I said, these cattle'd come from the big runs where they weren't used of fences so they're more likely to get their horns hooked up in the wire, which will cause them to panic and then the whole lot will go. They'll rush.

Anyhow this mob wouldn't lay down like usual, and that's a bad sign because it means they're worried about something. And on this particular occasion there must've been some kangaroos fighting either side of the fence down aways because the fence wire twanged and it frightened them. So they panicked and they jumped. And when bullocks jump like that the whole ground sounds like it's all thunder underneath. So they took off at about two in the morning and they took a good part of the fence—wire, posts, the whole lot. Luckily for us, out from the fenced area was pretty open country and, with a couple of night horses, it was easy to wheel them around and block them up.

But then, the next morning when we counted them, we found that we were a hundred bullocks short. So we sort of patched up what was left of the fence in the hopes that the cocky wouldn't come across the damage until we were long gone. Then I left the cook and the horsetailer to go and get the missing bullocks while we moved on.

So we drove our eight hundred into this little cocky place, and he had a bore drain. Why it's called a bore drain is that when the water comes out of the bore it flows down a man-made creek, sort of thing. Now these bore drains, they're only about a foot wide and the cockies have this tractor that straddles the drain and it keeps it very nice and neat and clean of grass for about two foot either side. Like I said, nice and neat. Because these sheep, if you ever see them, they come tippytoeing down to the bore drain and they have a little sip and then they tippytoeing back to the gidgee.

Anyhow it comes along to dinnertime and these Gulf bullocks are looking for a drink. But see, they've never tasted bore water before. They're used to monsoonal water and waterholes. So there's

Camping on a bore drain.

my eight hundred trudging up through this bore drain, hock deep, making a real mess of it. Like they'd have a bit of a drink and they wouldn't like the taste so they'd walk up along the bore drain, hoping the water might be better further along, which it wasn't.

Anyhow, just in case the cocky who owned the place arrived and saw the mess we were making, I sang out to the fella that was on the dinner watch, 'Hey, bring 'em back outa the bore drain and put 'em back on camp again.'

But then, just as he was doing that, down came the cocky and, I tell you, he was your typical chief cocky. He had braces. His bottle of Stockholm tar was in his saddlebag. He had a pair of hand shears to crutch any old maggoty sheep he come across. He had a bit of wire around his saddle and a straining fork. Anyhow, he's come down with his kid and he's giving me a real serve for messing up this bore drain of his and, blow me down, who shouldn't appear but the horsetailer and the cook, along with the missing hundred head. And I tell you, these bullocks, they're not only turning his bore drain into an absolute, complete mess but they're also dragging fence posts and they've got wire strung out all around them.

'What happened there?' the cocky says.

'Oh,' I said, 'we had a rush the other night out at the Millungera horse paddock and these fellers are just bringing 'em in.'

Now the Millungera horse paddock was the only place I could think of that was nearby and had a fence around it, other than the cocky's place, of course. But I wasn't going to tell him that. But anyhow, it's enough to get him going again. He gets on his soapbox and he's going crook about how the drovers from the Gulf are bullying all the little fellers like him, and how rotten they are, and about all the damage they cause, and so forth and so on.

Anyway all this whingeing got to me, so I said, 'Look mate,' I said, 'how big's this little cocky farm of yours?'

And I can remember it as if it was yesterday. He stuck his thumbs in his braces, puffed out his chest, and he said, 'This place is 66,000 acres.'

And I said to him, 'Blimey, 66,000 acres, is it?'

'Yes, it is,' he said.

'Well,' I said, 'that's just about as big as the night horse paddock back on Vanrook Station.' So that put him back in place, a bit. Then I said, 'Look mate, you're getting on me goat and right now they're getting another mob of bullocks ready for me to bring down this way and if I hear that any of me droving mates have trouble with you, then the next time I come through, I'll bring a pocket full of grasshoppers and I'll let 'em go right here, and they'll eat yer out in a week.'

And that's what the drovers used to do. If any of those small cockies gave us a bad time, we'd burn them out. It's what they call letting the red bull go, or the red steer. Burning him out. Sometimes you can put the wind up these cockies by just asking them if they've got a box of matches because then they know that they can't push you around or you'll 'let the red bull go'.

Anyhow, boy, didn't that shut this cocky up. After that he saw us to the boundary gate, as quiet as a lamb, and when most of the mob had gone through he turned around and rode away.

Then just as he disappeared, down trots this big fat bullock to have a stickybeak at our cattle. It was on his property so, obviously, it was his. And he was fat. Anyway, to cut a long story short, we run this cocky's bullock into our mob and we knocked him off the next day and we ate him. Beautiful he was, too. Beautiful.

Like Bloody Hell

No one knows *when* I was born, not even my old Aboriginal people. But they do know *where* I was born, and that was under a mulga tree on Finniss Springs Station, about 60 mile out from Marree, in the far north-east of South Australia. And that old mulga tree's still standing. So it must be a good old bloody tree, aye. So then what happened was, on the day I walked into school, what the school teacher done was, he called that me birthday, then he back-dated it ten years. So when I got the job here in Port Augusta I got it registered as 28 October 1935.

Finniss Springs was taken over in about 1922 by me grandfather, an old white Scottish bloke, Francis Dunbar-Warren, and he was me mum's father and he sort of grew us all up. Mum had about ten or eleven kids and Grandfather had about five children himself.

But Grandfather didn't want us kids taken away, so seeing that there was so many of us, he got a school up there. And the first person who come up was old Daisy Bates. Daisy Bates, yeah, all them years ago. I remember old Daisy very well. She'd come in on an old horse-drawn buggy, or sulky, or whatever they called them, and we'd chase after her horse and that. But I wasn't in school then. I was too young.

Then later on, Grandfather got a mission up there. I even wanted to go to high school in Adelaide but he wouldn't let me. That man was so close to us and we were close to him as well. And the best part of it all was that he paid for it all by himself, not like nowadays. He built the school and he built the houses for the missionaries. And it all come out of his own pocket. Oh, he was just a marvellous man. Then when I'd grown up a bit more, I said to him that I'd like to go working somewhere else. So the first place I went was Andamooka Station, and I was only getting five shillings a week. But in those days we didn't worry about bloody money.

So I was at Andamooka for about six months and, during that time, Grandfather kept writing for me to come home. So I went back for a while and then I heard about this droving. Like, me eldest brother, he was a drover for somebody else. So I told Grandfather how I'd like to go droving and he said, 'Very well, but it's hard yakka.'

'That's okay,' I said.

So I took off droving with an old white bloke by the name of Jack Sullivan. Jack was as hard as old salt beef, you know, but he did look after me even if he was a drunken old cow. Every pub we'd come to he'd say, 'You take over the cattle and I'll catch up in a couple of days time.' Then a couple of days would turn out to be a week or so. But he was a great old bloke and I stayed with him for quite a while.

But on the first job with old Jack, we went over the border into the north-west of Western Australia, to a place called Billiluna, and we came down the Canning Stock Route, down to Wiluna. That was in '48 or '49. Then after we done that, old Jack went elsewhere so I went back to Billiluna and I got a job there for a couple of weeks, just mucking around. Then old Jack come back in an old army blitz and he said, 'Let's go droving again.'

'Okay,' I said, and I jumped in the old blitz. I never said nothing to the boss in at Billiluna. I just took off, because I was only a kid, aye.

And that was it, you know. I stayed droving with old Jack then, and we went to Alice Springs and over to the old railhead at Burban, up from Brewarrina, up the top of New South Wales. That's where the narrow gauge railway line started. Then after we done that we went back to Pine Creek, between Katherine and Darwin, and we travelled out to a place called Douglas Station, on the Daly River, and we were there for about two months, mustering all the wild cattle.

But I'll tell you this one. I was only a bloody kid, like. But at Douglas Station there was this old Aboriginal bloke and, one day, he said to me, 'Oh, we'll go fishing.' Now, coming from the dry country, I didn't know nothing about fishing. So we went down the river and he said, 'Watch out, there's a lota crocodiles here.' And you know, he put the fear in me; it give me the bloody shits.

Anyhow this old Aboriginal bloke had a three-legged dog, okay, and he was just so attached to this old dog. So I was sitting high on the bank because I didn't want to go any more down near the water, and this dog was lying down there next to the old bloke who was fishing. And he's just got an old 'cock-rag' on; a bit like undies. Then the next bloody minute this old bloke pulls a fish up and, at that exact same time, out comes this big croc and *whoosh* . . . it grabs his dog from off the bank.

And do you know what this man did? He had this long knife and he just jumped in the river and he turned that croc inside out. And without a word of a lie, he got that dog out. And he didn't kill that croc. He didn't even touch it with the knife. He could've, but he didn't, because I asked him, 'How did yer get the croc to let go of the dog?'

'I just poked in his eyes,' he said.

And I said, 'Then why did yer take the knife?'

'Well,' he said, 'if he'd a grabbed me I would'a ripped 'im apart with it.'

And I don't know how many times I've told me old wife, but that was the most amazing thing I ever seen a man do.

So anyhow, after that we started droving from Douglas Station and we came down to Katherine then on to Newcastle Waters, which is up from the centre of the Northern Territory. Then before we got to the Barkly Stock Route . . . firstly, have you heard of Edna Ziggenbaum? I met Edna near Newcastle Waters, at a place called Elliott. She was young and I was still only young too, and that's where I met her. And I met the old bloke as well, old Harry Ziggenbaum. To me it was a very big name and I worshipped old Harry, being a big drover and all. And I remember saying to old Jack, 'One of these days I'll be a drover.'

And he said, 'Well, yer've got the potential.'

So anyhow, from Elliott we got onto the Barkly Stock Route and we delivered at Camooweal, just inside the Queensland border.

Then after that, in about '57, I went with a Kidman drover called old Billy Braden. He's deceased now. They used to call him

'Todd Morton Willy', and he was the one what recommended me to Kidman as a drover.

'I'll be too young,' I said.

And he said, 'Oh, you'll be okay.'

So he pushed me age up a bit and that's how I got the job as Kidman's drover. I was one of the youngest he ever had. And he didn't have too many Aboriginal drovers. He had plenty of black stockmen and ringers but not many drovers. There was only old Bill Gorring and Harry Gorring and there was Roger Murray and there was a bloke who just died not long ago. So there were a few, but that's about all.

And the Kidmans were very good to me. Though I never actually got to meet Sir Sidney, I did meet the late John Ayres and an old bloke by the name of Ernie Spencer. John Ayres was a great bloke, and old Ernie was the travelling manager. Ernie was as hard as nails but he was a great bloke as well. The only time he come to me was when Kidman wanted something done. Other than that, he never worried me. He knew I looked after the cattle and he knew exactly what sort of person I was.

And they were the happiest years of me life. I liked cattle work. And I liked the responsibility, you know, of getting the cattle to market or to the railhead, in good spirit and in good condition. They knew that. And I wouldn't allow grog in the camp. I made that a very strict rule, so I had no problems with my men at all, not like the others. See, the grog's no good because the worst part was when old Ernie'd ring me up on the radio and say, 'Look, can you go and relieve so-and-so of their cattle.'

'Why's that?' I'd say.

'Well,' he'd say, 'he's out there at Thargomindah and the cattle are all out in the paddock.'

And I just knew they'd been on the piss, you know. And relieving me mates of their cattle was something I didn't like doing. But I had a job to do. I had responsibilities. But that happened too many times, especially with me Aboriginal mates. They were head drover but they had no control with the men and the grog, so they'd call on me.

Sir Sidney Kidman with James Robertson Chisolm, a business partner.

And I also made it a rule how we were not to use stockwhips with the cattle, especially when we were taking them to market. We'd have the whips strapped across our shoulders, of course, just in case. And I'm not bragging, but every cattle I took for Kidmans into Bourke, Tankreds bought, you know. Every one. Because they knew that I looked after them. In fact, one day Tankred come out and he said, 'These bloody cattle, they're too bloody fat for us.'

'Well,' I said, 'I get paid to look after 'em so that's the way it is.'

He was only joking, of course, because like I said, Tankreds took every cattle I had, every time, and that's what made me one of Kidman's ace drovers.

But I only came down the Birdsville Track twice and that was a bit hard because I wanted to come down more than that. There was once when I was coming down with a mob from Duri Station and old Billy Brown, he came up and he said, 'Look, I got some bad news.'

'What's that?' I said.

And he said, 'The manager at Glengyle, old Harry Crombie, well, he says the drover won't be able to handle the Glengyle cattle over to Quilpie.'

'Well, he's gotta put up with it,' I said.

'Oh no,' he said. 'Kidman wants you to go up and take the mob over.'

And oh, they were wild bloody cattle. But cattle do settle down. It may be just a matter of a couple of days, or even a week, but they will eventually fall into place. See, all you do is give them a big day. That's the way to go. Then anyway, while we were on the road, old Ernie Spencer turned up with old Harry and Harry said, 'I cannot believe how you got these cattle as quiet as this.'

'Well, that's me job,' I said.

Then by the time we got to Quilpie they were the best-behaved mob on the road. And I must say that it's tough delivering cattle like that, especially after you'd been nursing them for six or seven bloody weeks, you know. You just get so close to them. And we always had a habit of naming the cattle, so we knew the leaders and the tailers. Then all we had to do was to sing out 'Go back', or whatever, and they'd just fall into place. No whip. And at night when you had the fires lit they'd come in around the camp with you. Oh, you do get attached to them.

But the worst part, like I said, was when I was asked to take cattle away from me mates—like when Roger Murray was going around the bore tracks around Innaminka, taking a mob to

Quinyambie Station, a Kidman property just out from Broken Hill. And in them days the bore track was just that, a track—no graded road, nothing, you know. And the bore water was just bloody salty water, as salty as the sea.

So this was near summer and old Ernie Spencer come and he said to me, 'Even though you're younger than Roger, he hasn't got your experience, so give him some advice.'

Anyhow, there was this big stage of 60 mile with no water. So I said, 'Roger, yer've got number three bore. Camp there a while, give 'em a late drink then go out, say, five or six mile, and the next day make it one big dry day. Then the day after that yer'll get into water around lunch. By that time they'll be screaming for it.'

That was my advice. Then a while later, bloody Ernie Spencer turned up again and he said, 'Get a couple'a boys and go out around the bore track.'

'Why's that?' I said.

'Well,' he said, 'Roger didn't take your advice and he just poked along, doing his eight mile a day, and now he's lost two hundred head.'

So these poor bloody cattle hadn't had no water for three whole bloody days. And they'd lost two hundred head and quite a few horses as well. So I grabbed a couple of the boys and we went out, and there were all these dead cattle, all over the place. But a few live ones were still scattered around, and I knew there was a bore just inside New South Wales, so I cut the bloody fence and I shoved them in there. Then we went and saw the bloke who owned the property and he said, 'No that's all right.'

And that was one of the worst experiences. It was Roger Murray's last trip. He's passed on now. But he was a great old mate of mine, too. They were all good mates, but it was just sad. They were good fat cattle, too.

So that's the reason why I was a Kidman ace drover, because I treated the cattle so well. And nowadays I reckon I'd be pretty close to being the last Kidman drover around, especially up this way. Most of me old mates have passed away now. But I just loved droving. I loved the cattle. And I've still got the saddles I used and

the elastic-sided boots and the old spurs—you know the old ones—
and the old bridle. And I said to the old woman, 'When I go yer may
as well throw 'em all in the grave with me.'

And she said, 'Like bloody hell.'

Lock, Stock and Barrel

I'm of Aboriginal descent. My father was born in 1885, as a three-quarter-caste. My mother was born in 1895 or 1894 and was part Aboriginal and part Afghan; the Afghans being prevalent in those days. Both my parents came from around Charleville way, in the south-west of Queensland. My father was from the Warrego area and my mother from the Paroo area. I was born in Charleville in 1915, so I'm getting on a bit. So that's the background.

Now I'm going to clear a point up, straight away. You know how these Aboriginals say that they were taken away and 'stolen', when they were born. Well my father was taken away and he was 'adopted'. See, some call it 'stolen' but I say 'adopted', because I'm personally in favour of those poor children being taken because they were saved from suffering in poverty and despair for the rest of their lives. So that's my point, and I want it to be made clear.

So my father was taken by Albert Hart, a Scottish teamster, and he was reared with Albert's four children—two daughters and two sons. That's how my father became known as William Hart, at five years old. I don't know my mother's background other than her maiden name was Topsy Wells.

Anyway, with my father being a horse breaker, as well as a stockman and a noted buck-jump rider, he went and he broke in horses for Gowrie Station. Gowrie was what's called a 'State Station', meaning that the Queensland government owned it. Back then Gowrie went halfway up to Augathella and right down south, around Charleville. So that's where my father spotted my mother, and I suppose, being a wild young buck, that was it.

I was the first-born and we lived out of a wagonette and a tent, on the bore drains and that, around Gowrie Station. I was followed by my brother, Bill, who was two and a half years behind me. My other brother, George, he came much later. Then with my father not being able to read or write and my mother not being much better, my parents assured I had a good education. So when I was about five or so, we went to live on the fringe of Charleville, to be nearer a school. Then I got a scholarship and I went through schooling from 1922 to 1930. So I had a good education. I done bookkeeping, shorthand, typing, business method and all that.

My father followed on being a horse breaker and a stockman until he became associated with a family called the Drennans. The father's name was Jack and the son was also Jack. With the Drennans, my father also done a bit of droving.

But when I left school at fifteen, the Great Depression had started. There were people carrying their swags everywhere and there was no possibility of me getting work, so my father took me on a droving trip for Jack Drennan's brother-in-law. We took 1000 mixed cattle from the head of the Warrego River, out across to Cunnamulla, to Eulo, down to Thargomindah, out through Bulloo Downs, and down to Adelaide Gates, on the border of New South Wales, north of White Cliffs.

Now on our way to the market at White Cliffs, we happened to go past a property called Cobham Lakes, and though we didn't know it at the time, the owners of Cobham had just bought these cattle. So when the news got to us, we had to turn around and go back and deliver to Cobham before heading home to Charleville. That was back in 1930 and I got no money for that. It was just a learning experience. I mean, they clothed and fed me but that was all. So after that I was, more or less, left to battle against the odds, with the Depression and all.

Then in 1933 we hooked up with Dougal Cameron. Dougal had two droving plants and my father became his leading hand and run one of the plants. Dougal was more of what you'd call a 'gentleman drover'. He never soiled his hands. He just used to take the contracts and supply the droving plants and the horses and the men, then he'd inspect them like he was a king cocky. Dougal was always well groomed.

One time we had 3000 bullocks in two mobs. My father took the main mob. Now while we were on camp out at Morestone, on the

During the depression many a swagman walked the outback in search of work.

Queensland–Northern Territory border, a funny thing happened. My father said, 'I fergot to buy the bullets, so who's gonna volunteer to catch 'n' kill one'a the bullocks fer somethin' to eat?'

Anyhow, nobody volunteered. So the cook . . . Tom was his name. Tom was a huge, raw-boned bloke, real wild, big moustache, and a born liar to boot. At night-time he always kept a bucket of melted dripping nearby so that if the cattle rushed in his direction, he could throw the dripping over the fire and it'd explode and scare them off.

'So, Billy,' this Tom said to my father, 'a nice lota stockmen yer got 'ere. Hows about yer run a bullock out in the morning, Billy,' he said, 'and I'll show yer's all how to turn his pissle to the stars.' His pissle being his penis.

So in the morning this Tom, he chased this bullock up and down until it jumped over the border fence, over into the Northern Territory—from one state to another—leaving Tom on the Queensland side. It was only a rabbit-netting fence.

'I'll put the bullock back over the fence,' I said. 'Now you be ready, Tom.'

So I chased the bullock until it fell back over the fence again, into Queensland. It changed states, again. Then while it was on the ground, Tom ran in to kill it. Anyhow he got a couple of paces from this bullock and it suddenly got up. And it took one look at Tom and it didn't like what it saw, so it decided to charge him. So Tom, he's off, and the bull's off after him. Down along the fence they go, with this bull gaining on him, quick. So Tom realised that the only way to escape the bull was to jump the fence, back over into the Northern Territory. So that's what he done.

Anyway, this's all a great lark, so I'm laughing and going on and the old man goes crook at me. 'Well,' he says. 'You go 'n' do somethin'.'

'Okay,' I said. So I chased after this bullock until I got hold of its tail. And when I latched onto him he kept charging around and around in circles, trying to get at me. So I hung on for dear life until he got giddy and fell over. And that was the end of him, then. I hooked the tail around his hind legs and turned him on his back and run him through his brain with the butcher's knife. So we had something to eat then. But laugh, I tell you.

Then after that we went down the Cooper Creek to the Windorah area, in the south-west of Queensland, where the cattle were sold at the market. So that was 1933.

Well in '34 a drought was all over Queensland and most of the stock was moved by train, doing the long trips away for pastures. And that's when I hooked up with a drover called Claude Burns. Now Claude's father, old Tom, had been the head stockman on Gowrie Station, back when my father was the horse breaker there and I would've been just a twinkle in me father's eye. So we had a long association with the Burns family. So I worked for Claude and we took a mob of cattle from up near Springsure, in central Queensland, south to Tara, on the New South Wales border, then on to Goodooga.

Anyhow, after we dropped the cattle off we stayed around Tara for two or three months, shepherding 6000 sheep before we put them on the train at Goondiwindi. And talk about cold. The temperature got so low at Tara that, in the morning, you'd think you'd lost half the sheep because they were packed so tight in the sheep break, trying to protect themselves from the cold. Gee it was cold. We were freezing to death, ourselves. Oh, it was terrible. I never went back in that area. Never.

Then after we delivered the sheep, we went back north and we picked up another mob of cattle and we took them down to Goondiwindi, then over into New South Wales, to Boggabilla, and we put them on the train as well. But I was away for nine months that time, first with the cattle, then with the sheep, then with the other mob of cattle.

Then in '35, when I was nineteen, we went on another trip with Dougal Cameron. Now Dougal had reared two Normanton black boys, Kidman and Johnny. They were absolute Aboriginals. So this Kidman and Johnny and a white cook by the name of Cliff Brown, they went ahead with the wagonette, over to Wave Hill, a Vesteys property, in the central west of the Northern Territory.

Anyway, Dougal Cameron had a Chrysler car and, later on, he

took off with my father and a white stockman. After that, I flew out with Qantas, from Charleville to Camooweal. Qantas was only just beginning and, back then, it was only an eight-seater passenger plane made out of galvanised iron—the small-ribbed corrugated iron. And oh, it was a frightening trip, what, with the air pockets and all. We were all sick, all of us, including the pilot and his offsider.

The first night we camped at Cloncurry and the next day they dropped me off at Camooweal, then they went on to Darwin. And in those days, with the telephones you could send a message, so I got a lift out and I caught up with the Chrysler car. Then when we got to Wave Hill, Dougal dropped us off and he turned around and he drove the Chrysler back home to Charleville. Like I said, Dougal wasn't much of a 'hand's-on' type of drover.

Anyway we took 1525 bullocks over from Wave Hill. There was my father and myself and another half-caste boy who was the same age as me. He was born on Brunette Downs. Then there was Kidman and Johnny, and we had the white stockman, plus the cook, Cliff Brown. Cliff was from Charleville.

But I tell you, none of us ever dreamed that it'd turn out as bad as it did. Now I don't know how long it took Cliff, Kidman and Johnny to get that wagonette all the way from Charleville. In those days, back in '35, the Murranji was only drovers' tracks and they'd just put the first two bores down. One was named after the sinker and the other one was named after the surveyor.

Anyway, we came across the Townsend. It's not a big river, and we headed to the Murranji Stock Route. Now the Murranji's full of bulwaddi and lancewood scrub. There's also a lot of chalky ground so when your cattle rush it sounds like a thousand bloody native drums. It's deafening. The ground explodes and shakes, just like you'd imagine an earthquake.

But my father was one of the best stockmen I've ever known. Even though he couldn't read or write, he was a very astute man; he had a great knowledge of reading signs and tracks and knowing what to do with stock. So he'd avoid camping near this chalky ground and he didn't like camping near the bulwaddi either, because it grows over like an umbrella, almost back down to the ground. And once they got into that, you had a terrible time getting them back out. Oh, it's terrible stuff. And we never lost one beast on that trip. In actual fact we found a few with the Wave Hill brand, so we added them to our mob. Like, it wasn't illegal or anything because they were just roaming about out there, anyway.

But at the first bore we came to, I almost got killed. See, the drinking trough could only water twenty-five to thirty head at the one time. And when you've got over 1500 head you've got to keep them away from the windy side of the bore. If they smell the water, you'll lose them and they'll just go straight for the water.

So we cut out the first twenty-five and, once the others saw them going, they wanted to go as well. Anyway, I was chopping them off on a special breed of stockhorse called a 'clumper'. He's solid; built for strength, though he's not a harness horse. So I was on this clumper and the ground gave away and he fell over on top of me and crushed my foot. So I'm on the ground with my foot caught in the right-side stirrup iron. Then when he stood up and realised he was dragging something he panicked and he started to jog. So I'm being dragged along and I'm talking to him, trying to calm him down.

Then somehow I got my left leg underneath me and heaved myself up and managed to grab the saddle leather. Now, I've seen men get dragged by horses and it's not a likely experience, so whenever I went droving I always got a cold chisel and, where the stirrup leather goes in the stirrup iron, I used to lift it off the saddle and hammer it. By doing that I could pull my stirrup leather on and off at any time. Anyhow I ripped my stirrup leather off the saddle hook and that's what saved my leg.

But if I'd had a real bad accident I don't know what would've happened. The Murranji was such an isolated place. There was no transport. Nobody lived in that area. And if I'd have been killed, my father would've just had to bury me there and leave me.

So I thanked my lucky stars and we got to Newcastle Waters. Then we went down through Eva Downs, along the Barkly Stock Route to Anthony Lagoon, then through Brunette Downs, along the Ranken Stock Route to Alexandria, then on to Ranken. In those days, on the dried-up Ranken River, there was a combined pub and a store, so they called it a 'pubble'.

From Ranken, we followed the river down until it ran into the Georgina, and we followed that to Lake Nash and into Queensland, to Urandanji. Then down a bit, the Georgina takes the biggest bend you've ever seen. It looks like how you bend your elbow. So we cut across and we came out on the Georgina again before heading for the Parapitui Waterhole, south of Boulia.

There was no grazing properties across that way. It's what's called a dry stock route. So we gave our cattle their last water at Glengyle, a Kidman station, then we went all the next day without water. But my father always camped within easy access of grass so in the early morning you let the cattle meander off to eat the grass with the dew on it. That's how they got their water, off the dewy grass. Then they went all that next day without water and, I tell you, they were very anxious by nightfall. Then the next morning we headed for Parapitui and we eventually got there about ten on the morning of the third day.

But the Parapitui's a magnificent waterhole. At the top there's a break and, about half a mile further up, it's as salty as the sea. Yet further down it's clear, crystal, fresh water. And we always carried fishing lines to catch a feed of fish there. After that we swung into Boulia, then across to Winton, following the grass because by that time they'd had storms.

Now a funny thing happened about 6 mile outside of Winton, at a place called Western Creek, which is actually a series of wide little creeks. We were feeding the cattle and up come a white man, riding a horse. He was a local, a stockman or whatever, and he saw my old man sitting on his horse. Now my father was quite a sight. He was a podgy bloke; pretty dark, and he had this big heavy grey beard all over his face and he wore a Tom Mix cowboy hat. So up rides this whitefeller and he addresses my dad in his best pidgin blackfella language. 'G'day,' he says. 'You see horsey-horsey long creek wid' tinkle-tinkle on neck and jingle-jingle on legs?'

And the old man looks this feller up and down, and he eyes him off, then he says, 'Now, look here yer white bastard, if yer'd speak the King's bloody English I'd be able ta understand what the hell yer was talkin' about.'

Well this bloke, he near fell off his horse, he was that shocked. 'Oh, I apologise,' he said. 'It's just that I'm used of talking that way to the Aboriginal boys out here.'

Anyway, from Winton we went over the open plains to Longreach, across the Min-Min Light country, then down the Thomson River before we came out near Windorah, heading to Quilpie. From there we went down to Cunnamulla and across through Hungerford, on the Queensland–New South Wales border. Then to finish off a long story and an even longer droving trip, we ended up at Walgett, in the central north of New South Wales, and we dropped the cattle off there, at a property.

That trip took nine months. But the thing was, when we finished we still had the same number of bullocks we started off with. And people said, 'How did you get along for meat?'

'Well, we killed our own,' we said.

But remember how we picked up those Wave Hill strays along the Murranji. That's what we ate along the way.

But at the end of that trip I was so worn out, tired and weary, that I became very ill. I had what they called bad tonsils so when I got back to Charleville I had an operation. But I was a bleeder and I bled internally, and by the time they found out, I was unconscious. And when I came to, two weeks later, the doctor said, 'We were very lucky to save you,' he said. 'I got a cup of congealed blood out of your stomach and that's what saved your life.'

And he told me that the nursing staff had just left me. See, in those days, being Aboriginal, or even a half-caste like I was, there was a lot of neglect in that line of business. But anyhow, I survived.

Then in 1936, we were about to start droving for Dougal Cameron again. He had a grazing property on the river, south of Charleville. Anyhow, Dougal was connected with a racehorse and early one morning in winter he went up to clock it at the training track and he had pneumonia and he died.

But as it turned out, Dougal Cameron had made a will out and in it he gave everything to my father. All my dad had to pay was two

pound a head for each horse. Everything else was free—the wagonette, pack saddles, all the paraphernalia, the tents, the tarpaulins,
the camping gear. So that's how highly Dougal Cameron thought of
my father. He left him the whole lot, lock, stock and barrel.

Looking into the Heavens

You could say that my first experience of droving was when I was just a kid of about twelve, when we were living on a 100 acre property, down near Midland Junction, about 12 mile north-east of Perth. We didn't own the place, we just lived there. Anyhow, Midland Junction had a big abattoirs and saleyards, and I loved horses so I bought a pony, an ex-brumby, and I started poking around there.

Nobody told me to do it. I was just drawn there. And that's where I picked up with an old bloke who was employed by the William Angliss company—very big butchers and station owners, they were. But this bloke used to drove the sheep and cattle from the saleyards out to the holding paddocks and from the paddocks back into the abattoirs. It was all sheep and cattle. We had nothing to do with the pigs. So I holed up with him and give him a hand.

Now I worked with him for eight or nine months and I really enjoyed it. Then, I'm not exactly sure when I left but it was coming on summer time when he could handle the droving by himself, because of the more daylight hours. So I decided to go back to school after that. Like, being only twelve or so I hadn't officially left, yet. I just hadn't turned up for those months because I'd found something far more interesting to do.

Anyhow, I went to the headmaster. 'Can I come back to school?' I said.

'No problem,' he said. 'Back you come.'

So I went back to school. But that was a mistake because by the end of the year I was browned off again. So I said, 'No, forget it,' and I left.

Then on me mother's insistence I got a job in a grocery store, weighing up potatoes and onions and all that jazz. That was like purgatory. But around that same time, the property we were living on got sold and the new owners evicted us.

Now for a single mother, struggling on a widow's pension, with a son and two daughters, being evicted was a big problem. See, we didn't have a dad. He was a casualty during World War I and he'd died with related ailments. Then to make matters worse the Housing Commission hadn't started up by then, so we suddenly found ourselves homeless.

Anyhow, we were eventually allocated a house in Perth and we had to go there. By that stage the grandparents had retired, down to a beach suburb, so when my eldest sister got work she went to live with them to help make costs pan out. Now the eldest sister was working for a steel and saw manufacturer and she convinced them that I'd be useful. It was more like useless really, though I did learn how to handle and sharpen a saw.

But there was a bloke working there, Orb Miller was his name. He was in his late fifties, and at his father's instigation Orb'd followed the profession for years, becoming a saw doctor for the meatworks and the like, meaning he was able to travel until he got married. Orb'd go up the far north of Western Australia to Wyndham and places around there and he'd go over into Queensland, wherever. Now Orb was very fatherly to me and he kept saying, 'Come on, get a trade just like me. Settle down and make something of yer life.'

But all Orb's talk had the opposite effect, see, because all that stuff about caution and settling down and making something of life . . . well, I didn't even listen to that. That went by the by. But what did get me looking into the heavens was that Orb got me imagining all these places he'd visited. And the more I imagined them the more I wanted to go and see them. But just how I was going to get there I hadn't a clue, though it definitely wasn't going to be as a saw sharpener, that's for sure.

See, I'd lived without the influences of a father and as far as I could see, I was still alive and kicking. I'd got this far okay. I still had ten toes and fingers like, so I believed I could do anything. There was no limits.

'Don't patronise fear,' I say. 'Just go for it.'

Anyhow, near where we were living there happened to be a dairy. And the owners of the dairy gave kids the job of running their cattle out into the scrub and looking after them. So I jumped at that. I'd grab one of the horses and help take the cows out to graze after their early morning milking. And I really enjoyed doing that; far more than working at the saw factory.

What I didn't realise, of course, was that it was training for later on, when I went droving. You know, if you walked the legs off them through the scrub, you soon got a kick in the bum because they wouldn't give much milk. But if you poked them through, nice and easy, they'd be more relaxed, they'd eat better, and so when they come back for their afternoon milking the old dairyman'd give them the once-over and he'd say, 'Yer lookin' after 'em real good. See, yer got 'em nice 'n' full today. Yer good boys.'

Then around that time there was another feller who lived up the road. He had a Housing Commission house too, and his son'd been killed in a bus accident a year or two before. Now he'd been a shearer and by that stage he was pretty browned off with working in the suburban sphere, so he got a job in a shearing team. So he asked my mother if I could go too because he'd told the contractor he'd get a couple of roustabouts. Now I jumped at that because my father was a shearer back in the twenties.

'Okay,' Mum said. 'At least yer've got someone to keep an eye on yer.'

So I went out with this shearing team. I was fourteen, going on fifteen, and that's when I left home. And I just loved the bush. Then later on I met a bloke in Darwin—Rum Jungle to be exact. He owned Dunmarra Station and I went to do his mustering.

Now this bloke'd taken the property over from his father-in-law but he'd hardly had any stock experience. It was of my mind that he hadn't sold anything other than grog at the pub. He might've even been its best customer. So it soon became obvious that prospects there weren't too bright. But he had a couple of blokes working there, breaking in horses, and they were going on the road with a mate, droving.

'This looks like the go,' I said.

So we teamed up and we picked up a mob from Willeroo, which is west of Katherine, in the Northern Territory, and we went down the Dry River Road to Top Springs, then down the Murranji Stock Route and out onto the Barkly Tablelands, in north-western Queensland.

And that was it. Oh, I've done lots of other things. You have to, to survive. I've been a ringer, a head stockman, mechanic, roustabout, shearer, did fencing and land clearing; I've worked in a pine forest and I was a cattle stud groom, though I proved not to be diplomatic enough because I've got a habit of saying what I mean. And oh, I even had shares in an oyster lease at one stage. So you name it, I've done it.

But it was the droving that I loved. And it's funny, isn't it. All those unrelated childhood experiences just fell into place—the love of horses, the working for the bloke who took the sheep and cattle to and from the saleyards and abattoirs, learning how to move the dairy cattle through the scrub, the love of the bush.

Young ringers dreaming of the future.

And there I was, as a young kid, looking into the heavens, wondering how I could get to see all those places that Orb Miller was talking about. And all that time the answer was right before my very eyes, and it fell into place when I went droving.

Lost

Gee, it's been about twenty-six years since I done a droving trip and that was only with the wife and a young bloke, and two other young chaps. It was during the drought time and we took a mob of Kidman cattle from off Tickalara Station, in south-western Queensland, and we let them go down on the Cooper. There was plenty of water and feed down there then and there was nothing back on Tickalara.

But I've done lots of droving with lots of different fellers. I've been down the Birdsville Track. I done one trip with old Bland Oldfield. Bland's related to the feller, Eric Oldfield, who's doing that big re-enacting droving trip now. Then I also done one with another old feller, and I done quite a few with Harry Thompson. Harry's passed away now.

Then there was one with Red Fred Rousch. They called him Red Fred because of his temper. Oh, he had a bad temper. I'd better not swear but, Red Fred, he was a real mad bugger, especially when he got wild. He was good for knocking fellers down, you know, young ringers. He used to reckon that it kept them in place. But no, he was a very bad-tempered feller.

And I also done the droving with Dick Nunn. He was a good man, Dick. One trip in '50 or '51 I'll never forget. I was cooking and horsetailing and we took a mob of cattle from off Durham Downs, just when droving was finishing. Then we went out to Thargomindah and down through Hungerford, on the Queensland–New South Wales border, and on to the meatworks at Bourke.

Now there was a tale going around out there about how a mob of cattle rushed one night and when the fellers went out to bring them back, they got lost, and when they sent a search party out looking for them, the search party didn't find a trace of anything—not of the cattle, nor of the men, nor the horses, not even the wagonette. They'd all disappeared. Now I reckon that's all very hard to believe,

Keeping the stock moving.

though, mind you, on this trip with Dick, one of our fellers got lost
out there.

See, we got to just near Hungerford and it was about to pour
down with rain so I got all the packs and swags and I covered them
over with this great big tarp. Then I got as much wood as I could
and I stacked it up in heaps and got a big fire going.

And I'll never forget that night—lightning, thunder, rain, the lot. It was terrible. And we had this young feller with us, George Tankred. His father and uncles owned the meatworks in Bourke for years. George would've only been about eighteen in them days; pretty new to the game too, he was. So I came off watch and I got George to go on.

'George,' I said, 'it's rainy and sloshy and there's one lone bullock what's laying out on his own. Just leave him there,' I said. 'Don't upset him or he could cause trouble.'

'Okay.' So off he went to do the watch.

Now as I said, I had a big fire going. With the weather being as bad as it was, the cattle were very unsettled and I knew that if the bullocks took off they wouldn't go through the fire. So I was safe.

Then I'd just gotten into bed and Dick said, 'How're they going?'

'Oh,' I said, 'they're on their feet and they're moving around and there's one lone bullock—' Then the next thing, away they went, see, just like that. This's about half past ten at night and young George's out there on his own. Anyway, we had the night horses ready, so off we went after them. But then by three or four in the morning we realised that we hadn't see hide nor hair of this George Tankred. So I went up to Dick and I said, 'Wonder where George is?'

'Don't know,' Dick said, 'but if he hasn't turned up by morning, we'll go and have a look around for him.'

So daylight comes and there's still no sign of young George. And of course, we're getting a bit worried. So we tracked the cattle as far as we could in the mud and, no, we couldn't find him. This's funny, I thought. Then at about nine o'clock in the morning he turns up. And oh, he was in a state, crying and carrying on.

'I tried to stop 'em Dick,' he sobbed, 'but I couldn't. I just couldn't.'

I mean, the thing was, we had 650 head of bullocks and this young George'd tried to stop them in the middle of a thunderstorm, you know. But try as he might, he couldn't. Then while he was out there he got completely lost in the dark. So in the morning, he followed the cattle tracks back to camp and when he seen the fire, you know, that was it. But oh, he was upset.

Now, it took us something like five or six days to get all those cattle back together and, when we did, we'd only lost one. And we were just wondering where that one had gotten to when an old boundary rider came over and told Dick that he'd seen a bullock who'd either broken a leg or a shoulder.

'Go 'n' get him,' Dick said to me. 'Yer might get some meat off him.'

So we stayed there that day, just to get the bullocks settled. Then the next day we got going again. And after that, them cattle never moved once. But you had to feel for this young George. He reckoned how it was all his fault and then he went and got lost, to boot. But oh, he was upset.

Mick 'n' the All Blacks

The late Ed Casey, the Labor MP and one-time Deputy Leader of the Opposition in Queensland, he came out one time to see me and he said, 'Mick,' he said, 'just how many Aboriginals do you have working here?'

And I said, 'Hey Ed, have a bloody look around. They call me none other than Mick Gallagher 'n' the All Blacks.'

That's what I said, and it was about right too. Just about all my droving was done with Aboriginals, or 'black boys', as they were called. And most of them were very good stockmen too, better than the whites in most cases, though, I can tell you, we did have our odd drama.

There was one time we started out with some Dunbar bullocks. Dunbar's on the Gulf side of Cape York Peninsula, north of Normanton. This was with all Aboriginal boys. So we get a week on the road and a couple of the blackfellas, they pulled out.

Now back in them days there wasn't any telephones, only telegrams. So if something happened, you went to the nearest station and you sent a telegram back to the manager at your home station. Anyway, the manager of Dunbar brought out another two black boys and one of these boys'd been drinking too much and he got the DTs and he went into the horrors so bad that he kept everyone awake with his talking and carrying on. Then at about two in the morning, this fella up and he walked out into the cattle, still yabbering and going on, and he frightened the mob and they jumped up and they rushed off. We were just lucky that it was a bright moonlight night and they didn't go too far.

Anyhow, I was on watch so I sorted the cattle out then I come back down to this fella and I took him back into the camp. But the thing was, you know, he was still carrying on and wanting

Mustering camp.

to walk away. He was that bad. That's what the DTs do to you. And this fella, he didn't have a bloody clue where he was.

And with him being that bad, I knew that if he did wander off then he'd have gotten lost out there and, of course, with all these cattle to look after we just couldn't afford to go out looking for him. So to stop him walking, I got this heavy-duty dog chain, the one that's got a steel bar that you put through the ring so that a dog or an animal can't undo it. So I put the chain around his ankle and I squeezed the clip together with the pliers. Then I led this boy over to a tree and I tied him up there for the night.

Now when I squeezed the clip with the pliers, I must've cracked the metal or something because he somehow untwisted the chain and he broke it. Away he walked again, still yabbering and carrying on, so I up and after him on the horse and grabbed him and brought him back. But this time, when I put the chain on him, I put number eight wire on it and I tied the ends off so that he couldn't get his fingers under. I mean, he must've had pretty bloody strong fingers in the first place. So then I tied him back to the tree and this time he did stay there for the rest of the night.

Then the next morning we were going on with the cattle, so I said to the cook fella, 'Look, you'd better take this boy back to Gamboola 'n' get the Flying Doctor to come out 'n' take him over to the hospital in Cairns.' Gamboola's up on the Mitchell River; an out-station of Wrotham Park. Then I said, 'If they won't come out, well, just bring him back 'n' we'll keep him tied up fer a couple of days till he comes out of his bloody horrors.'

Anyhow, I led the boy over to the old Toyota—it was one of those with a hand-holder above the dashboard of the passenger's side—and I put the chain around his wrist and up through the hand-holder. Then just in case he broke free and jumped out of the vehicle while it was travelling along, I doubled it back up through again.

So the cook took him back to Gamboola and they called the Flying Doctor who came out and took him back to Cairns. But the thing was, he was only in Cairns for a day before they stuck him back on a plane and flew him back home again, back over to Normanton. Anyhow, by that stage, the manager had brought another boy out to us. So we delivered that mob, then we had to go back to Dunbar and get another mob.

Now all these blackfellas, they've never got any money, see, and they've never got any clothes. So what you did was, just before you went out droving, you went and bought all their gear for them. I mean, you're up for a new swag, clothes, everything. I know because I was the boss drover and I used to have hundreds and hundreds of dollars of clothes and things booked up every season for the men.

Anyhow this fella, the one that'd gotten in the horrors, I took him back out again that next time. Like, he owed me a lot of bloody money by then so I had to take him out again to get it back out of him. And anyhow, this time he hadn't been drinking as heavy and he was no trouble on that droving trip, no trouble at all.

But with the money . . . see, they lived in there, on the reserve in Normanton. This's between '65 and '81. So before you went out on a droving trip you'd just go in and whoever was around you'd ask, 'Do you want a job? Do you want a job?'

'Yeah, right-o. Yeah, right-o.'

So then you'd go down to the store and you'd buy all their gear and away you'd go, pretty much straight away, because if you left it any longer they'd sell the lot to buy grog. That's why you never stayed in town the night before you left, because they'd have nothing left in the morning, apart from a hangover.

But I had quite a few of them go in the horrors during the time I was droving, and you'd just take them out of town and sober them up as you went along. I mean, you'd take a bottle of rum along so that you could needle them with it; break them out of it slowly.

Like, you'd go out for three months or whatever and they'd get a real health kick out of it. And it probably kept a lot of them alive, at least for a while, because so many have died since; just drunk themselves to death. And a lot of them died young, too. One kid in '74, he was only fifteen then, well, he's dead now. He went out on the grog. It's pretty sad really, in a lot of ways. But they just can't handle the grog. That's what it amounts to.

And it's only going to get worse too, because they haven't got the work these days to support them. Take Miranda Station, for example. There would've been about thirty blackfellas working out there in '69, around the time I was droving, and now there's probably only six. There's no jobs for all these people. Like, one time you'd have a few young blackfellas and they'd have the good men teaching them and, of course, you'd have your half a dozen or so no-hopers.

But now all the stations are going for contract workers. Take musterers—they'll turn up with ten good men, get the job done, and they're gone the next day. And that's what's going to ruin it for these blackfellas, because there's nothing like a twelve-month job any more. Like, back then, they'd muster up until September or October and when that finished they'd go fencing or yard building or even just chopping wood. They were kept on. Even if it was mundane jobs, they were still kept on, and away from the towns.

But you just can't live on a six-month job. No one can. That's why these blackfellas end up in the towns. And that's the end of a lot of them then. They haven't got any work. They're bored. They're living near a pub so they hit the grog. That's it then. Oh, some of them might get a job on the councils or whatever, but then they go and spend their pay on grog or their mates come and bite them, then these so-called mates of theirs go and spend it on grog. They'll be broke in the morning anyway, no matter what happens. If they've got any money at all, everyone bites them. That's just the way they are.

I had one black boy: we had a few days off before we went out droving again so I paid him up and he always wanted to buy a wireless to take out with him. So he bought this wireless and the next day he come around to my place and he says, 'Me father sold that wireless ta the publican fer grog 'n' I want it back 'cause I wanta take it out when we go drovin'.'

So I went down and I saw old Bill, the publican, and I said, 'I know the boy bought his wireless from the store for seventy or eighty dollars 'n' he reckons that his father sold it to you for ten dollars, then he spent it all on grog.'

'That's right,' said old Bill.

Then I said, 'Well, I wanta buy it back.'

'Right-o,' old Bill says.

So I gave him the ten dollars and he give me the wireless back. I mean, it was getting to be an expensive wireless by this stage. Then a couple of days later, we go out droving and there's no wireless. So I said to the boy, 'Where's yer wireless?'

'Oh,' he said, 'I sold it fer grog.'

So I got in touch with the wife. 'Get in 'n' see old Bill to see if yer can buy that wireless back again.'

I mean, it was a bloody new wireless. It wasn't even out of its plastic. But old Bill wouldn't sell it back that second time. Anyhow, he'd probably already sold it to someone else for fifty dollars. But that was old Bill. He used to buy gear off them all the time, then they'd spend the money in his pub, buying grog. And what's more, old Bill'd get rid of the gear like nothing. It was a pretty good racket he had going.

So then in '81 I finished the droving and I went contract mustering. And in that same year we bought our first property. So that was about the end of it for me then. And also it was about the end of the droving up there as well. Some even reckon that I was the one who shut down the stock routes. And it might appear that way too, because I was the last person to drove cattle to Forsayth. And back in '73, the bridge over the Delaney River at Forsayth got washed away and no more cattle were drove that way. So I was the last one through there.

I was also the last one to drove Miranda bullocks to Mount Surprise; but only by a week, mind you, because John Curley was ahead of me with 1000 bullocks. I had 1000 more. So I was the last one to go there. Then the road trains started to take over because the Miranda cattle had a history of TB and you weren't allowed to take 'dirty' cattle through clean country anymore.

The same thing happened to Dunbar Station, so I was the last one to take Dunbar bullocks. They were the only ones going into Mungana, which is north-west of Dimbulah, up near Chillagoe. That was in '81, and that was because of the TB, as well. The same thing happened to the Vanrook cattle into Julia Creek. In '77 I went to Julia Creek and I was last by a week. Keith Campbell was a week ahead of me.

But with the TB, they started road-training them all, then. Like, they still sold them but a lot of places'd gone to the trouble of getting their herds cleaned up and the Gulf was about the last pocket that still had the TB. So naturally, they were worried that the drovers might lose some along the way and they'd mix in with their clean cattle and infect them. So though I wasn't the first drover on the scene in the Gulf, by far, I reckon I was about the last.

Mirage

If a horse has never seen a camel before, he'll go mad. That's true. Oh, those camels, they've got that look about them. And they've got a stink about them, too. There's even been known cases of horses dropping dead at their first sight of a camel. One look—a heart attack—and plop, down they go. True. But that's only in the rare cases, of course, because, usually, if horses are brought up with camels, they're all right with them. They don't mind each other. And actually, when we were droving down the Canning Stock Route, the camel boy always rode the horse that led the pack camels.

And that's where camels do come in handy—not for the actual droving but mainly as pack animals. Like, when we'd start off from Halls Creek, well, you had to take along enough rations for at least twenty weeks which meant that you'd need thirty or forty horse packs and the horses to carry them. But if you used the camels, you could put the whole lot on about six or seven of them. So no, we never drove cattle with camels, but they were excellent pack animals and they were also very good when it came to pulling the water out of the wells.

In actual fact—and here's a story for you—the only time I went with camels, we nearly perished. I was the camel-tailer with teamsters, carting wool. There were four of us: the old boss bloke Jimmy Oslington, myself and two others. Then we had three wagons, two drays and about sixty camels. I forget how many bales of wool we carried, though it was a lot. But we only had two horses on that trip and they were mostly tied up behind the wagons and were only used in the morning when I'd ride out to muster up the camels to put in the wagons.

Anyhow, we were going out to a place called Granite Peak, out the back of Wiluna, which is at the bottom of the Canning Stock Route, and one of the wells we come to was dry and the next one was burnt right out. So we couldn't get nothing out of either of them. By that stage the camels had already gone for a couple or three days without water, so they were pretty thirsty. Anyhow, the manager of Granite Peak, he happened along in a motor car and he told us where this big lagoon was that had plenty of water in it.

'Just saw it recently,' he said.

So me and another feller, a half-caste Afghan bloke, we jumped on the horses and we led all these camels out to where this big lake was, about twenty or thirty mile further out, to give them a drink.

Anyway when we got there, to look at it, it looked like there was miles and miles of water in it. But the further we went towards this

Sharing out the last of the water.

water, the further it moved away from us. Of course it turned out to be a mirage, but because this feller'd told us that there definitely was water out there, we kept going. And also, because we'd only thought that it was going to be an overnight trip, there and back, we'd only taken our dinner and we had just this one small canteen of water between us. So we used that up as we continued on into the second day, looking for this water.

This was at the end of November, early December, and it gets mighty hot in that country, I can tell you. Still, we kept going with these camels right out into this lagoon and still we couldn't find water. Then we come across a dried creek so we went up there, but that turned out to be dry, too.

So by our second night we'd pretty much decided we'd gone far enough. We'd run out of water and our tongues were pretty dry and the camels were also getting harder to handle. See, if a camel goes without water for too long it'll start to go blind and stagger around, falling over trees and that. And that's what these fellers were doing, and we couldn't do nothing with them, so we had to let them go.

A few of the camels followed us back but a lot of them wandered off and they would've perished. Some might've even found their way back to the last water but then they would've had a great big drink straight away and gotten cramps and died, anyway.

Anyhow it was about thirty-nine hours from the time we went out until the time we got back and, by then, our tongues were swollen up so bad we couldn't talk. But still, old Jimmy Oslington, the boss, he wouldn't let us have a big drink. He knew it'd kill us. So he just wet our mouths and then he made us spit it out. Then we had another go and we spat that out, too. So it was probably a couple of hours before we had a proper drink. Our horses were no better, neither. They also took three or four days to get over it.

Then when we finally got to Granite Peak, this Jimmy Oslington, well, didn't he go crook at the manager feller for telling us there was water out there. And this manager still swore, black and blue, that there was. But see, he never went out across the lagoon to find it. He just had one look and said, 'Oh yeah, there's plenty of water there.'

But there wasn't. It was only a mirage.

Mothering

Emily was four months old when we went into central New South Wales to pick up a mob of cattle. And it couldn't have been a much harder trip for both of us because, when we walked them towards Nyngan, we got caught in the April 1990 floods.

But with Emily, I was lucky because for the first three months I was at home at our base, in south-eastern Queensland, and there was an old bush nursing sister there who gave me lots of tips on how to cope when I took Emily on the road. So even before we set out I'd read a lot of books, and also my husband's mother was fantastic. If I was really having a bad time I only had to ring her. That's if we were anywhere near a phone, of course. So I'd read a lot and, when I could, I made lots of phone calls. But basically, on the road, I just had to cope on my own.

There was one time when Emily got a very bad case of bronchitis. Of course there weren't any mobile phones back then and, as usual, it was raining, so we were stuck and we couldn't go anywhere for help. But I just put some Vicks in a bucket of hot water and made up a vaporiser to try and clear her head so she could breathe a bit easier. Then when we got into Narromine the doctor said that I'd done the right thing because it helped to loosen everything up in her chest.

And we always used disposable nappies. I know they're not very good for the environment, but when you haven't got much water on board, thank God for disposables, I say. I mean, there was plenty of water laying all about the place but we couldn't carry much in the caravan. It was a case of water, water everywhere and not too much to bath in, so most of the time we'd recycle the water. I'd bathe Emily then I'd have a wash in the water and so forth. Then whenever we came to a creek or something we'd all have a good wash-up and I'd wash all our clothes.

So anyway, after we got caught in the floods around Nyngan we walked the cattle up to Brewarrina, which is east of Bourke, and we came back the Belt and Buckle Route, back to Duck Creek, then back to Nyngan again, where we ended up putting them on agistment for a while. But to start with there was only my husband and me and Emily on that trip because our usual jackaroo was busy on another job. Then he came to help us after the first month, which made it a bit easier.

But talk about mothering; we had 800 cows and 650 calves on that trip and a lot of the cows were calving along the way, which made it even more difficult. Now, with the newly born calves, what the old fellers used to do was to just knock them on the head and skin them and take the skins along for the old cow to smell so that she wouldn't get too upset. But we couldn't do that with these because they were stud Brafords (Brahman-Hereford cross) and we had to keep the calves with them.

So what we did was, we'd load the newly born calves on the truck each morning. And oddly enough, the old cows didn't seem to worry about it too much. They'd just stand there and watch us putting them in the truck. Then as soon as we got to the lunch camp all the mothers came across, bellowing, so we'd unload the calves and they'd have a feed.

Then when it was time for us to load them back onto the truck again the cows would nudge them toward us. It's amazing how they were so happy for us to cart their calves along. It was like they realised what the problem was and what the alternatives might've been. Then on night camp we'd unload the calves again and they'd spend the night with their mothers.

But after the calves were about three days old they'd usually be strong enough to walk. Then if one of them got tired, we'd just come along and pick it up and hang it over the horse with its head over one way and the tail over the other. And they didn't seem to mind that, either.

But during those first few weeks when we couldn't get the young bloke to help us, it was all hands on deck and I'd put Emily in a joey pouch. It was one of those snuggle pouches that you wear on your front. And I'd be up on the horse, working the cattle, with her snuggled down in this joey pouch. And because it was so cold and wet, I had this great big jacket that I'd put over the top of her and zip it up.

So Emily would be all snuggled down in the joey pouch and you'd get these tourists coming along and taking photos of us droving the cattle. Then they'd see my jacket start jiggling about so I'd unzip it and Emily would stick her head out and she'd be looking around. She was such a tiny little thing.

'Oh, there's a baby in there!' they'd all say.

They were amazed to see a little baby out on a horse with her mother, droving all these cattle along. But oh, it was so wet those early years with Emily. Those four years around 1990 were very wet. Everywhere we went in New South Wales it seemed to rain, and we always seemed to be getting caught in floods.

Murder

When we started droving for the Schmidt brothers, they owned Alroy Downs Station, over there in the north-east of the Northern Territory. Brunette Downs was on the north side, Alexandria was on the east side and Rockhampton Downs was on the north-western side, going towards Tennant Creek.

Alroy was only a 35,000 head property, while Brunette Downs was 50–60,000 head. Alexandria held 60–70,000 head of cattle. They were big properties in them days. Charlie Johnson was the manger of Alexandria. A feller called Barnes was the manager of Brunette and one of the Schmidt brothers was the manager and a part owner of Alroy. He was the one that give my father the droving contract when we took his cattle down to the Cooper Creek, to one of their other properties, South Galway, down there in the south-west of Queensland, near Windorah.

Drover at the Queensland–Northern Territory border.

So we drove for the Schmidts from 1936, up until the war started. Then when the war came, all the young stockmen went to the war and the elder ones were getting beyond it, and that's when my father packed it in. I tried to enlist but they said that I was committed to stay with the industry. Otherwise I'd have gone. So I stayed with the Schmidt family until after the war was over. That was at Alroy, South Galway, and at another one of their properties down near Cunnamulla. All the Schmidt family have passed on now, the senior ones anyway, bar one lady who's a couple of years younger than me. I'm eighty-seven and she's eighty-five.

But the worst droving trip that I ever done was when we took 1500 head from Alroy to Twin Hill Station. Mind you, these were supposed to be dry cows. That's what we'd been told, anyway. But they weren't. These were all calving. Now we had no calf cart on that trip so what happened was that we had to kill the calves when they were born, otherwise we would've gotten nowhere. We'd have been just stuck out there.

Anyway, it turned out to be my job to kill these calves. Then at night I had to tie the cows down—the mothers—so that they couldn't go back looking for their calves. Now I was only eight stone at the time, maybe eight four, and I had to throw these cows and tie their hind legs together so they couldn't walk. And what's more, I had ten to fifteen of these cows to tie down each night, and sometimes I had to tie them down for two nights until they forgot about that memory of their calf.

Then after I'd killed six hundred calves, I forgot to count them anymore. I just give up. And I told the boss when I run into him the next time, I said, 'What a terrible thing you done.'

And he said, 'I didn't do it. The manager done it. He was supposed to give yer dry cows.'

'Well,' I said, 'he should be tried for murder because all I done was murder over six hundred calves, 'n' the other man helped me.'

And that haunted my memory for weeks. Because those poor cows, you know, the sounds they made. I tell you, their mothering instinct was so wonderful, just to see how much they wanted their calves. But then, to know that I'd gone and murdered them, it was terrible.

Mysterious Happenings

Now all this happened down near the Victorian border. There was this feller, a drover. He was a mate of mine. Anyhow I seen him one time, not far from my farm, driving a mob of Hereford cattle along the road. He had a good mix of steers, cows and calves. So I give him a toot of the horn as I went by, off down to Echuca, where I spent most of the day.

Then when I was coming back, there he was on the road, 50 mile from where I'd seen him just that morning. Fifty mile. And he was riding the same piebald horse and, by all intents and purposes, he was moving the same bloody mob of cattle; the same number of Herefords. And I tell you, it really give me a bloody start.

'What the hell's going on here?' I said to meself, because he was quite a portly feller, one that you couldn't easily mistake.

So I drove about two mile up the road, and I just couldn't stand it any more. I thought I was going crackers. So I had to go back and find out.

Anyhow I pulled up and I said to him, 'Look,' I said, 'I must be mistaken but didn't I see you this morning down at Blighty with a mob of cattle?'

'Indeed you did,' he said.

'Then how the hell did you travel so far in such a short time?' I said.

And he said, 'Haven't you ever heard of a wife, a car and a bloody horse float?'

Well, blow me. I mean, they were Herefords again, and about the same number. But it was a different mob. As it turned out, his wife'd gone up with the horse float and picked him and his horse up and there he was, 50 mile further down the road. But gee, it gave me a shock.

Native Affairs

In 1955 I tangled with the bloody Native Affairs and they black-balled me from the Northern Territory for twelve months. So I come inside again. The blackballing was nothing. It doesn't matter. But anyway the people that should've supported me, well, they didn't. And after all what I did for them they should've supported me because I put me life on the line for them more times than not. But we won't go into that, not this time. We'll just leave sleeping dogs lie on that, okay?

But anyway, with that Native Affairs mob, in my days, if you wanted to work some black boys then you had to apply for what was called a 'dog licence'. Now I know that sounds pretty bad but it's what they called it. And you paid ten bob for one of these licences which enabled you to use the labour of, what the Native Affairs described as, a 'native'.

Now if you didn't have that licence you couldn't even give the black boys—natives—a pannikin of tea or a drink of water. So all that other bit about the ringers and drovers chasing the gins and all that, that's all rubbish. I get stuck up at old Ted about that. I mean, we're good friends and that but the blacks' camps were so far away from the stock routes that it's not funny. You wouldn't even know they were there unless you knew the area very well.

And anyway, if you were going up past Alexandria Station or Brunette Downs, for instance, and you left your cattle and went over to the blacks' camp and the bloody station manager found out, well, he'd put a bullet in you. I mean, you just didn't go around messing with somebody else's blackfellas. It just wasn't done. It was worse than patting another man's dog. Oh, Christ yes.

What's more, you never ever spoke to another man's blackfella unless you come up to him and he was on his own and you said, 'Where's the drover?' or whatever the case might be. And it was only then that he'd give you the information. But you just wouldn't sit there and have a conversation with him unless, of course, you were like me and you'd known him all your life or you'd been piccaninnies together or something. I mean, there's times when he might come over and offer you a bite of his plug of tobacco which, of course, you did because it was the done thing to do. It was good manners.

So that sort of thing went on right up into the '50s and into the '60s. But we treated our blacks okay, I think. I just told them, 'If you keep yourself clean, then you'll be treated that way. But if you don't, well, that's the way you'll get bloody treated.'

So they kept themselves clean. And that's another thing. We used to give them that old Lifebuoy soap, the carbolic soap. And once they got near the water, they'd use the whole cake to have a bath with.

I remember one time I was out on Killarney Station, in the central west of the Northern Territory, and I was down on the ramp, knocking the nuts out of a big Micky, a big bull, and this black boy was holding back its leg and I just happened to glance over at him and, gees, didn't he have mobile dandruff (lice). Oh, it was shocking. So I stopped everything and I got all the boys together and I cut

Knocking the nuts out of a big Micky.

their bloody hair off and I burnt it and I shaved their heads and smothered their scones in kerosene and fat. Then for good measure, I put a bottle of Californian Poppy all over them, just so they'd smell good.

And you should've seen their hair when it grew. Oh, when they took their hats off and they shook their hair it was all curly and glossy. And they were that bloody proud of it.

So like I said, I think we treated our boys pretty well. And they treated us well, too. On the whole they were good workers and they were very good with the stock. I had a black boy droving with me, Johnny was his name, and he was just marvellous with horses in particular. I've had a horse in the yard that'd virtually eat you and Johnny'd slip through and he'd just stand there against the rail. He wouldn't move. And you'd see that bloody horse; all of a sudden it'd start to simmer down and its ears'd be going forward and back and eventually it'd come over to Johnny and it'd smell him. Then before long, it'd be all over the boy.

But Johnny never once approached the horses. Never. He'd just stand there and the horse'd come up to him. And when he touched the horse, he always used the back of his hand. Never the front; always the back. And I don't know why, it's got me beat, but the horses were all over him in a few minutes. Oh, it was marvellous to see the boy working. It really was.

Now this thing with Johnny goes back fifty odd bloody years. See, he come from a Myall tribe, which is a word that describes an Aboriginal living in a traditional way. They're not educated people. He's just a wild blackfella, or his father was anyway.

But Johnny joined us when I was in the Northern Territory, heading over Western Australia way. I pulled up at Alexandria Station and I asked the station manager who was there at the time, Billy Young—'Bellowing Billy' they used to call him—I asked Billy if he had a certain size horseshoe because I had a horse that had a little foot.

Anyway, Bellowing Billy said, 'Go 'n' see Rankine. He'll give 'em to yer even if I say so or not.' And he would've too.

But I didn't see the boy at all; I didn't see Johnny. Anyway we were travelling out empty, on our way out to pick up some cattle, and I'd camped a day's stage away from Alexandria and one of the other boys that was with me called out, 'Yarraman (horseman) coming.'

So I looked up and I see this Johnny coming. I hadn't seen him in a long time but I recognised him. And he come up and he didn't get off his horse. He just sat there and he had what we called a bagman's plant, which is just a pack and a couple of horses. And Johnny said to me, 'Before,' he said—I wont speak in pidgin because it'll only bugger you up—'Before,' he said, 'when you wanted me to go with you droving, my father wouldn't let me because you didn't have any beard. Now,' he said, 'you got a black beard and I got a black beard so I'm coming to go droving with you.'

'Well,' I said, 'you'd better get off yer horse and the cook'll give yer a feed.'

So he got off and he fixed up his horses first, before he come over and had a feed. And I had him for two droving seasons and only then it was partly my fault when he left us. It was very sad to lose him. Still, it was just something that happened. We gave him a lot of horses over the time he was with us so he ended up with a bloody good plant of horses. And we knew he'd look after them. He loved horses. As I said, he just had a way with them.

I remember another time, we had a big chestnut horse. Now, what did I call that bugger? Starlight or something. I forget just now but he was a big, liver-coloured chestnut. And oh gee, he was a touchy bastard. I bought him off a selector, just out of Mount Isa, along with half-a-dozen other horses.

Anyway, Johnny said to me, 'I'll make a night horse outa that feller fer you.'

'Pig's arse, yer will,' I said.

'No, no. He'll be all right,' he said. 'I'll ride him.'

'Well you'd better because no other bugger will, I can tell yer,' I said.

Anyway, sure as anything, the first night we were out with the cattle, he had that horse out on watch. But he was a touchy big bugger—the horse, that is—and thanks to Johnny he eventually come good. That boy settled him down.

Never

Unfortunately, like many drovers, I never had a real education. See, there were eleven of us children and things got very difficult at home so, when I was thirteen, my parents decided that it was time for me to help bring in an income. So they sent me out bush to help my brother-in-law, timber-cutting and driving a team of horses. From that I got into ringing and then the droving. And I soon found out that I wasn't the only young kid in my sort of situation. Lots of other young fellers had also been forced to go out bush and work to help their parents feed their other kids.

These days, of course, people romanticise it all. But it was a bloody hard life. There's no denying that. A lot of the treatment that us kids got was tough; too tough for some. There were the beltings and the suicides; young kids that just couldn't take it. And I've seen fellers killed. Then one time, at the Quilpie trucking yards, I had to help fish a dead shearer from out of a water trough. And when you're only a kid yourself, that sort of thing's hard to shake. It's hard to forget.

But we didn't know any better. And anyway, where could you go for help? You couldn't run back home to your parents or you'd be in strife. And if you went to the cops, they'd more than likely belt you up, too. And you'd belt them up as well, if you got half a chance. That's just how it was. I remember when Bobby Woods and me got belted up by the cops. We were coming out of Queensland with a mob of Chatsworth bullocks. Alan Remfey was our boss drover, and we got over the border into Bourke and we let the bullocks go on the common. Then Alan said to Bobby and me, 'You two blokes can go into town but don't get drunk 'n' don't get into a fight.'

Well I didn't drink anyway, so we were pretty safe there. So off we go into Bourke. Now Bobby came from Hillston, in south-western New South Wales, and while we were in the café we came across some part Aborigines who were also from Hillston. Anyway, we all got chatting and the cops came in and they arrested us for talking to these fellas. I mean, we spent our whole life droving with Aborigines and, all of a sudden, here we are getting arrested for talking to some of them.

Anyhow they took us back to the cop shop and they said to Bobby, 'What's yer name?'

And Bobby said, 'Me name's Bobby Woods.' And one of the coppers give him one up the kidneys. *Thwack!* Just like that. Then he give me one for good measure.

So the sergeant asked Bobby again and Bobby said, 'Fair dinkum, me name's Bobby Woods.' And the copper give him another one. *Thwack!* Oh, he was a rough bastard, he was. Then this copper said that he was after his real name. So then Bobby said, 'Oh, it's Robert so-and-so Woods' and the copper didn't hit him.

Anyhow, they locked us up and they didn't treat us real good; always having a go at us and that. Then when Alan come in the next morning and he seen the mess we were in, he wanted to know what the hell was going on, and this copper told him how we'd been caught talking to blacks.

And Alan just couldn't believe it. 'Well,' he said, 'we've got two Aborigines droving with us 'n', what's more, we're all going down to Victoria together, so what, aren't we supposed to talk to them neither?'

Anyway the cop told Alan that he was supposed to get some sort of special permit if he wanted to keep the black boys with us. I don't know exactly what it was, but he got it. Then when we were being booked out, Bobby said to the copper, 'Don't let me see you up the track, old feller.'

And the copper pointed to the cell and he said, 'Don't get smart, sonny, or yer'll go back in there.'

'Like hell I will, old feller,' Bobby said. 'There's three of us here, 'n' now there's only one of you.'

Anyhow, we left Bourke after that. Then later on, with these two Aborigines that were on the droving trip with us, when we got further down into New South Wales, we stayed at a cattle station.

I won't mention the name of the place but we had to spell the bullocks there for a fortnight because they'd had it pretty rough coming out of Queensland, with the drought and all. Then while we were staying at this place, they were going to tail the bullocks and rest the horses. But that gave us the chance to sleep in the empty men's quarters, in proper bunks, which was a rare thing because we were all used to camping out together in swags or whatever.

We were really looking forward to that, so we went into the men's quarters; a beautiful big quarters it was too. And we were about to get settled when the cook came in and he said, 'The boys have to camp over at the woodheap.' By 'the boys' he meant these two black boys that we had droving with us.

'Why?' we asked.

'It's company policy,' he said.

'Look here,' Alan said, 'we've just come all the way down from Queensland with these two fellas and, if they wanted to, any night of the week they could've put the bullocks over us,' he said.

'It's still company policy,' the cook said.

'Well,' said Alan, 'bugger you, we'll all go over 'n' camp at the woodheap, then.'

So we stayed over at the woodheap with the two boys, which was some sort of an education, I suppose. But those boys were as black as black. I don't know where they come from but, by gee, they were black. And as Alan said, when they were out doing their night watch, they'd be riding around the bullocks while we were asleep in our swags and, if they wanted to, it wouldn't have taken much for them to put 1500 head of bullocks over our camp. And that would've been the end of us.

So when you're droving, there's a hell of a lot of trust built up between the whites and the blacks. And for us to go and sleep in the men's quarters and leave them to camp out in the bloody woodheap—my God, how would you feel?

But the company used them as cheap labour. It made the contract cheaper. That's why we had them. But really, the Aborigines were exploited, as were a lot of us ringers. Like, we were good enough to take thousands and thousands of pounds' worth of

A drover required a special permit when using aboriginal labour.

cattle halfway across Australia but we weren't considered good enough to even walk into the garden at the station homestead. Now that tells you something, doesn't it?

But what else could you do in those days? There was no dole and you were too young to do a grown man's job. So if you could ride a horse, that's what you did. And even though a lot of your wage was paid in tobacco, and I didn't smoke, I still sent money home. Though, for me, the money wasn't such a big thing, really. You got your cheque at the end of the trip. You'd fix your swag up. You made sure you had blankets, boots, and that you had trousers. Then you sent the rest of your money home. I mean, the boss drover looked after you. Well, most of the time he did.

But I didn't even drink on a trip, where a lot of them hit the grog when they were near a town. Like, we got to Boulia once and I was out with the horses, horsetailing. Then when I come back into camp the ringers were all drunk and fighting. These were white-fellers. And we had 1500 head of bullocks and about eighty or ninety horses to look after, and there they were, drunk and going on at each other. So I just rode the bloody horses over them. That pulled them up pretty quick, I can tell you.

Then the next morning those ringers pulled out, which left Alan and me to look after all the bullocks and horses; the whole lot. But the thing was, we couldn't wait around for more ringers to come out because we still had to do so many miles per day. That was the law. So we put the horses in with the bullocks and we headed out. Then of an afternoon, I'd pick the horses out and I'd go on and set up camp and make up a bit of a dinner and hobble the horses out. Then Alan and me, we'd half-night the bullocks. Like, I'd do watch for half the night and Alan did the next half. And we did that for a fortnight, until the agents got a couple of ringers out to help us. That's when Bobby Woods joined us. By then we were right down near the Diamantina.

So that was a bit of a bummer, a bit tough, because it was all with packhorses and I was also doing the cooking. And I hated cooking. I can't even boil water. I just wanted to be a horsetailer. But the bulls were good by then. They'd come a long way and they were as quiet as milking cows. Then we finally delivered them down on the New South Wales side of the Murray River, somewhere near Echuca. I'm not real sure of the station. See, us ringers weren't a very important item in the organisation of things so we never knew what station we were going to or where we were picking up from. We just went.

Then after we delivered, Alan said to Bobby Woods and me, 'Youse can take the plant back to Cloncurry.' And he went over to Sydney while we took the plant back up to north-western Queensland. The plant's all the horses and all the gear. Then by the time we got back, Alan met us again and we went back to Chatsworth to pick up another mob of bullocks and we headed off again. But I didn't finish that second trip because I got smashed up down in Brewarrina, in central-northern New South Wales. I got dragged in a stirrup and I got all me ribs and head kicked in. I was unconscious for three days in hospital. Then I was pretty crook for a while after that so I went back home to recover.

But Alan Remfey was a good boss; at heart he was a good boss. You know, he'd punch you in the head as quick as look at you. And you had to look after his horses, or else. But some of the longer trips I done with him were up to thirty-two weeks. That was seven days a week. You never had a day off. But I did two trips with him as his horsetailer so I was pretty pleased about that. But Alan was tough, and he was a wild bastard too. You didn't ever want to get on the wrong side of him.

Like, there was one time we got down into New South Wales. There was big long feed and the cattle started to put on some condition so we were taking them easy; we were bludging. But the station owners and the stock inspectors must've had an eye on us. Oh, they were a pain in the arse, they were. Those stock inspectors were always checking to make sure that you did your mileage each day. Then out of the blue, Alan got a summons for 'loitering'.

'Shit,' I said, 'what're you gonna do now?'

'She'll be right, Nugget,' he said. 'Don't worry, I'll fix those bastards. I'll use it as toilet paper, then I'll post it back in.'

And that's true. That's what he did. He used it as shit paper and he sent it back into them. And the stock inspector didn't come out again after that and we never heard any more about it. But they were good trips. Hard though. Like I said, Alan'd sooner punch you in the head as look at you.

Then when I got a bit older, I thought that if I didn't come in from the west I'd end up in a real bad way. You know, a lot of the ringers ended up being either crippled or drunks, or both, and I didn't want that to happen. So that's what I did, I came in and I went cane cutting and fruit picking and I met my wife, Margaret, and now we've got property and we're into tick serum and breeding Droughtmaster cattle, among other things.

So things have turned out okay. I've got a Mercedes now that's only got 9000 ks on it. So I can't complain. As I was just telling George, it's certainly a bit different from the days when we never had the money for the train fare so we'd throw our swags up and jump on the Flying Flea, there at Charleville. Then just before we got to the railway bridge at Quilpie we'd jump off, in case the coppers got us and give us a real belting.

That's true. I can still remember being stuck in at the Quilpie trucking yards with Ronny and Colin Millard and we didn't have a brass razoo between us. And in those days, if you didn't have five bob on you, you could be jailed for vagrancy. Anyhow, we were too frightened to go over the railway line into town to look for a job because we knew that the cops were waiting for us and they'd belt us up. So there we were, we didn't have any bloody food and no money. But the galahs were coming in to eat the grain so we ended up stoning them, and we'd boil them up and then we'd eat these bloody galahs.

And now, like I said, I'm pretty well off. So I guess it's all turned out okay for a thirteen year old who was sent out to earn a wage to try and keep his family going. And like George was saying, 'We might've just been kids but we grew up quick and we learnt a hell of a lot.'

But there's one thing: I never, ever forget that, as a kid, I humped my bloody swag and I didn't have a penny in my pocket, not one penny. I never forget that. Never.

Old Claude Kidman

My name is Azzie Zilla Fazulla. I was born in 1926, which makes me seventy-six in this August, and what keeps me going is that I've got a young wife. She's fifty in July and we've been together for twenty-six years. They said it wouldn't last but, on Monday, it'll be twenty-four years since we've been married. So there you go.

My background is that my father come from the Punjab, in India. He was more of the Afghan. Then my mother was Irish, and I was born in Broken Hill, in western New South Wales. So what do you reckon all that makes me? I don't know, even myself.

After my father came to Australia he used to cart with pack camels from Broken Hill up to places like Innaminka and Tibooburra, and to Cordillo Downs Station. He did that for years. He'd cart supplies and bore casings out and he'd cart wool and all that stuff back. Cordillo Downs was a very big wool place back then. And you just wouldn't believe how they loaded them camels up.

Now I never worked with dad because we had to make a quid so, when we were kids, the eldest brother and me, we got into droving. That brother died just the other day—well, three weeks ago to be exact. He was seventy-eight. But we first went droving around 1939, and we moved a lot of sheep from all around the Broken Hill area. Then we started to drove sheep down into Victoria. And after that we started to go up to places like Longreach, in central western Queensland, and into south-western Queensland, and we'd bring sheep or cattle back down to Cockburn where they'd be trucked to Adelaide. Cockburn was a very big place for trucking at one time.

But there was a lot of droving back in them days. In a good season, you'd go down the Tibooburra road and there'd be cattle 6 mile apart and there'd be sheep 6 mile apart, mob after mob after mob. And now, fair dinkum, you hardly see a mob. Everything travels on trucks these days. It's the same down the Birdsville Track to Marree. One time you never even saw a motor car along there, not one, just cattle, mob after mob. And these days, yes, you see the mobs, but they're all on trucks.

So I've done quite a bit of droving around the tracks but I've never been right up the Top End. I'll admit that. Like I said, I've been up to Longreach but I've only drove them from there, not to there, if you get my meaning. Like, we'd take them over from Longreach and we'd walk them back down to Marree or we'd walk them to cattle stations down in New South Wales and South Australia. That was mainly with the Kidmans.

Now I first worked for the Kidmans on Quinyambie Station, which is just over the New South Wales border, in the north-east of South Australia. That was when I was only young. Then when the war was over they cut all that country up for the returned diggers. But we used to drove for that old Claude Kidman. He was some sort of relation to Sir Sidney Kidman. But Claude did a lot of droving off Quinyambie, and we'd take mobs of cattle down to Cockburn to be trucked. And he'd come along with us. He didn't stay at home, not old Claude.

And also, here's another interesting thing that you mightn't know: with Sir Sidney, he used to get the young city blokes sent out. The ones that'd been put in homes. You know, like, when they played up they'd be put into a home, in detention, instead off going to a jail. So Sir Sidney got some of them out to work on his stations. They sent them out to other places, too. They were sent to everywhere.

And the Kidmans were bloody good with them young fellers. Old Claude'd get something like three of them and he'd put them together with someone who was either experienced with the horse-tailing or the cooking. And by the time he'd done one droving trip with them boys, say, from Quinyambie to Cockburn, well, by the time old Claude got to Cockburn, them boys were broken in real good. It might've only been a three-week trip but it done them boys wonders. And some of them went on to managing places, too, later on in their years.

Sir Sidney Kidman with aboriginal 'boys'.

Kevin Johns was one. I remember Kevin as plain as day. He put in about twelve months on the road, droving with old Claude Kidman. Then after he finished droving he got on to Bill Bowman's daughter, and he married her. Bill was managing a property out there. Then when Bill retired, Kevin took over the manager's job. And Kevin was only fifteen when he come out from one of them homes and he was about twenty-five or twenty-six when he took over from Bill. Kevin only died a few years back, in Marree or somewhere.

And with them same fellers—with the ones that came out on the road with me—well, after the droving some of them went working out on stations, around and about, and some of them ended up being head stockmen and managers too. So that just goes to show you, aye.

So I would've been . . . I forget how old I was, exactly . . . but it was back in the 1940s, I guess, when I first went droving with old Claude. He would've been in his sixties or seventies, even back in them days. And he could still ride a horse all day, and he smoked a

171

big old pipe. I remember how he'd sit on the horse, humped right over, smoking on his pipe. That was old Claude. And he'd still get up at the right time and do his two-hour watch. A big, tall, raw-boned bloke, he was.

Old Shinny and the Saddle

Because I came from a family of drovers I got into the game when I was only a little jibber. So they first took me away back in about 1950. And for a while there we used to get a couple of good black boys to come along with us. They were mainly from places around the centre of the Northern Territory, like Philip Creek, or there was the old Alroy Downs boys. The Alroy boys, they'd sort of mated up with the older brother, George. George was the boss, but don't call him 'the boss drover' for Christ's sake. It's drover-in-charge. That's what you call him. Anyhow those boys liked George so they sort of come along with us.

But back in them days, well, up equal against man to man—that's white and black—I don't think you'd find a slacker among them black boys. We never did, anyway. They always pulled their weight when they were with us.

So that was back then, but now they've sort of buggered the system up, somehow. It's a bloody shame to see the way the country's gone. You go to Mt Isa and they're always in town there, hanging around. And the thing is, you know full well that they could be out there, equal beside you, ringing or throwing a bull or tying a horse or whatever. So I don't know what's happened, but as I said, it's a damn shame.

And track; we had a one-eyed blackfella called Old Shinny. I think he might've had a skinny shinbone or something. But Old Shinny, he could track an ant, that bloke, even with the one eye. He once tracked me across the bloody desert, when we were on our way to Wave Hill, after my horse give up on me when I was chasing clumpers. Wave Hill's right over there near the West Australian border.

See, we used to take these big clumper fellers, these Clydesdale horses, out of the Territory and George'd trade them with the black boys for broken-in saddle horses to use in our droving plant. For one of these clumpers they'd give George three, or maybe even five, broken-in horses. And these clumpers were mad; real wild. So we'd trade them. Then when we come back from a droving trip, you'd see the blacks going walkabout with them. They'd have broken them in and they'd hook them up to their two-wheel carts and they'd stack all their kids and piccaninnies and their gins all in the cart and away they'd go.

And if we ever got one of these clumpers back off the black boys, they'd be real cagey with us because they weren't used of the smell of a white man. Sometimes you had to be like a sand goanna to catch them. You'd have to sort of sneak along the ground to rope them on the front foot or you had to rope them out of a tree. But once you got them under control they were pretty handy horses. I don't think we ever got a dud off the black boys, not that I can ever say.

So anyway, there we were this time, going to Wave Hill and I decided to go out and get some of these clumpers. And I had this big,

Horse breaking.

bay, West Australian horse that I could ride to hell and back. That's how tough and fit he was. But the boys must've been riding him, chasing something or other, because they'd run him down. They'd overheated him, sort of. But they never said nothing about it to me, see, so I just got on the old feller and I went out after these clumpers.

So there I was, away out in this semi-desert with no water and the old feller, this horse, wasn't there when I wanted him. He sort of knocked up and he couldn't go no further. He chucked the towel in so I hopped off and I rubbed him down and I just left him there. That's all I could do.

But I had this brand new saddle on him, see. I'd just bought it off a feller called Johnny McDonald, a couple of days before I come home from the Curry (Cloncurry). Now I wasn't going to lose that, so I strapped it on me back. Like I had the girth around the belly and behind me, and I carried it with the pommel against me ear. It was like a turtle shell, sort of, and it protected me. A fair weight too, it was, but I wasn't going to part with it.

Then somewhere along the line, back at camp they twigged that something'd gone wrong. So George got Old Shinny and they come out looking for me. Old Shinny done the tracking, you know.

I wasn't lost, like, but while I was walking everything sort of got a bit funny. The saddle was getting weighty so I took my shirt off. And after a while longer, I started to chuck me clothes away. Then I started to get blisters and things from my riding boots so I took them off and I left them. So I was barefoot then, and that made it a bit harder for Old Shinny, until he seen where I started to do the wobbles. See, me feet weren't making no more sense so I started to move like that—shuffling.

And George reckoned that when Old Shinny saw the shuffle marks he said, 'The little feller, his a little bit gone funny in the head, boss. We mightn't find 'im alive.'

So George and Old Shinny kept tracking me because they thought there was still a bit of hope. See, they all reckon that when you start doing the circle you're near enough finished—you know, near enough to dead. Well I hadn't done the circle yet, but I was getting pretty wobbly and I was shuffling a lot.

So I was out there, in this desert, for probably about three days and, as I said, I didn't have any water. No water, and nothing to eat. And in that country it don't matter what sort of tree you climb up, everything looks the same. There was nothing out there, only those stinking, mongrel, bloody mosquitoes. Mosquitoes; jeez, you've never seen anything like them. They nearly drove me mad.

Then they finally found me. Well, me sister-in-law found me first. I was somehow coming down past the camp and George and Old Shinny was pretty close behind. But apparently, when I got near camp all my tummy and tongue was all swelled up and I was trying to drink at the waterhole and the sister-in-law, she tried to grab me by the hair and she pull me back out of the water and, apparently, I punched her and hooked her. So then George and Old Shinny, they come along and then they had to strap me down for a couple of days because they reckoned I went a bit funny in the head. I must've been delirious, aye. So they fed me on a bit of broth and then I finally come back to my senses, sort of.

But I got the saddle back okay. I reckoned I wasn't going to part with that. I bought it off old Johnny McDonald. But because of what happened, even these days, I still can't wear a shirt. I know that I've got a shirt on now, but normally, if I'm doing anything with a shirt on I get, sort of, claustrophobia. Like, when I'm working at home I always get down to a singlet. It don't matter how cold it is or what the weather is, I still wear only the singlet.

One Day while Counting Sheep

I used to be in the navy many years ago. Anyway, we were steaming up the coast one time and, with nothing better to do, we were sitting up in the quarterdeck, bullshitting away to each other. This would've been in '59 or thereabouts.

Anyway, there was this bloke with us whose surname was Poor, so obviously we'd nicknamed him 'Pissy', as in Piss Poor. Pissy hailed from right out the back blocks of western New South Wales, and every mid-year leave and Christmas leave he used to go home, up the bush. So he came back from leave this time and, like I said, there we were spinning bullshit in the quarterdeck and Pissy told us this droving story about the largest mob of sheep he'd ever seen. And what's more, he swore that it was true. And knowing Pissy . . . Well, you can make up your own mind.

Now when Pissy spoke, he talked in a real slow, laconic manner, so you've gotta imagine that, and you've also gotta imagine that Pissy's brother, having never been out of the bush in his life, talked even slower.

Anyway, Pissy and his brother were having a quiet beer or two, out on the front verandah of the pub, near where they lived. It was about ten o'clock in the morning, and they were sitting there, when this mob of sheep began meandering down the main street, past the pub, heading on their way out of town to wherever they were going. Then once each hour or so, a half-starved, flea bitten looking kelpie would happen to drift by, walking more with the mob than keeping them in any tight sheepdog order.

So with not too much else going on in town at the time, the two brothers grabbed another beer and they sat down again to watch this passing parade. Then a couple of hours later this mob of sheep was still wandering down the main street, past the pub, heading on their way out of town to wherever they were going.

Talking bullshit.

By this time Pissy and his brother had had a few more beers and they were feeling a bit peckish so they decided to go inside the pub to have a counter lunch. And it was while they were having lunch that Pissy happened to remark to his brother, 'That's a fairly big

mob'a sheep goin' past, aye?' To which the brother gave the statement a lot of thought while he ate another chop and had another
beer.

'Reckon yer might be right,' the brother eventually replied.

Anyhow, after lunch they grabbed another beer and they went
back out on the verandah only to find this mob of sheep was still
coming down the main street, past the pub, heading on their way
out of town to wherever they were going. So with nothing better to
do they took up their seats again to watch some more sheep drift
by. And like I said, once each hour or so a half-starved, flea bitten-
looking kelpie would aimlessly wander past with the mob. Now why
Pissy made a point of mentioning about the dog was because it was
something that his brother was to suddenly remark on.

'There goes another dog,' Pissy's brother said, seemingly fascinated by how the occasional, half-starved dog broke the monotony
of colour; the dogs being brownish and the sheep being a dirty
white-grey-reddish colour.

Anyway, they had a few more beers and at about four o'clock in
the afternoon they were still there, watching this mob coming down
the main street, past the pub, heading on their way out of town.

So Pissy and his brother had a few more beers and it was just
coming on sunset when a horse and sulky appeared in the
distance. Now, mind you, this sulky wasn't bringing up the rear of
the mob because it still looked like there were thousands of sheep
coming up along behind it.

So they waited a while longer and had a few more beers and,
when the bloke with the horse and sulky finally got close enough,
Pissy and his brother noticed that the sulky was loaded to the hilt
with pots and pans and cooking gear of all shapes and sizes.
Loaded to overflowing it was, with all this cooking gear.

'I reckon that bloke's the camp cook,' Pissy said to his brother,
to which his brother contemplated the statement while he finished
off his beer, lifted his hat, and scratched his head.

'Reckon yer might be right,' he said.

Now, by this stage, this almost ten-hour parade of sheep had
started to get to Pissy's brother, and his highly inquisitive brain

began a complex mathematical process of trying to work out just how many bloody sheep there were in this mob. So when the cook got near enough to the pub, Pissy's brother grabbed his beer and wandered through the sheep and over to the sulky, which, as I said, was loaded to the hilt with pots and pans and cooking gear of all shapes and sizes.

'Mate,' he said to the cook, 'just how many head'a sheep do yer reckon yer got?'

'Buggered if I know,' the bloke replied. 'I just cook fer the bloody dogs 'n' I've lost count'a them.'

Red

I want to tell you about me father who bought a dog.

We were always looking for good sheepdogs on the farm because to train a dog up, it took a long time. Then, of course, we never had the continual work to keep a young dog practised. So if we spent a lot of time training a dog up, and then we didn't have the work, it'd soon lose the knack of it. It wouldn't be so sharp.

Anyway, being an old-timer around the place, Dad drank a lot in the local pub and he sort of got to know all the townspeople and the farmers and the drovers that came through the place. This was in the late '40s, just after the war.

So Dad was in the pub one day and he got talking to this drover feller and Dad happened to mention how he was looking for a good sheepdog to work out on our farm.

'Got just the thing,' the drover said.

Now some of these drovers were pretty shifty characters and the old man didn't just want to take this drover's word for it, so he asked, 'Can I see the dog work?'

'Yeah,' the drover said. 'The young lad's with the dog working a mob'a sheep out on the road so how's about we go out 'n' I'll show him to yer.'

Anyway they get out there and the drover says, 'This's the dog here. His name's Red.'

Then the old man looks this Red over and he seems okay—a kelpie, he was. So the drover's going on, telling the old man about just what a good worker this dog is and just how obedient he is, and the dog's sitting right there at the drover's feet, looking up at him as if he knows he's being talked about and he's waiting for an order so that he can go and prove just how good he really is.

Anyhow, by this stage there were sheep all over the road, and just then a car came along, so the drover called out, 'Red! Split 'em.' And Red went straight up through the mob of sheep and he split them either side of the road so that the car could get through. Almost perfect, it was. Then Red come back and he sat down again, right at the drover's feet, looking up as if he was keen for more work; maybe something a bit more difficult this time.

'Jesus,' the old man thought, 'the drover's right. This Red's a bloody good sheepdog.'

Anyhow the old man ended up paying something like twenty-five quid for the dog, which was a hell of a lot of money in them days, a hell of a lot. So then Dad brought Red home and he said to me, 'Come 'n' see the new dog I just bought.'

So I did. I had a look at him and he seemed okay. Then we tied him up for a couple of days just to get him settled into his new surroundings. So that was that. It was all settled. Then a week later, when we had to move some sheep, we took this Red out with us. So there we were, us, the sheep and the dog, and the old man shouted, 'Red!'

Red in action.

And the instant the old man shouted, 'Red,' this dog shot straight up and he split that mob of sheep clean down the middle; almost perfect, it was. Then he come back and he sat down again, right at Dad's feet, looking up as if he was keen for more work. And that's when we found out that that's all this Red could do. He'd been on the road for so long with the drover that it'd become his job to go up the road and split the sheep whenever a car come along. That was his forte. That was his job. And that's all he could do.

Right on Cue

After the war I did my first droving trip for the Delta Pastoral Company. That was from up in the Gulf, at Miranda Downs, down to a place called Nulla Nulla, which is up behind Charters Towers there in north-western Queensland.

Now the thing was, with them being my first mob after the war, I knew only too well that if I buggered it up, it may have been the end of it as far as my droving went. Because, with all them old drovers already being so well established, I had to prove myself all over again.

And oh, they were the worst bloody mob I ever had. See normally, you've either got all cows or all bullocks and when they're separated like that they're pretty good to handle. But in this mob there was five hundred cows and five hundred bullocks, and the bullocks were up chasing the cows all night. They never let up. And these were spayed cows, too, meaning that they'd had their ovaries taken out so they couldn't breed no more. But it didn't matter to these bullocks. They were like a mob of young boys chasing after young girls, you know. It's all the same. But oh, they were a real bastard of a mob.

Then to make matters worse, they'd been living up in the Gulf, in the bloody swamp country, so they were very soft in the feet. So when we hit the stony country up through Einasleigh, a number of them started to wear their hoof down to the sole of their feet. Then we had to cue them.

Now what cueing is, it's putting half a horseshoe on the hoof of a cow or bullock. In this case, it was mostly cows. There might be another letter in the word 'cue', but I'm not sure. But anyway, that's near enough because I don't think there'd be too may buggers who'd know about cueing these days, anyway.

But luckily, I'd been through that country before the war, so before we left Normanton, I went around and I picked up a lot of old horseshoes. You don't want big heavy ones. A good old thin, worn-out, horseshoe is the go because cattle have smaller hooves than horses do. Then in your plant, you always had one packhorse that carried all your shoeing gear anyway because, naturally, you had to shoe all your bloody horses on the droving trip as well.

So when we were out on camp, we'd sit up all bloody night carving these old horseshoes up with an old wood axe. You'd cut the shoe in halves or thirds and shape it to fit the back, outside claw of a cow's hoof. That was the only place where they went sore because, when they walk, they must screw their back foot a bit. We never had one go in the front.

Now there were six of us on that trip. I was the boss drover and I had two young nephews, one good black boy, an old, worn-out blackfella, and then there was this bloody cook who could just manage to sit on a horse. A Thursday Islander, he was. Apparently he used to be a pearl diver.

See, when the war broke out, because they thought the Japs'd take over the place, they cleaned out all the Thursday Islanders from over there and they put them into stations around Normanton. And this cook was one of them. There was all sorts of breeds in them, Jap and Chinamen, and Christ's knows what else. Anyhow this cook feller, he was pretty bloody rough, I can tell you. He didn't know much to start with, but I guess he turned out alright in the end because he, at least, learned how to boil the billy, make a rough damper, build up a bit of a stew and cook a bit of corned beef.

The blacks we used were Myalls. They couldn't read or write. But they were reared in the stock camps so they were good horsemen and they were very good with the cattle. The only time you had to take them a bit steady was when they came out of the scrub country and onto them big open plains; out of their own country. See, those boys weren't used of big open plains.

Even the old blackfella, he was a bit like that and he'd done the trip a few times before. But gee, he was a worn-out, poor old bastard, he was. Still, he paid his way all right. After we'd move off camp of a morning, all the sore-footed ones'd soon drop behind and this old blackfella, he'd just poke them along all day, on his own, nice and steady. And the cook'd pack him some tucker so it didn't matter what time he got them on camp at night.

But back to this cueing business—oh, it's a terrible job. See, without much hoof to put a nail through you could only use those little, fine, shoeing nails. Bait nails, they called them. And by gee, you had to be careful because if you ever went in on the quick, well, that's the bloody end of them then. Their foot'd go all septic and it'd fall off.

If you found some stockyards, it made the job a bit easier because you could poke the sore-footed ones into the yard. Then once they were up in the crush you'd just lasso them and lash them onto a rail and get into them, you know. But if you weren't near stockyards, you'd have to use a tree. You'd rope them off with one of them good old bronco horses, then you'd pull them down, put a leg rope on them, pull the leg from under them and let the horse sit back and take the weight. So you'd cue them then. And the next day you'd see them walking along as good as ever. It was marvellous what it did for them.

Lashing a bullock onto the rail.

Anyway, it took us a fortnight longer than any other drover but we delivered our full number. That was the main thing: we didn't lose any. So I proved myself. Then I was right from there on. I got all the droving I wanted.

Salted Meat and Damper

I've got a thick skin so I don't mind if you use my name. It's John Davies and I was born in 1931, which makes me seventy-one this year. Luckily though, I'm in good health because I could've been dead yesterday, and there's plenty of my old mates who've died, and a lot younger than me.

Anyway, I started off breaking in horses when I was very young. But I got a bit jack of that so I picked up with some one-horse drovers around Warren, in western New South Wales. Then I picked up with some other fellers and we went out west, between Coolabah and Byrock, to a station at Glenariff Siding, halfway between Nyngan and Bourke. So I was there for three and half years, maybe four, doing droving and stock work. That was in 1948, when I was seventeen.

I also did some droving for a feller, Jackie Malloy, from Forbes. He was a ex-rodeo rider. Now I never wanted to try my living at buck-jumping but I was a good hand with animals and we also used to educate a lot of horses for station owners. They'd have a toey horse, something a bit snorty and lively, and they'd say, 'Look, take him with yer fer a while then bring him back when yer've fixed him.'

Of course, if the horse was any good you lost him, sort of, and he never went back. Same with the dogs. We'd get a lot of dogs to work and if they turned out any good, well, we'd sort of lose them too. It wasn't dishonesty. It's just that the good ones seemed to wander, somehow. Strange that, aye.

Anyhow, from there I went up to Birdsville and on to the Diamantina. See, it was a great dream for us horsey blokes to go into the Channel Country. It was the pick of Queensland in those days. You could fatten bullocks there like nothing. Unbelievable.

A packhorse drover.

But it was all horse work. That's what got me. I would not have stayed anywhere without horses and stock. And it was all outside; open camps, working out in the bush. I mean, in those days, if we got into town once every three months we were laughing, really laughing. But you didn't give a bugger. We loved the work. We wanted it. We loved the horses, and the money was completely bloody unimportant because, when you went droving, all you got was one pound a day, plus keep. This was in '47, maybe '48. And you never got paid while you were going out with the boss drover. You only got paid from the time he took delivery of the cattle, up until they were delivered. That's all. No travel, out and back.

Then at times, the cooks were very flighty. Out on the stations they went into dispute very quick. You could have a cook for two or three months or you might only have him for a day or two before he cleared off. They were like that. I mean, all those stories you hear about crooked, drunken, and cantankerous cooks are pretty true.

There was one cook—only a little feller, just like me. And see, you'd come in and you'd pick your meal up off the counter, then you'd go and sit down to eat. Anyhow, this cook used to serve up some very bloody ordinary meals. And of a night-time he'd always put out custard for sweets. That's all, just bloody custard.

So there's eight or ten of us there one night and I said, 'Can't yer serve anything else other than bloody custard, or at least put something in the stuff to give it some taste?'

Well, didn't he have a snap at me.

Then the next night, up comes this bloody custard again, so I had another go at him. 'Can't yer cook anything else?' I said.

By this time, I'd sat down. Anyhow, this cook, he grabbed a big boning knife and he came flying around the table, straight at me. But instead of stabbing me, he flicked the knife in the bowl and out came this piddly bloody apricot. I mean, the animal had gone and stuck this half apricot in the bottom of the bowl and then he'd smothered it with custard. Of course, I hadn't seen the bloody thing. Neither had anybody else. But holy shit, the whole lot of us were out through that bloody door in a shot. I tell you, nobody had any sweets that night. We disappeared.

But with the droving, I did a lot of the cooking myself. And cooking in a drover's camp's hard bloody work. It's a hell of a job. See, depending on how many men you had, you'd kill a beast every week or so. That's because you'd only be able to keep fresh meat for a couple of days before it went off, then you salted as much as you could.

See what happened was, you shot and bled him. Then you'd skin from a bit over halfway down the backbone to the gut, across the front and back legs, then you'd peel the hide back. Now because you only had two tucker packs to carry fresh meat, you'd keep a bit of the good steak and also some for stewing. Then you laid all the meat that you were going to salt, out on bushes—mulga or whatever—and you rubbed the salt into that and packed it away the next morning. But because bloody salted meat sweats something terrible, you had to lay it out again every night, to cool it; air it. I mean, this stuff's not like the corned meat you get at the butcher's. It's not like that at all.

Then at breakfast you had a bit of damper, because that's all there was. And sometimes you might have some of the leftover stew or curry from the night before, to go with the damper. That'd be done in the camp oven or bedourie. Anyway, you never ate much of a morning because you'd be up early getting your horses ready then, by piccaninny daylight, you'd leave camp.

But it was real damper. There wasn't bread in those days. That only came in later. Mind you, this was at the end of the war when things were still rationed. People don't realise that tea, sugar and clothes were rationed for a long time. I can still remember sending butter and clothing coupons to my mother and she'd send back tea coupons. Tea was scarce. You rarely had tea, so we drank coffee, and the coffee was horrible. You boiled it in a billy and, Holy Jesus, it was dreadful bloody stuff.

Then on the odd occasion we got macaroni and vermicelli. Oh God, when that happened, you'd think you were in bloody heaven. You'd cook it up with powdered milk and you'd put sugar on it. What a treat that was, I can tell you. But you never saw vegetables. I mean, they might throw in a pumpkin or a few potatoes when you first started out but, after those were gone, that was it. You never saw vegetables again. And there wasn't any canned stuff in those days. That only came later, in the '50s.

So basically we lived on salted meat and damper. And because of that, we used to get Barcoo rot. It's like scurvy and it's brought about because we ate no vitamins. See, how people lived later on, after the unions come in with all their rules about how you were supposed to live and what you were supposed to eat, well, there were no bloody rules like that when we were out there. If you didn't like it, you just got the bloody sack and you pissed off. That's all there was to it.

But jeez, it got cold. People think that just because you're travelling through a desert it gets hot. Well it might get hot in the summer but in winter it's bloody freezing. So much so that, in the morning, you had to let your camp sheet and swag thaw out before you could roll them up.

And we used those green-hide hobbles; peg hobbles, about a foot long and doubled over with a wooden peg through one end, and the other end had a slit in it where you pushed the peg through to lock it. I mean, they were soft enough of a night, when you put them on, but by morning they'd be frozen stiff. And also, you'd get back to camp and your hands were frozen, and if you put them near the fire they hurt bloody worse. Then if you put them in hot water, it hurt worse still. So it was a matter of belting them against your side until they thawed out.

But it was a magic life, so we didn't care. I mean, I wouldn't have given a stuff if me hands had fallen off because you just loved the work.

And also with the cold; see, most of our work was done around the sandhills, where you got big lumps of spinifex, so we'd throw a wax match into that and it'd flare up like crazy. And it didn't even frighten the horses. It was that bloody cold that they'd push in around the fire to warm themselves up, as well.

But with the food; because we ate so much salted meat and damper, we'd get constipated something terrible. Anyhow, with the constipation, you may remember that old saying about how you had to 'shift the bun'. Well fresh meat'd do that in a flash. See, on the nights you killed a beast, we all cooked our own meal. The cook didn't do anything. So if you wanted a bit of liver or kidney or the ribs or whatever, you just cut that off the beast and you cooked it yourself.

So after you had fresh meat that night, then again for breakfast, by jeez, you'd go gastric. And you'd feel it coming on and you'd get off your horse, and when the others saw you, they'd ride ahead and, of course, your horse'd want to follow them. So there you'd be, hanging onto the reins, struggling to go to the toilet, with your bloody pants down around your ankles and the bloody horses pulling away and you'd be shitting all over the sandhills.

And that's true. A while back, I put all that into the oral history at the National Museum in Canberra, and the feller from there asked me, 'How did you get on for toilets?'

'There was no worries,' I said. 'We had 50,000 square miles of them.'

'But,' he asked, 'did you dig holes or anything?'

'Not really,' I said. 'We just went when we went.'

But you could always tell the boss drover because he'd have a roll of toilet paper in his bloody pack while the rest of us had nothing but a handful of spinifex. And I mean, have you ever felt that spinifex? It's dangerous stuff, I tell you.

So Close, So Far

My name's Jack Goldsmith and I was born in the Blue Mountains of New South Wales, at a place called Springwood. Those days, Springwood was a little bush town, now it's a suburb of Sydney, or just abouts. But with me, I had a rough time with the stepmother so I cleared out when I was sixteen and I headed out west, rabbit trapping, out at a place called Gulargambone. That was in the late '40s, and I ended up going to the little cocky places around the Tamworth area.

Then when the Korean War broke out, I tried to get over there but I was three months too young and by the time I was old enough, the war was starting to wind down so they weren't taking any more volunteers. So I decided to head up to Boulia, in the central west of Queensland, and I went boundary riding out from there on a little place which was only around 150 or 200 square miles.

That's where I first done the droving, taking sheep to Charleville. It was quite a short trip, only around 50 or 60 miles. And I also took a mob to Muckadilla, 150 mile or so further on. But I found that sheep were too slow and it was like I was getting nowhere, so I went up around Cloncurry to work on a few cattle stations.

After that I headed for the Gulf of Carpentaria, where I worked myself into shares of a small place just outside Normanton. By small, I mean it was only 72 square mile. And to make any sort of a living off such a small property, we had to go over into the bigger stations to muster up some of their cattle and bring them back over into our place. See, our neighbour, Reg Quilty, had 1800 square mile. The Quiltys were well known up that way. Reg was Tom Quilty's brother.

Of course, if you want to put a finer point on it, in actual fact what we were doing was cattleduffing. But to use the words 'pinching' or 'thieving', that'd be a bit strong because it was the accepted thing up there in the Gulf. Everyone done it. So that's what we did to survive.

But I mean, we tried everything. We had to. I even done a bit of fighting—boxing—as well. And that hooks into droving and duffing in a funny sort of way, too. See, there's one exploit what happened in me life that got mentioned in quite a lot of newspapers and books and things. Because I had a bit of a rep for handling meself around the Gulf, like, one time I got organised to fight a bloke they called 'The King of the Gulf'. Now the King of the Gulf was a feller called Tom Edwards. We were mates really but, anyway, I rode off to Normanton to scrap with Tom, alias the King of the Gulf, at Larry Del Hunty's boxing troupe.

Now the township of Normanton was over the other side of the Norman River from me. So I comes in, and there's a yard there for the horse and a thing there to put the feed in, and there's also a great big brass bell. Now when you ring this bell, the feller's supposed to come over in the punt and pick you up. So I ring the bell and the feller sticks his head out from his hut and sees me and he thinks to himself, 'Oh, it's only Goldie,' then he goes back and sits down or whatever. So I'm still ringing the bell and he's not doing nothing. He's completely ignoring me.

'Well, stuff yer then,' I said and I took the boots and clothes off and I tied them to me head with the belt I was wearing and I started to swim across the river.

Now I measured the Norman River the last time I was up there and it's pretty wide—very wide, in fact. So I'm halfway across and I'm starting to feel sorry that I even began, you know, because I was getting knocked up and I didn't seem to be getting nowhere.

Anyway, I eventually got across, and they ended up calling the scrap a draw after a feller stopped it, because all me and Tom were doing was cutting each other up. But the thing was, there was another feller, George Byrnes. He done some droving as well, and just three days later, George was swimming about forty or fifty bullocks across the river, right where I'd swam, and a big croc took one of his bullocks. Fair dinkum. Right where I swam. And they still talk about that in Normanton.

But the point of the story is, up until the time I'd done it, only two other people had swam the Norman River. One was a feller called Norman Smith. He swum it for a bet. Then the other person that swam it was a feller called Harry Readford, and if you know your history, you'll know that Harry was also known as Captain Starlight. Now there's a well-known drover for you, and a cattle-duffer too, I might add. Yeah, Captain Starlight was the other one that swam the Norman River. So I'm in pretty good company, aye. And that's been written up in newspapers and all, so it's true. I'll show you the piece out of the paper, if you like.

But when it come to the droving, I done quite a few trips. I done droving, like, from the Gulf, off places like Vanrook Station. There was a cattle buyer up that way by the name of Tom Wheelan and he'd buy off the little fellers—two hundred head here, a hundred there and three hundred somewhere else—and by the time he bought all these cattle he'd have about 1000 head, so we'd take them down to the trucking yards at Julia Creek.

Then I also done a couple of trips with a feller . . . I forget his name right now, but we went from right up on the Gulf, at Burke-town, and we took them along the Leichhardt River, down to Kajabbi. What was his name, now? I know him well. He was only one of two jockeys in the Commonwealth to ride every winner at a race meeting and the Queen presented him with a saddle with this big brass thing on it. The other jockey got the same thing. That's right. His name's Findlay, Ray Findlay. Anyway, Ray had a place outside Kajabbi and he wanted me to go up into the Gulf with him to get a few poddies—duff them, like. Then I also done a few trips from Kowanyama. That's halfway up Cape York Penin-sula, on the left-hand side, and I took them down the Mungana Stock Route.

But I'll never forget one trip, and this's the thing I really liked about droving. I took a hundred Hereford bulls from Julia Creek up to the Gulf. And bull droving, oh, I tell you, look, it's absolutely fantastic. I mean, you had to watch them for the first few nights but after that they settle down beautiful. You'd feed them up on the camp and there you'd be, you'd have them all around the fire and you'd be right there in the middle of them, you know. It was fantastic.

And once they settled, every bullock walks in the same spot in the mob. You've got your tail-enders what might be a little lame or not as long-legged. Then the long-legged fellers—the great big pikers, the big cock-horned fellers—they'll stride out the front. Then there's the bullocks that've been reared up together as calves. They remain mates for life, you know, so you might get four or five in a little mob like that and they'll stick together. And if there's a rush and the next morning you glance your eye over the mob and one of these little bullocks what's always been with his mates, well, he'll be looking around. 'Mooo! Moooo!' he'll be going, singing out for his mates. And of course, if he doesn't get an answer then you'll know there's a good chance that his mates are still lost out there somewhere; they're still missing.

Then as you get further on in the trip, you get to be real good mates with the bullocks too, and you can get off your horse and walk along with them. There was one Hereford bullock on that trip and I had him broke in so tame that I could ride him. He'd carry me along. And I felt like I wanted to buy him, you know, for a pet. I just got on so well with him. Oh, they're terrific. You just can't help it. After a while you get so close to them, you do. And when they're in camp, in the morning they'll just hang around, waiting for you to crack the whip or whatever, to let them know that it's time to walk off again.

But see, droving's all different. There'll be other times when you can sense trouble. I don't know. It's a feeling you get. Sometimes, if they've had a hard day and they don't feed properly, they're unsettled and they'd be laying there dreaming and a possum might come down and jump on one. And when one bullock goes, the whole lot go.

That's why you always camp near the fire and close to a tree because, if they rush, the fire'll split the mob which might give you just enough time to jump out of your swag and get behind the tree. True. I've been behind a tree when a rush's happened and the bark of the tree's been all torn where they've gone past you.

'Sometimes you get so close to the bulls.'

And sometimes, when they've rushed together, you see them hanging up in the fork of a tree with broken necks. And I've seen broken horns, broken legs, the lot. Terrible, it is.

Then also, when it's raining, with lightning around, or even just lightning, you never lay in your swag. You put two men on the watch then, on the night horses, and you get behind a tree. And you're on tenterhooks, waiting for them to go. They don't always go, mind you, but you can't take the risk because, if they come your way, you'd be trampled to death. That's true. I've had them come through the camp and there's flour everywhere and they've smashed all the pack bags.

And other times they rush for no real reason. Not one you can pinpoint, anyway. They're funny, you know. Something will upset them and away they'll go, just like that. It depends a lot on what sort of day they've had. That's why, when they're on the waterhole or the government bore or whatever, you must give them a great big gutful of water at night before you spread them out to feed. As a rule, the bigger the gutful they get, the bigger they'll feed and the better they'll settle.

But the ones in the mob that you've really got to watch are the milkers' poddies. They're the poddies that've been reared up by hand, around the station. Sometimes you've got to put a bell around them because they get homesick and they try and sneak off of at night to head back home. And when that happens, the other bullocks see them walking away and they want to follow as well. They're a damn nuisance them milkers' poddies. Any drover'll tell you that.

But as I said, usually the bullocks get so broke in after a while that, when they see the camp in the distance, they'll just drop their heads and they'll spread out. And here's another funny thing, a bullock will always camp in the same spot, every night. And like I said, I like my bullocks real close to the fire, only ten feet away. Then they get used of you walking around, singing or talking or whatever. It's also security for them.

But when you're moving them along, the main thing is that you've got to keep both wings straight. And when they're broke in, and they're strung out, and you see the lead starting to swing over, all you've got to do is to ride up halfway along and call out, 'Move over boys.' And they will. Or if that doesn't work then you might just have to crack the whip and the whole two hundred head up front will swing right over. You get them so broke in, you know, they're almost tame. Like I said, after you spend a lot of time together, you just get so close to them.

And here's a story: there's a mate of mine from Murrurundi, Viv Walsh, he won't talk much. He's very quiet. He's very quiet and he's got a very dry sense of humour. Well, Viv had a contract once to bring bullocks down from a place called Frogmore and over to Singleton, in the Hunter Valley of New South Wales. He had that trip every year, and it took him about four months.

Then one year, he took this eight hundred head over to Singleton, but when he got there, the owner said, 'Look, there's no sale here, take 'em down to Wangaratta.' Now Wangaratta's a long way away, right down there, over into Victoria. It's near on 500 miles as the crow flies, and Viv wasn't flying by no means because now he had eight hundred head of cattle to negotiate over the Great Dividing Range.

So that's what he does. But when he finally gets to Wangaratta there's a telegram waiting for him which says—'Take them to Forbes.' So he turns around and he marches them up to Forbes, in central New South Wales.

Anyhow, by the time Viv got to Forbes, the whole trip'd taken him eighteen months and eleven days. So the next time I saw him, I said, 'I don't know about you, Viv, but sometimes I get so close to the bulls that I don't like letting them go, aye.'

And he said, 'Not this mob,' he said. 'To tell yer the truth, after eighteen months 'n' eleven days, I were a little bit keen on getting home.'

Some Might Call it Duffing

Dad bought a droving plant and I hooked up with him. That's how I got into droving. I was only a kid, like, but I didn't really have too much choice because it was just after the war and men were hard to get. So Dad ended up with me, and he also got Kelly Timmins and Tommy Bowman. We were the shepherds. Kelly would've been about eighteen or nineteen and Tommy, well, he'd just come back from World War II.

So Dad bought this plant—the whole works—and for a hell of a lot of money too: one hundred pound. I mean, at that time a man's wage was bugger-all really, somewhere around one pound for a seven-day week and keep; plus his tax and tobacco, of course. I mean, five hundred quid back in them days'd buy you a home—house, land, the whole bloody lot. So that'll give you some idea.

Now this actual droving plant consisted of a wagonette, six harness horses, eight saddle horses, three black kelpies, tarpaulins and a break. The break consisted of the ropes and things that was used to set up a makeshift yard to hold in the sheep or cattle at night. Oh, and of course, there was the harnesses for the horses, plus the saddles and all that.

But Dad started out, more or less, as a freelance drover, up in the central north of New South Wales, around the Collarenebri area, which is up there near the Queensland border. Most of his droving was done when the mobs needed walking for grass. See when it was dry, the cockies just put their stock out on the road for food, and they needed someone to look after them, like.

A lot of Dad's work came through the local Stock and Station Agent, a chap called Hugie Gill. Hugie handled most of the freelance droving, and the companies'd get in touch with Hugie; places like AML&F, who me uncle drove for. Then there was Goldsborough Mort and Australian Estates. They were the main three Dad worked for. Oh, we also done a bit for Australian Mercantile Land Finance. Another mob was the Australian Pastoral Company. That was owned by the bloody queen. Well, actually it was a king at the time. His company only drove mobs to market, mainly bullocks. They were a bit big for the likes of us because when they went droving they'd take six to eight men, plus a huge wagonette that took six horses to pull it, so they needed about forty or fifty horses in all.

But a lot of the big station companies employed their own full-time drovers. Fellers like Kidman, he had his own drovers, and they used to go from up the top of the Gulf, right down to Adelaide, and anywhere in-between. That was the Kidman way.

Then later on I drove with a feller called Pearl Tye. Pearl originally came from around Gunnedah way, and I hooked up with him in Boggabilla, up on the Macintyre River. Pearl was a packhorse drover. He never had the wagonette like me dad did, so everything was carried on horses. Pearl had about six fellers with him and he used to drove for Keith Buffield, a cattle dealer from Moree.

But one time when I was droving with Pearl, we came across a place called Gin's Leap, just outside of Boggabri. You might've seen it in your travels. There's a big waterhole right at the foot of it, and the story goes that a buck was chasing a young gin and rather than get caught, she jumped right off the top of the cliff and she landed down on the rocks and she died. And this's not a cock-'n'-bull story or nothing but cattle just won't camp there. They will not camp there. Pearl and me tried but we were up all bloody night trying to hold the bastards. And they reckon it's because of that, because of the gin dying there. But it's an ideal spot. Beautiful feed, and the water's crystal clear, everything, but cattle just will not camp at Gin's Leap.

I mean, there's a lot you learn about when you're droving. Out the other side of Moree, going to Narrabri, there's no wood, only gorse, and you've gotta boil the billy with cow shit because there's not a stick to be found. True. I've crossed it in the middle of summer and I've crossed it in the middle of bloody winter and it's been a bastard every time. But cow shit's okay. Oh, she'll cook up. She'll hold the heat. You can cook damper, brownies, anything. You just bundle her

Hardly a tree to be found.

up and she'll start just like tinder. The old camp oven goes good on it too, just beautiful. It's surprising how much heat them cow pats hold, and they're good also for keeping the mozzies away.

But you've gotta have the know-how. Like, when you're building the fire, you build her up on the high side, not the low side, because if your tucker gets smothered in the smoke from the cow shit, she don't taste too good. You get a real bitter taste. So that's one you just learn. You put them pats on the top side. Or if you've got a shovel, you dig a hole, which is better still, because the ground holds the heat. And baked spuds, you just drop them in, skin and all. Bake them in their jackets, like. Then when they're good and ready you pull them out and get into them; just beautiful. Mind you, they've got a bit of a different flavour but they go down all right, especially if you're hungry.

But you get used of all that sort of stuff when you're out droving. I mean, when you get to a waterhole in the middle of summer and she's almost dried up and the cattle or sheep have been shitting and pissing in it, well, you don't worry about that neither. You're so bloody thirsty that you just brush all the crap aside and put your head down and you go for it. Oh, you'll do anything if you're thirsty, I can tell you.

Then later on I went out west, and I remember there was a feller called Joe Grosvenor. Well, Joe and me took a mob of cattle down from Brighton Downs to Diamantina Lakes, right along the Diamantina River. And down that way there was nothing to eat apart from the blue bush, and all our horses, they lost calcium and they went blind from eating this bloody blue bush. Then later on some of them got their sight back after they got back on the good grass. And buckle grass's another one what takes the calcium out of them. I've seen a mare break her pelvis giving birth to a foal because she were so brittle. True. She went down and had the foal but she couldn't get back up again, just like that. Take your brood mares off buckle grass, I say, because it takes away all the calcium.

Anyhow on that trip with Joe Grosvenor, the water was so crook in places that we had to clear it with carbide and ashes. Carbide stinks like hell. She's a chalky sort of cake, like sandstone, and when you put water on it, she gasses. I mean, the old carbide light used to be all the go in the shearing sheds. They came in, in place of the kerosene lamp because they're a brighter light. Then the pressure lights came in after that.

But the old carbide light took a bit of blowing out, I can tell you. They still keep flaming even in a windstorm. But the thing was, they reacted with the water. I mean, toss them in the river and you'd blow the fish right out of the water, just like gelly. True. We used to make bombs out of them to catch the fish. You never went without a feed when you was on the river and you had some carbide with you, I can tell you.

So you learn all that sort of stuff when you're out droving. I mean, at school they don't teach you how to cook spuds in a cowshit fire, do they, or how to blow fish out of water with carbide? But you'd be well and truly buggered if you didn't know it, aye.

But gee, we used to get up to some tricks. Like, you were supposed to make sure that your stock stayed to a three chain lane along the stock route. But we didn't keep to that, not if we could get away with it. We just sort of looked the other way and let the mob spread out a little and you'd leave it up to the cocky's station hand to chase them back in.

'Oh shit, sorry about that, mate,' you'd say. 'The buggers must'a wandered off on me.'

But see, we knew they'd get a better feed outside the three chain lane, and so did the cockies, so that's why they sent the station hand down to keep an eye on us. Oh, there was lots of things we got up to. Everyone did. I mean, sometimes you'd wait until it was good and dark and you'd wander over and cut the cocky's fence and let your mob in to have a good feed on his lot for a while. Then you'd be up and away before daylight.

And you never, ever, killed one of your own beasts. Never. You'd be going through a place and when you saw that no one was looking, well, you send the dog out a bit wide and he'd bring back a few of the cocky's stock and they were your killers. Some might call it duffing but everyone done it. True. I mean, it's a bit hard to read the brand on a lamb roast or a hunk of steak, aye.

But I do remember one stampede when I was with Dad. We had over a thousand bullocks what we'd picked up from Collarenebri, in the central north of New South Wales. So we were out the other side of Walgett and we'd ordered some bread to be brought out on the mail truck. And when it arrived it was dark, like, and the bullocks were all resting.

Anyhow this bread was wrapped up in brown paper and the cook was unrolling it to put it into the tucker box and a gust of wind came along and it took a strip of that paper straight over, into the mob. Now there was hardly a bullock on its feet before that time but, in a blink of an eye, they were gone. True. And what's more, they took 7 mile of fence with them. And of course, the thing was, we had to wait until they tailed off before we could follow them through the fence, and every time we tried to head them off they went straight back through again. They crossed that fence four times before we headed them. Seven bloody mile they took.

In the end we ended up losing about fifty or sixty bullocks who was either killed or we had to kill them ourselves because they was crippled up with broken legs and stuff. And I'll never forget it, like, I was only a fucking kid at the time but this one bullock, he ran straight into a tree with the butt of his head. *Bang!* And his front legs wrapped around the tree, just like that. And I was sitting on me bloody horse, just looking, and there was this bullock looking like he was cuddling the tree.

And that was one of the biggest rushes I ever had. So you've always gotta be on your guard. And you've gotta look after them, too, because drovers got paid on delivery. I mean, if you started out with 1000 head and you ended up with nine hundred and fifty, you only got paid for the nine hundred and fifty. That's why we also tried to pick up a few along the way; cleanskins, as they was called. But they mixed up pretty well. I mean, it takes a pretty good bloody eye to pick a few bullocks or sheep out of a mob of, say, 1200 or 1500 head, aye.

But it was a tough life, all right. I mean, take Dad for instance. He'd take a mob of sheep for, say, 10 pound a day and out of that he had to pay the shepherds, then there was their tucker, plus his own, and he had to pay for the upkeep of all the gear. Then he had to take responsibility for all the stock, and he also had to somehow make a bloody quid for himself. So the size of the mob's what got most drovers through. There was never a mob that come through this way that was under a thousand head. That'd be the average. But you always tried to pick up a few extras along the way. Everyone did.

Sooner or Later

I did droving trips through the Northern Territory quite a few times. Then I also worked on some of the big properties up there, as a stockman between the droving times.

Anyway, while I was up there one time we had twelve station black boys, and we had a cook, and there was this head stockman, a feller called Lewis. Now, there's no doubting that he was a smart type of stockman, no doubting that at all. But he did have this thing in his head about blacks and he used to call the black stockmen all the names under the sun. You know, 'black niggers' and 'boongs' and all that sort of thing, right into their faces.

'Oh, yer bloody boong,' he'd say, 'get over there 'n' do that.'

Then another time there was this flour and it had weevils all through it and this feller Lewis said, 'Just make some damper out'a it 'n' give it to the boongs.' So he'd give them all the rough food, the bad food, because he didn't care.

So the boys were getting pretty upset about all this bad treatment and one day I said to him, 'Look,' I said, 'yer'd better go easy on them boys or they'll git yer. Just remember what happened to Tommy Nevins.'

Now just about everyone'd heard about Tommy Nevins. Tommy Nevins was a drover's cook and he also cooked out in the stock camps. He was a big, wild, rough bugger, middle-aged, around thirty or forty. And Tommy was one of them blokes who also had a real bad attitude towards the blacks, and he was specially noted for chasing the gins.

I first met Tommy up at Newcastle Waters when I was on a droving trip out of Wave Hill, which is a place over near the West Australian border. And I've seen Tommy working on it and, oh jeez, he wasn't fussed over whatever he had. So I'd seen Tommy and, when you've been in that sort of wild territory for a while and you've been knocking the gins around, you've gotta be very careful because the blacks will get you. They might take a while but, sooner or later, they'll get you.

Now a couple of years before, Tommy got caught mucking around with the gins. Then one afternoon they come back to camp and they found him dead. And at the time, I said to the policeman—it was only an outpost police station—I said to him, 'So what happened to Tommy Nevins, then?'

'Oh,' he said, 'Tommy stood on the wrong end of a long-handled shovel 'n' it come up 'n' hit him over the temple and it killed him.'

Now that was a load of bull because we all knew how Tommy'd been caught with the gins. So in other words, this policeman he didn't want to tell me the truth about how it was the blacks who'd took to Tommy with a long-handled shovel and they'd killed him. That was the fact. But I accepted what he said.

So I reminded this feller Lewis about what they did to Tommy Nevins and he answered me by saying, 'Them boongs haven't got the guts to have a go at me.'

Now I'm a half-caste, myself, but I was brought up in a town. But still and all, I just knew that those black boys could only take so much. Anyone'd only be able to take so much of that sort of a bad thing. Anyhow, that was that. I'd warned him.

Then Lewis, he said to me, 'You go around so-and-so waterhole 'n' bring them cattle back to the yard, up the so-and-so.'

'Right-o,' I said.

Then Lewis said, 'I'll send Tommy 'n' Jackie up with yer,' he said. 'They'll give yer some help.'

Now I just forget what their exact names were now, but all the black boys in those camps was called names like Tommy and Jackie. So he said, 'I'll send Tommy 'n' Jackie up with yer. They'll follow yer up.'

Anyhow I got on me horse and I'd gone about a quarter of a mile and I realised that nobody was coming with me. There was no sign of either Jackie or Tommy. And just then I had this terrible gut feeling that something was wrong; that there was some trouble or other. So I turned around and I galloped back as fast as I could.

And when I got there, there were the twelve black boys, gathered around in a ring and they've got this Lewis in the middle and they've got lumps of dried gidgee wood, and two of them were moving in, about to swing the wood into his brain.

Anyway, I cracked the stockwhip. Then I rode into them, still cracking me stockwhip, and they kept jabbering away at me in their blackfella language because, you know, they didn't have any argument with me, whatsoever.

So I said to them, 'You hurt this man 'n' big-feller Crouch . . .' —Jack Crouch was the station manager and, by gee, he was a tough boss. They were all frightened of him, all the blacks were. So I said, 'Big-feller Crouch, he come in with rifle and he go bang, bang and there be no more gin and there be no more piccaninny. You won't see your family no more. He'll shoot you all if you kill him.'

So anyway, they were arguing about it and they sort of trusted me because, like I said, I'm a half-caste myself, and they didn't have any argument with me.

'You'll be all right now,' I said. 'I'll fix it up. No more bad chat. No more bad food. Only good stuff from now on for youse fellas.'

Anyway they settled down after that. So then I went up and I told this feller Lewis, I said, 'You haven't got long to live if yer stay in this place.' And he left not long after.

And another story I heard when I was out there droving was about a bloke called Baker. Now he was a half-caste, and a few years beforehand he come across a white bloke knocking his gin off and he chased this white bloke with his rifle and the bloke went in through the door of the men's quarters. 'Hold that door shut,' the white bloke said to another white ringer feller, who was inside. So the ringer did. And while the ringer was holding the door shut, the feller that was knocking off Baker's gin, he jumped out through the back window and he took off so he wouldn't get caught.

Then when Baker come to the door, he tried to get in but he couldn't, see, so he shot off the rifle right through the door and the white ringer was still there, hanging onto the door, wondering what the hell all the fuss was, and he copped the bullet right through his throat. This Baker feller shot him through the throat, and it killed this white ringer. But it was the wrong bloke. And Baker, he ended up in Fanny Bay jail, up in Darwin, for that.

So all this was happening back in the early '30s. Oh, they were really touchy about the gins. I was only a young feller and any gin or half-caste gin or yellow gin, as they called them what's mixed with the Afghans, well, you just kept well away because, if the blackfellas didn't have them, then one of the white men on that station had them.

Oh yes, they were all touchy. But I'm not sure what happened later on because that was back in the early days when I was droving.

But I kept on my side of the fence and I left them to their own. I just went on with my droving and I did my stock work. My way of thinking about it was, if they wanted to act like that and behave like that, then there was going to be real big problems.

Streaker's Corner

*Back in March '89 we were coming down from the north with sheep,
doing a trip to Bourke. And gee, it was hot, very hot. Anyway, we'd
just picked up a Dutch backpacker who needed a lift to Cunnamulla.
So this was her first day out with us and she didn't know us too
well. Anyhow, it was still around 45 degrees when we got the sheep
to camp, and there's a stock trough there. Blow this heat, I thought,
so I stripped down to my knickers and bra and I jumped into the
stock trough to cool down.*

*So you can imagine this girl. Shock, horror, she goes. She's all the
way from Holland, she'd only known us for a short time, and here I
am stripping down and jumping into the dirty old stock trough that
all the sheep'd been drinking from. What's more, it was right there
beside the Cunnamulla to Bourke highway, with the traffic and all.
But then the heat started to get to this girl and she saw the sense in
what I was doing. So the next thing, she's stripped down and she's
in there with me, too.*

*So if you can imagine the scene; there's these two women perched
up in a stock trough, beside the Cunnamulla to Bourke highway,
stripped down to the bare necessities, with all these cars and trucks
going by tooting their horns and going on.*

I don't think she'll ever forget that.

Talk about stripping down. Back in '88 we were going through
that same area, again with sheep. They'd recently been shorn so
they were a bit 'stir-y', unsettled. Anyhow, we'd left the Bourke
highway and we went east until we got to what's called the Widgeegoara Creek, then we headed north, up the creek, to the Bollon
to Cunnamulla road, on Camden Station. This wasn't in summer.
It was during the winter, and it was freezing.

Anyhow, we were just about to go across the Camden Plains—
they're about 6 mile across; big and open—but right on the edge of

the plain there's some very thick gidgee, and that's where we decided to set camp for the night. So we put up the sheep break and we put the mob in there.

Now on that trip we had about eighteen dogs, ten horses, one motorbike, the caravan, and a truck that carried the break and all the gear. As I said, this was winter and it was frosty, so frosty in fact that, even at eleven o'clock in the daytime there'd still be ice in the shade of the trees. There'd even be ice in the trees. That's how cold it got.

Now every drover I've ever talked to since says that they've always had trouble getting their stock to settle in that particular area. It's just one of those spots. But, of course, at that time, I didn't know anything about it. So we set camp and we got the sheep settled and I went to sleep in the caravan where it was a good bit warmer. Then about midnight the sheep decided to take the break. It might've

'On that trip we had about eighteen dogs, ten horses, one motorbike, the caravan and a truck.'

been pigs, kangaroos, foxes, dingoes, wild dogs, any number of things. I don't know what it was, but anyhow, away they went.

Now when sheep take the break, you've got to be straight after them. You can't hang around. So if you're sleeping with no clothes on, you can't worry about it. You just jump out of bed, you race out, let your dogs go, jump on the motorbike and you're after them. And that's what I did. Off I went after these sheep, on my motorbike, without a stitch of clothing on and, eventually, I got the sheep back together.

So that was all right. Now as I said, that particular area was very thick with gidgee scrub, and the following morning I just followed through to have a look around to see if I'd missed any sheep. And for the life of me, I couldn't believe how I'd gotten the motorbike between the trees in some of the places where I'd been the previous night.

'How the hell did I get through that in the dark?' I kept saying.

Now I never said anything to anybody about it, about me going out on the bike with no clothes on. And the only other person who knew we were there was the bloke that owned that bit of country, and when I seen him I only told him about the sheep taking the break, nothing else, and he said, 'Oh, I'm mustering in that paddock in a couple'a days and if I find any of your sheep I'll let you know.'

Then I would've only been a bit up the road when he come up and he seen me and he said, 'No, there was no stock of yours there.'

So we done pretty well out there in the dark. But the odd thing was, the next time I passed through that way again there was this story going around about how on one particular freezing winter's night a mob of sheep had taken the break and the drover had jumped on his motorbike and he'd taken off after them . . . in the nude. And what's more, they'd gone and named the area Streaker's Corner.

Sweat

As tractors came in, a lot of the farmers virtually started giving their working horses away. So Lionel Evans, Lorry Jones and them jokers went over the west coast, here in South Australia, and they picked up a mob of these horses. This was back when horsemeat was selling pretty well for pet food.

So at any rate, these jokers were bringing these horses back, you see, and I was crutching down here in the shed and a joker from over Crystal Brook rang me up. I think his name was Shunkey or something. That's right, Jack Shunkey. He was in that stock and station agents, you know, Bennett's Fisher. Anyhow, Jack said, 'I got some horses for yer,' he said, 'but they're on the road, so if yer want 'em, yer'll have to go and get 'em.'

'Gee, I don't know so much about that,' I said.

'Look, come over,' he said, 'and I'll run yer out there to have a look at 'em.'

By this time they were up near the top of Eyre Peninsula, this side of Whyalla. So Jack took me up there to have a look at these horses. At any rate, when we got there they're not in too good condition, see, and these jokers wanted five pounds for them, so I said, 'I'll give yer four-fifty, take it or leave it.'

'No,' they said.

So I said, 'Come on, Jack,' I said, 'we're going home. I got work to do.'

'Look,' Jack said, 'they're in a bit of strife and they've gotta sell 'em.'

So he went back and he had a chat and they said, 'Okay then, take 'em.'

At any rate, they were pretty glad to get rid of these horses, see, because they'd already shot quite a few when they'd gotten sore-footed and also the bloody cops and the RSPCA were chasing them. But anyway, I bought these 320 or so horses at my price.

'Okay, we've made the deal,' I said. 'I'll take delivery in the yards at Wilmington, so yer've gotta take 'em through the Wilmington Pass.' The pass goes through from Port Augusta.

So that was alright. They agreed to that. So I come home and I got a state lad who was working for us, young Johnny Mudge, to come with me. Now these state kids were wards of the state. When Mum was alive she used to look after them like a mother. They were good kids, mostly white boys and girls, without any homes. Like, their mothers couldn't control them or whatever, so they was always on the street, getting into trouble and that sort of thing.

Any rate I had a ute here, see. So I left crutching one day and I packed up the old tucker box—oh, it's been thousands of miles with me—and away we went, me, Johnny, who was about fifteen, and a neighbour, Peter Brooks. Peter had his licence so he must've been about seventeen. So we went up to Wilmington and we counted the horses, and that was all right. Then we bought a couple of their broken-in horses off them for us to ride.

So we got out along the dirt tracks, down from Wilmington, with these horses. Any rate we were coming past Melrose Railway Station and I went inside, purposely, and I said to this bloody idiot who was behind the box, I said, 'Is there any trains coming through in the next hour or so?'

'No,' he said. 'There's no trains coming.'

Now why I asked that was because there was a chain road going three mile or so, straight down along the railway line, and that's where we were taking these horses. So I thought we were safe. So I sent the ute ahead and Johnny and me were bringing the horses up the back. Then the next thing, this goddamn goods train come. And these horses'd never seen a train before. At first they just froze, you see. Then after they froze they turned around and they took off, straight back towards us. And the pace they come was unreal.

So I said to Johnny, I said, 'We'll turn the leaders.'

Any rate, there we were stuck halfway down this chain road and all we had was our stockwhips to try and turn them back, and that was proving impossible, so I called out to Johnny, 'Git behind me.'

Then I backed towards the fence and I headed me horse at them and I was belting them over the snout with the short handle of the stockwhip, trying to turn them away from us.

'Keep behind me Johnny or yer'll get killed,' I shouted.

And if ever I had a fright in life, that was it. If you can imagine three hundred horses coming straight at you, it was near bloody murder. The earth was moving like thunder. We had no show. Hell it was a frightening situation. I'll never forget it.

So when they finally went past, we chased them up the road for a couple of mile until we got ahead of them. But then—and this's what I wanted to tell you—when we got them together, all the bays, the chestnuts, all the different colours, well, every one of them had turned snow white with the sweat and froth of fright. Snow white, they were.

Then the next morning, when we lit the bloody billy, the bloody dried sweat that was on them, it smelt so bad that I started to spew. So that set things going. We just couldn't eat our breakfast. I tell you, the vilest smell that you can possibly get is dried horse sweat. If you don't believe me, you try it.

That's the Problem

I always say that Banjo Paterson got it a bit wrong when he wrote, 'For the drover's life has pleasures that the townsfolk never know'. See, the way I look at it, it should've been, 'The drover's life has pleasures that the townsfolk know not of'. That's the way I say it— 'know not of'—if you get my meaning, and that's true.

But anyhow, I was born in 1918 at Gundagai and I lived at a little village named Brungle, which is on the Tumut River between Tumut and Gundagai, on the south-western slopes of New South Wales. And oh hell, back in them days, in spring, the drovers used to come through with thousands and thousands of sheep and cattle, taking them up into the northern parts of what's now the national park. It was all freehold then and later on snow lease country. And this stock came from everywhere; from all around the Monaro and from around the Riverina, below Narrandera and Jerilderie. Some even came down from the northern, central and western areas of New South Wales.

These days, of course, no stock goes up into the mountains. The park's all shut up. But back then there were around six or seven drovers in Tumut and that's all they done, go up in the spring and come back in the autumn. Oh I tell you, it was a pretty busy thing.

But when I was a kid there was a bloke, Bill Jones, living not far from us and he had a lease up in the park and I used to go up with him. I did the droving and he did the cooking. Then after that I started going up there for other fellers, fellers like Fred Bye. We took stock from down Jerilderie way, at Coonbil Station, and when I first went up with Fred, I done the cooking, then later on I was droving with him.

Then I started droving for Coonbil, by myself, like. That was in about '38 or '39. I'm not too sure of the dates now, they're that far away, but I mustn't have been much more than eighteen or

Droving sheep up into the snow lease country.

nineteen. By then they had big snow lease country up in the mountains. So I sort of got into it pretty early, and what helped was that I got recommended by fellers. That's what really gives you a kick along.

But one of the biggest jobs I had was when I went up to Warren, in central New South Wales, to pick up six hundred Northern Territory bullocks. I took the horses up on the train that time. Mostly we didn't, but that time we did. Anyhow, I got to Warren and it was nearly 90 mile out to where I had to muster these bullocks from out of the lignum swamps. But what got me was that, at Warren, it was 114 degrees in the shade and I'd been up on top of the mountains over the Christmas–New Year and it'd been snowing. By gee, I nearly died, I did. And the mosquitoes. Holy ghost, you talk about mosquitoes. They'd eat you. They didn't hurt the cattle so much but they ate us and they also caned up the horses something terrible, too.

Anyhow, I mustered these bullocks out of the bloody swamps and then I had to ring the owners up to let them know how many were fat enough to go to Sydney. But there wasn't any fats and, what's more, there wasn't anything for them to eat out on the road, so I suggested that they truck the lot of them home and give them the chance to pick up a bit of condition. So they eventually trucked them down, to just out of Tumut.

So if you do the right thing then fellers'll recommend you. Another feller was Alec Webb. Alec was terrific. He was a bush feller, like, and he recommended me to different ones and that's how I started with Arthur Cochrane. Now even though Arthur owned the cattle, he liked going out with the drovers, and this time he was up in the north-east of New South Wales, this side of Tenterfield, coming down with eight hundred head, and the local drover he had with him didn't want to come down this far. So I rode me horse all the way up there and we come back down through Tumut together, and up to his property. Then when they got fatter, what he'd do was, he'd send them down to Corryong, on the Murray, or further down the river to Wodonga, or he'd go to Bairnsdale, in the Gippsland area of Victoria. That's where he sold a lot of his cattle.

But Arthur, he was a terrific feller. As I said, even though he owned the stock, he just liked to go with the drovers. And he never interfered. He wouldn't tell the men anything. He'd say, 'French's the boss, not me.' That's how he worked. When we were droving, I was the boss and he was the worker. So they're some of the fellers that gave me a kick along.

But there's one thing I'll say, when I was droving I always liked a good dog with me and I always liked a good horse. And I've had some of the best dogs I've ever seen and I've had some good horses too, you know. As a matter of fact the first feller I did the droving for, Bill Jones, well, he give me a very good dog, a black-barb.

Then I got another dog as a pup, a red baldy. He was a black-barb, border collie cross, and he was red and white. His eyes were a bit light which a lot of them don't like, but he was the best dog I ever seen. When I used to go down the Snowy River way, down to the Murray and into Victoria, he done more than three or four blokes, you know. And I don't know how many fellers got pups from the bitches he had along the way. So them fellers got some good dogs out of him, aye.

And now, it's only been in the last few weeks that I haven't had a dog. The last one was another border collie. In actual fact I got him from old Bill Jones' son, a good while back. But he was getting old and when he got a bit frightened he was biting kids and people, you know. He wasn't too well, either, so I got rid of him. So I haven't got a dog now and that's pretty hard; it's very hard, you know, especially when you're used of having one around all the time.

And also I haven't had a ride on a horse for two or three years now, either. I've still got a couple but I don't ride them. I'm getting a bit old so I can't get on. That's the problem.

The Canning Stock Route:
An Overview

The History

In 1900, to prevent the spread of tick fever into the Pilbara and Murchison areas, a total movement ban was placed on the Kimberley cattle by the West Australian government. Subsequently, during 1906, the station owners in the Kimberleys banded together to pressure for an inland stock route rather than to continue the expensive shipping of cattle down the West Australian coast. Although previous explorers including Forrest, Giles, Carnegie and Warburton advised against the idea, the then Minister for Mines, Mr H. Gregory, agreed to send a survey party, led by Alfred Canning, to examine the possibility of a stock route between Wiluna and Halls Creek.

On the 30 October 1908, the first well was constructed at the Wiluna end. Then exactly two years after setting out, the expedition party arrived back in Wiluna to a fine welcome from the townspeople. It is said that upon arrival, Canning casually walked into the post office and sent the following telegram to the Under-secretary of Mines: 'Work completed. Canning.'

In 1911, Shoesmith, Thompson and Fred Terroni set off from Mabel Downs Station, in the east Kimberleys, for Wiluna, with the first mob of two hundred bullocks. Fred Terroni suffered from conjunctivitis in the early stages and had to find his own way back to Halls Creek. The other members of the party continued south and were murdered by local natives at Well 37.

Between 1911 and 1958 it was estimated that forty to fifty drovers came down the Canning Stock Route with a total of 30,000 head of cattle. Bullocks on the drove from the bottom end of Billiluna to Wiluna walked 960 miles, some taking the long way via

Carnegie Station to drop off their tail (lighter-conditioned bullocks) and to pick up fats.

From the Wiluna trucking yards, south to the Midland trucking yards, near Perth, was one of the state's longest and poorest maintained rail links. The loaded cattle wagons swayed, lurched and jerked along the 712 miles of railway line for two nights and three days.

Most drovers returned with unbroken horses for sale. These brumbies were trapped on Wongawol and Windidda and were fitted with shin-tappers and tailed around with quiet station horses to make them manageable.

The last mob of cattle was taken down the Canning by Mal Brown in 1958. He had great difficulty during the trip because of deteriorated well conditions. Latter-day drovers were Ben Taylor, Wally Dowling and George Lannigan. Ilene Lannigan was the only known white woman to go down the stock route when, in 1940, as the cook, she came down with her husband, George.

Conditions and Conflicts

The central deserts of Western Australia are harsh and inhospitable for man and beast. It was no place for the inexperienced and the unhealthy. Water was always of chief importance. The drover had to know the season and the capability of the wells. Knowing where poison plants occurred was also important. There was no white civilisation nor means of outside contact and the drover had to be self-sufficient for the greater part of the stock route. He had to know all the skills and measures necessary for his survival as well as that of the well-being of his stock.

Not all the mobs that started out completed the journey. Some drovers struck drought conditions further south and turned back rather than risk losing their cattle. Other drovers had stock boys who refused to continue past their tribal country after learning from smoke signals of tribal fighting and murder among southern Aboriginals. Over the stock route's historic period there were ten murders, a number of inflicted woundings and several deaths from internal complications of unknown origin.

The Cattle

The endurance of the stock, often under bone-chilling conditions along the 1839-mile journey, was to be admired. The cattle were of a breed that pioneered the open-range country and formed the basis of the leading herds in the northern pastoral beef enterprise for decades. They were never given the monument, yet they inspired and shaped the lives of those early cattlemen. They were the Shorthorns.

The average drover's mob was between five and six hundred bullocks. Bigger mobs were always split into two, travelling about three days apart. Not every well had sufficient capacity to recover in time to meet the mob's daily requirements, meaning that the drover had to move on once the well was empty.

The Wells

There are 51 wells along the stock route, with a smaller number of seasonal watering points. North of Well 51 the route follows the Sturt Creek, with permanent waterholes, before turning north-west then west to Flora Valley Station and up the Elvire River to Halls Creek.

The wells are an average of 15 miles apart, having a shaft 6 × 4 feet wide with an average depth of about 29 feet. The deepest well was 104 feet, the shallowest 4 feet 6 inches. Average well storage was approximately 3523 gallons, with the average capacity to deliver 1062 gallons per hour.

The quantity and quality of the water depended largely on seasonal conditions. Some wells replenished very fast while others remained always slow. Generally the water was good but some wells, if fouled by dead animals and the water was left standing for long periods, needed part of their contents pulled up by the whip-camel or horse and dumped. Other wells were always brackish but still had good water suitable for cooking and stock.

Water was pulled using a reverse-twist three-eight inch rope, fed from a 6-inch ground pulley and then fed up through a 12-inch spoked pulley-wheel mortised into the end of a leaning whip-pole, set 10 feet above the well. The rope was then shackled to a metal eye

Well boring.

on steel rings, supporting a double canvas hand-stitched 25-gallon bucket, with a green hide rim for protection. The bucket was dropped into the well and quickly sank to a calculated depth and was then pulled to the surface by the aid of the whip-camel or horse and emptied down a water chute into the drinking trough.

Most wells were timbered down their sides to 10 or 20 feet, depending on the conditions of the soil. Either desert bloodwood mulga or desert oak was used, the latter having a standard life of about forty years. The wells had steel-covered doors, a metal 12-gallon bucket and a wire rope fixed to the wooden windless, or whip-pole, with handles supporting the wooden uprights. The workmanship was excellent and the material was made to last.

The Environment

The drover's mob was confronted with countless sand ridges. According to Dr J. S. Baird, over a region of 470 miles, some 730 sand ridges lay along the stock route, containing enough material to cover the country evenly with sand to a depth of 3 feet. The biggest sand ridges are between Wells 41 and 42. When formed they are approximately a mile apart, averaging 60 feet in height, with a base of about 320 feet. Their prominent loose caps continually change shape due to the wind. Most of the sand ridges lay between Wells 45 and 46, where the camels and bullocks have to pad across 39 ridges.

The stock route follows the typical desert country with its erratic rainfall. The desert vegetation responds almost immediately to moisture. In 1942 George Lannigan went down the stock route with two mobs, seven days apart. He found the desert flourishing after an inland drenching. Rarely did he pull water as every small and large catchment held ample quantities for his stock. With the abundance of green feed, the bullocks put on additional weight and, at times, the camels had difficulty keeping their balance when stepping onto the succulent carpets of lavish growth.

The Economy and the Drovers

The economic contribution during the war years and the Depression was immense. The drovers were skilled men without pretension, and with acute judgment and perception. They were tough, athletic and charitable. Australia should be rightly proud of these people. Their huge roll has granted a rich and historic background to the pastoral industry. Now, sadly, only a few of these droving men and stock women are left.

The Good Life

Well, I met my husband down the river there near Longreach, in south-western Queensland, and we worked on a property for twelve months. Then virtually straight after that we started droving together. First we took a couple of lots of cattle but the drought broke in and then we mainly travelled stock for property owners, just for the feed and that.

One drought year we had about three thousand ewes on the road and they were lambing as we went along. But there was so little feed that we had to kill the lambs as they were born, the poor things. I mean, even if we'd have picked them up and put them on the truck they still would've died. To start with I used to sing out to one of the men to come back and kill the lambs. Then eventually they said, 'Either you learn to kill them or we'll leave them for the crows to pick their eyes out.'

And oh, I remember the first baby lamb I killed. I couldn't sleep that night. Oh, it was terrible. But you just had to do it because a lot of people in cities don't realise just how cruel crows are. They're terrible things. And what they do to lambs, well. So we had to be cruel to be kind.

But basically, my job was a jack-of-all-trades and master of none, and that included being a mother. I had three children. They were born in '53, '55 and '57. I did the ringing and the cooking too, though when a brother used to come out we'd take turns cooking and ringing, which was good.

And the kids loved it. They'd get up and they'd be straight on the horses and that. They didn't even wait for breakfast. We'd have to cook something and they'd canter up alongside the truck to eat it. Then they'd be off again, around the stock. We had two boys and a girl at that stage. Barbara was only three.

But all the children were born in Longreach and then I took

them back out on the road until they had to go to school. My youngest stayed in Barcaldine with his aunty for a couple of years while he went to primary school. Then with their high schooling they went into Longreach. And I remember when I'd go in to pick them up in the holidays, all the other kids in the street, they'd want to come out with us as well.

Back then we had a Morris five-tonner with a crate on it and my husband made it up so that we could lay out some wire stretchers, and we'd just tie them back up when we weren't using them. And we also had a canvas that we could pull out to make a shelter. Then your table sat on the rungs of the crate and you'd slip that out to have your meals on, and that.

Loaded and ready to go droving.

But the kids were happy out droving. They couldn't have cared less if they went into town. In fact, we had quite a few Christmases on the road. We'd buy them a few toys then the people whose stock we were looking after, well, they might bring out lollies and fruit. But we still had a baked dinner and that. I'd cook it in the camp oven. As a matter of fact, I've still got one of my old camp ovens. The *Courier-Mail* come out one year and interviewed me and they asked me to bring the camp oven out and pretend I was cleaning it. That was a bit of a laugh.

Then I lost my youngest son when he was twelve and a half. It was pretty tragic what happened. After that Norman, the eldest, got that way that he'd just sit there at school and stare into space, which was a big shame really, because even the headmaster said that he could've been a veterinary surgeon or anything. I mean, he was pretty bright and all that so there was nothing wrong with him. He could've won his scholarships. But he just couldn't learn any more. He couldn't concentrate. He was fourteen, I suppose; no a bit older than that, fourteen and a half, and eventually they just exempted him from school.

But it was a good life for the children. They really loved it. I remember the boy that I lost; well, one time we were with a mob of sheep and his pony fell and he skinned all his face. It was pretty dusty behind sheep and, at the time, it was winter so I tried to keep him in the truck. But he wouldn't stay. He wanted to be back out with the sheep and that. Oh, he might've stayed in for a day, but that's all. Then after that I'd have to bathe his face at night because he'd been out in all the dust.

Then my husband died, and it was awful. It was pretty tragic, really. I don't know if it all got too much for him. But see, it wasn't very nice because I lost six relations in eighteen months. I lost my husband in the February. I lost Dad in June and in October I lost my son. As a matter of fact, the father died first and then I lost my son about six months after that. Then after that the droving days stopped. I stayed in Longreach then. I don't remember what year it was but we still had the pony club going and I'd take the horses up and help them there. So I kept that up.

But thankfully, the daughter, Barbara, she stayed until we finished. But it just got too much and I had to get out. So that's when I come to Brisbane and I've been here ever since. But I was only saying, even though I got to the stage that I had to get out, I'm now at the stage where I want to go back. It was a good life, and I really do miss the horses. I left them with my son, out there. I think they'd be dead now. But you do miss the horses, and that sort of thing. So if I won the lottery, I'd go back to Longreach; back my roots.

The Night Horse

There's none of this droves or drives business. They're called trips. The only animals that were driven in Australia were rabbits, and that was back when they were in plague proportions and they were driven into nets and killed. Then, we call them a rush, a jump or a splash—*not* a stampede, as the Americans call them. And it doesn't matter whether you've got a truck or just packhorses, it's always classified as a plant.

Then as far as your personnel went, you had the boss drover or drover, and he looked after everything. There was the cook and the horsetailer. Your white men were known as ringers. Then there were the black boys, who were called 'boys' no matter what their age was. Even though they done the same job as the ringers, they were still called boys.

Now this's how you worked the boys on a trip. See a lot of drovers would leave, for example, Camooweal, in the far west of Queensland, and head off to pick up a mob from, say, Inverway, in the far west of the Northern Territory, or the Ord, which is just inside the West Australian border. Now on the way over, the drover'd probably just take a cook, a horsetailer and he might take a couple of ringers. That's all. And when they got over there he'd organise two or three boys to come along and help bring the cattle back.

Then when they got into the Territory—maybe they got as far as the centre, around Newcastle Waters—those boys'd want to go back home because they were too far out of their own country; out of their natural environment, you could say. So when that happened, you'd let them go and you'd go to a ration station like Phillip Creek or, if it was before then, you'd see the sergeant of police and he'd get you a couple of boys.

But if you got as far as the Barkly Tablelands most drovers'd say, 'Oh well, we can get away with just the ringers.' That's because it was far more open county than over in the west and the cattle were out of their natural environment as well, so you could usually handle them easier. And that's where the night horses became an imperative. Now the night horse is indicative of what it's called. It's a horse that works well at night. It's got a sixth sense in the dark, if you like. If there's a rush during the night, he's there, saddled up, ready to go.

Take the time I was up in the far north of West Australia, at Argyle Station, in about 1954, when they were going to put a mob from Argyle together with a mob from Newry Station, to do a trip. Anyhow, the Newry mob was camped on one side of the river and we were over the other side, about half a mile away. Then on the night before we left, the Newry cattle jumped and they took a run for some unknown reason. Oddly enough, our mob didn't even get up. They weren't even disturbed. Sometimes it happens like that. There's no rhyme nor reason.

Now in that particular case, if it hadn't been for the night horses it would've made things very difficult with the Newry mob. See, it's pretty rough country up that way and when the Newrys went, they rushed along between the scrub and the waterway and they crossed a lot of breakaways—steep, erosion-type gullies. And these night horses never missed a beat. They just flew down along the wing in the dead of the night, through all this scrub and gullies, until they managed to get the mob under control. So there.

But see, the night horse is an amazing creature. And the odd thing is that there's no way you can tell if a horse'll become a good night horse or not. It just happens. It doesn't fit a precise pattern so there's no way of breeding it into them. Though to the experienced drover, a night horse does have a few attributes that stand out. Firstly, they're very adaptable. They're usually sensible, meaning that when you teach him something, like to draft and so forth, it doesn't take long for him to express to you that he's keen to learn. His ears'll always be forward rather than back. He's not pulling and tugging and reefing or distracted. He's on the ball. He can distinguish depth of perception and gallop high in the anticipation of tussocks and stumps or for jumping gullies. And they have a sixth

sense of where the cattle are and what they're going to do. He antici-
pates. But even with all those attributes there's no guarantees. He's
still got to prove himself.

Now a decent drover'll have a number of night horses on a trip.
Then when you camp, you always tie a night horse up to a tree,
saddled and ready to go, and the drover or ringer rolls his swag right
out near his feet. That tree's what's called the night horse tree. If
you're out on the plains, where there aren't any trees, you put a
couple of steel posts into the ground.

And I've seen these horses standing there in the dead of the
night, sweating up until they're covered in foam, like somebody's
soaped him up for a car wash. Now to the untrained eye, that might
look like nerves. But it's not. They're not nervous in the context of
what's understood as nervous, which is a horse that fidgets and
dances around, trying to get loose. I mean, a drover wouldn't be
sleeping right next to him if he reckoned he was going to be walked
on, would he. No, because these horses, they stand very quiet
and still, sensing the cattle. That's what all the sweating's about—
anticipation. From a man's point of view, you could liken it to an
adrenaline rush.

Then when the cattle jump, you're out of your swag and up and
into the saddle like a shot, and you're after them. And you don't
ever pull a night horse back. Put your trust in him. If that horse
wants to go one way, go with him because he's got a damn good
reason for going that way. You mightn't be able to see it, but he
can, so go with him.

So anyway, that might put you right as to all the terms we use
and how it all works with the personnel and the black boys. And
that's why a good night horse's worth his weight in gold because,
if there's a rush at night, it's that horse you rely on, completely,
just like the time up at Argyle.

The People You Meet

In about '94 a drought started to move in here, just out of Young, on southern slopes of New South Wales. It was also bad out west. But I'd noted that it wasn't going east, into the Southern Highlands.

Now on our property at Murringo we mostly had merinos so, as things worsened, we began selling off stock. See, that's what you do during the drought times. You try and hang onto your best breeding stock and you sell the rest, then when the good times return at least you've kept the basis of your line. So that's what we did, and we sold down to the stage where we decided to leave some at home then do the great Australian thing and take the remaining two and a half thousand on the road for feed. It's just marvellous the way you can do that.

At that time we only had a little Subaru utility so I hunted around until I found a small caravan that it could easily pull; one that was self-contained and clean, because most I saw smelt pretty shocking. My husband decided to stay on at home to look after things here while me and my son, Angus, worked out that we'd share the droving. See, I still had to go over to my shop in Canberra for a couple of days a week, and when I came back, Angus then had the chance to take the weekend off.

Now because things still had to continue on at home, we didn't take all our dogs, then some neighbours were kind enough to loan us a couple of theirs. So we ended up with about five dogs. We didn't take horses. We just went with the Subaru, the caravan, and the dogs.

So we set off up into the Southern Highlands. And how we worked it was that each morning we'd take the dogs up to where we were going to camp that night and we'd tie them to posts or whatever—we left the road free for traffic, of course—then we'd come back and we'd let the sheep out of the break and they'd sort

Droving during the 1994 drought, into the Southern Highlands, with my son, Angus, the sheep dogs and our ute.

of run down to where the dogs were and they'd graze back. Then at night, we either had to make a sheep break or sometimes, when we came across an old reserve, we put the dogs around that and the sheep stayed in there. So that was the daily pattern of things and it was one that the sheep soon become very accustomed to.

So we were away from just before September '95, right up until Easter '96. And we spent all those months walking the various stock routes and laneways around towns like Boorowa, Rugby, Crookwell and up as far as a little school near Bigga, called Two Mile School or something. And as luck had it, it'd been thirty or forty years since any real droving had gone on through that area, so the sheep always had good feed and the water was good because there were quite a few little creeks. There were also the dams on the reserves.

But the thing I remember most about the trip was the people. And a mixed bag they were too, because a lot of the farmers up there weren't keen on us coming through. See, they liked to have the luxury of being able to let their own sheep out on the stock route. It was free feed. Like there was the time this farmer tried to scare Angus off from outside of his place by accusing us of letting our sheep on his dam.

So Angus said, 'No, I didn't.'

Then this chap told Angus that if he didn't move on he'd get the police. 'Well, if you don't, I will,' said Angus, and that was the end of it, then.

Anyhow, the fellow who owned the property down the road was a QC from Sydney, so I said to Angus, 'You'd better be careful going past him, Angus.' But anyhow, when he did, this QC came out and invited Angus in for dinner.

So mostly they were really good, you know. Angus was twenty-five or something and when I wasn't there they'd come out and offer to do his washing and that, or they'd ask him if he wanted to use their shower. So there was lots of generosity, while on the other hand, there were also those ones who were trying to protect themselves.

But the funniest incident was the time we left the sheep up a lane, on the stock route, because we had to go off to a funeral. Anyhow, there were these two brothers who had separate land-holdings and they didn't want us there, so they complained to the police about us having diseased sheep. I mean, it wasn't even a police matter at all. It was a Pastures Protection Board job and they should've contacted them because the inspector from Young had been out to see us every week, so he knew we were disease free.

Anyhow, I just happened to come home after the funeral and that's when the police rang. So we arranged this meeting, you know, back up where we'd left the sheep. There was the two brothers, the police, a couple of fellows from the PP Board and Angus and I. So they inspected our sheep and, of course, they were all right.

But as it turned out, these two brothers were having their own, private, family feud and during this meeting it all erupted and they had this big fight. So there they were screaming and yelling and so forth, accusing each other of having foot rot and we just stood there watching it all unfold. Oh, that was a lot of fuss, you know, with it ending up being this big feud. Anyhow there wasn't much we could do, so we left them to it and we went on our merry way. But gee, they were characters. The people you meet, aye.

So yes, it was wonderful to be able to save the sheep and bring them back, and with a bit of condition on them, too. It really saved our day.

The Red Spot Drover

Back when I was about seventeen or eighteen I worked on a couple of the big stations out in south-western Queensland. And it was a pretty good life too, you know, especially for someone my age. But after a while you find that you spend so much time on your own that it's hard to assimilate back into what's called 'normal society'. So by the stage this incident happened, I was virtually station droving and I guess that I'd spent about seven months by myself.

Now this particular property was about three-quarters of a million acres; ninety miles long and about thirty miles wide. I don't know whether those statistics work out but, the point I'm trying to make is that it was a bloody big place.

Anyhow, it was shearing time and my job was to ride out and pick up 2000 or 3000 sheep in, say, the north-west corner of the property and spend the next few days droving them back into the holding paddock, near the shearing shed, which had a rain-fed dam on it. Now this holding paddock was around a couple of thousand acres, just on its own.

So I'd stay in the holding paddock with the sheep to feed and water them, then each day I'd pull off 1000 or so and take them in for the next day's shearing. So I'd do that day in and day out.

Station droving at shearing time.

Then after they'd all been shorn I'd spend another few days droving them back out to their paddock before picking up another lot. So that's the life I was leading, and the whole process would take a week or so by the time I got the sheep there, they were shorn, and I returned them to whichever paddock the boss wanted them to go.

Now by this stage I'd been working for three or four weeks straight, so I was pretty knackered, and the dog I had with me, it didn't matter how much meat you fed the poor girl, she was pretty tired as well. Anyhow, I was moving these 2000 or 3000 shorn sheep back to their paddock—just me on my horse and my dog— and we were pushing them as tight as possible along the fence line so that there wasn't the need for any other riders to help with the droving. Then down the road a bit, I ran into a mate of mine, a grader driver. As I said, with working like I was, I'd spent several months of that year virtually by myself. It was a real occasion to run into someone I knew so, naturally, I stopped for a chat.

Then as we were chatting, my mate pulled out this bottle of Red Spot rum, and that was a dangerous thing to do. Anyhow, we got stuck into this stuff and before too long my mate'd gone to sleep propped up against the tyre of the grader, leaving me propped up beside him, drinking what was left of this rum. Then I must've drifted off because, when I woke up, the sheep were gone, the dog was gone, the horse was gone, and with the horse gone, what was left of my supply of water had gone with it.

On closer inspection I could see by the tracks that the sheep'd completely turned around and had headed off back down the fence, back toward the holding paddock, near the shearing shed. Obviously they were thirsty and that's where they knew they'd find water, in the dam there. And with the dog being so tired, when the sheep turned around, she just turned around as well and followed behind, pushing along the stragglers. Then the horse followed up the procession by just meandering behind the mob, too.

Anyway, I was pretty drunk and I was seeing about two of every-thing. But then I happened to look down the road and I saw a big cloud of dust and, on gathering my focus, I noticed that there was a white spot at the bottom of the dust. And even at just making out the white spot, I knew it was the boss's car. Well there was nothing I could do. I'd been caught 'red-spotted', so to speak.

When the boss arrived, he was pretty cool about it. He just wandered up and said, 'G'day, Mike. How are you?'

'Okay,' I slurred.

'Yer've been caught up by this bloke, have yer?' Meaning my mate.

'Yeah,' I said.

'Well, do yer know where yer mob is?' he asked.

'Reckon they mighta gone back toward the holding paddock where there's water.'

'Well then,' he said, 'yer'd better get down an get 'em,' he said, and then he jumped back into his vehicle and took off, leaving me wobbling on the spot.

Now it was a fair walk back to the holding paddock. When I started out it was about three o'clock in the afternoon. Remember, I didn't have any water and it was in the middle of summer, out in the south-west of Queensland. Anyway, I finally caught up with the horse and I knocked off the rest of my water. Then I worked out that the most sensible thing to do was to simply follow the dog and the sheep back to the holding paddock and settle them down for the night by the dam then start the whole process of taking them back out to their paddock the next day.

So that's what I did. But I tell you, after having drunk the best part of a bottle of Red Spot, followed by a hell of a walk in the hottest part of the day, I reckon that I drank more water out of that dam that night than the whole 2000 or 3000 head of sheep.

The Three Wethers

You always hear people talking about 'the good old days', you know, and I say to them that there are no 'good old days'. Mind you, I've got some very pleasant memories of things that happened back in me life. But oh, these days'll do me. These are 'the good days' not 'the good old days'. Things were too tough back then.

See I was born in 1904, near a little town called Isisford, away down on the Barcoo River, just west of Blackall, in south-western Queensland. Then when I was around eleven or twelve me father died and all us kids had to dig in and help out. But there wasn't much work out at Isisford so we moved into Blackall where I done a lot of cleaning, helping me mother out. Then when I come home from school on the Friday, I'd be running around town, bare foot, delivering pamphlets for an auctioneer. I got four bob for that. Then later on I started driving the horse-drawn baker's van and working in the baker's shop.

So you could say that I started work when I was about eleven or twelve. Then the droving came about because there was a great old bloke in Blackall called Billy Cuffer, and Billy might've known how things were tough at home, so one day he came around to see me mother. At that time we were living up near the railway station, and me mother used to clean the railway quarters out for the men, and Billy said, 'Would yer let me take Norman out on a droving trip? I'll look after him,' he said.

'Oh, all right then,' she said.

So Billy took me away and we were on the road for about five and a half weeks. In them days wages for a droving trip was about two pounds seven a week, along with your keep, but I was never worrying about that. I just reckoned that Billy was taking me away, just for a bit of company. Then when we came back we took the sheep out to old Sam Blacklock's property, then Billy said, 'Thanks,' he said. 'I'll see yer later on.'

'All right,' I said. 'See yer, then.'

Then about an hour later Billy come down home and he's singing out at me, from the front. So I goes out and he hands me a cheque. Blimey! So I raced inside and I grabbed me mother and I said, 'Look what's here,' I said. 'Look what's here.' I couldn't believe it. Billy'd paid me the full five weeks' wages at two pounds seven per week.

So I reckoned that droving was a bit of a lark after that, and I did quite a bit from then on, right up until the last trip I done. And there's a story in that too. See, I went droving into New South Wales with a big mob of wild brumby horses we'd mustered from a property out of the mountains at Spring Lea. And oh, we had an awful time with them.

Now the owner of the property told us that, under no circumstances were we allowed to sell any of these brumbies on the road because they were going down to Dubbo, in central New South Wales, where he reckoned he'd get a lot more money for them. That was his thinking.

Anyhow, we got them just outside Cunnamulla and we were held up by a big rain. Then by the time we got to Dubbo we'd missed the sale so we had to hold them for a month until the next sale. Anyway, with one thing and another we finished selling these horses, but by then they'd run completely out of condition and they were sold at an awful price.

But gee there were some beautiful animals in among them. I remember one beautiful grey horse. Oh, he was a villain. Up in Cunnamulla a feller wanted him real bad, he did, and he offered a hell of a lot of money for him. But we didn't sell him because, like I said, the boss feller told us not to sell them on the road. Then when we finally put him in the saleyard in Dubbo, he wasn't looking so good. And then he went mad and he put everyone off, so they ended up selling him for next to nothing. But he was a beautiful grey he was, just beautiful.

Then when we got paid, me and me mate, dear old Les Scupper, decided to go down to Sydney and have a good look around the big smoke. We'd heard about the place but we'd never been there before. Now our boss drover was a returned soldier, and he knew the ropes a bit and he also knew that we was just young fellers, not used of the city. So he rang some pub up in Sydney to organise things for us because we didn't know where to go or nothing, once we got off the train at Central Railway Station.

So we took the train down and we arrived in Sydney on the Good Friday. And I'll never forget. Jeez it's funny. You can't pick people, can you, aye. We got off the train at Central and all we had was a swag and a little bloody pack each. So we go outside and we get in a taxi and we tell the driver where we want to go. It was some little pub in Campbell Street or somewhere.

Well I swear that taxi driver drove us around for at least twenty minutes. Then when we got to the pub, we asked him how much the fare was for the taxi and it was some awful price—very expensive. But we didn't know so we just paid up. It almost broke us, it did. Then the next morning, we got up and had a bit of a walk around and I said to Les—Les was from Blackall—I said, 'Hey, Les, that looks like Central Railway Station just up there.'

And bugger me, there it was about ten minutes' walk away from the pub we were staying at. So this taxi driver had picked us out good and proper. I tell you, you can't trust them city fellers. They'll have you all right, every time.

So then we said, 'Bugger this.' So after we went to the races we packed up and we went back home, back to Blackall, where I did some wool pressing for a while, then I went back out and did the droving again.

But, of course, in them days, only the big properties had shearing sheds and there was lots of droving along the stock routes—beautiful green grass it was, too. Whip grass. Beautiful. Anyhow there used to be big mobs of sheep—eight to ten thousand—all travelling through the country. And they had to get shorn somewhere so they shore a lot of them in the community shearing sheds, along the stock route. There was a lot of them places back then, but now Blackall's the only one left and they've made it into a sort of heritage place.

Then later, I remember a bloke called Ned Furner and he wanted to work something like 14,000 head of sheep down past Longreach. Ned had a big property called Wanderoo Station, which was out near Winton. Anyhow, Ned was mates with a taxi driver in at Blackall, so he asked this taxi driver to gill him up some men and, as it happened, I lived next door to this taxi driver and I had a couple of real good dogs. So the bloke said, 'Do yer wanta go out with those dogs of yours?'

'Yes,' I said. So I went out with me dogs.

And I remember, when we got the sheep down to Longreach, you've gotta cross a bridge over a river to get into town—the Thomson River, out on the Winton road. Anyway I was saying to one of the other drovers, 'Even with me dogs,' I said, 'it'll take a hell of a time to get this mob'a sheep over that bridge, there tomorrow.'

'Yer won't need no dogs,' he reckoned.

Anyhow, there was an old feller by the name of Tommy someone. He was the town ranger, I think. I forget his other name just now but he used to live right near the bridge at Longreach. And Tommy had these three big wethers that had bells tied around their necks.

Sheep crossing the bridge.

So the next morning we split our 14,000 head of sheep into three lots, two drovers with each mob.

Then when we got to the river, old Tommy came down to the bridge with these three wethers. And you would've thought, so help me God, that somebody'd told these wethers exactly what to do. Because, when they got to the bridge, they left old Tommy behind and they just walked right on over and through the first mob of our sheep, all the way back to where me and me mate was standing, right behind them. Then they turned around and they walked back through the mob, with their bells, and they headed back over the bridge. And so help me God, all our sheep followed them, they did, just like that. And in five or ten minutes our mob of 4000 or so had walked over the bridge right behind old Tommy's three wethers, and we followed them too, like.

Then once we got about half a mile or so up the track these three wethers come out of the pack as large as life and they just stood there beside the road, waiting. And the old feller, Tommy—Tommy Wolfe, that's what his name was—well old Tommy, he came back up the track and he had a bit of a talk to his three wethers and they followed him back to the bridge. Then they walked back over the bridge, right through the next mob of sheep, and they did the exact same thing. Oh, it was a work of art, I can tell you. It was wonderful to watch. No trouble at all, you know. I didn't need me dogs at all because those three wethers got the 14,000 head of sheep over that bridge inside the hour.

So that was early on in the year. Then later I got a job at Moscow Station and they brought 10,000 wethers down from Northampton Downs to Longreach and the same thing happened. Out came old Tommy Wolfe with his three wethers, with their bells on, and they did the exact same thing. You wouldn't credit it, would you.

But oh, the grass, the grass was this high back then. Whip grass. But there's no droving like that any more. It's all done by truck now. When they have the stock sales in Longreach, you can hear the trucks going all night. Drive you mad, it does. It's a shame, really. They really put pay to old Tommy Wolfe and his three wethers, they did.

The Tired Drover

My name is Jim Travers. I'm the son of Ambrose Travers who was the eldest of three brothers. Bill, or William, Travers was the second eldest. He was the drover. Then there was Hillary Travers, the youngest.

The brothers grew up at a place called Coothidie, which is near Jamestown, about two and a half hours' drive north of Adelaide. Coothidie was up on the hills just above . . . now, what's that town just north of Jamestown on the way to Orroroo, the one with the hotel that's been empty for fifty years—a big two-storey place? Anyhow, it's out that way.

Hillary, the youngest, died when he was twenty-one. That's right, the hotel was the Yatina Hotel. Yatina was only a small place, sort of halfway between Jamestown and Orroroo. And one of the things about it was that it was flat for about 8 to 10 miles each side of the road. Anyhow, the local Catholics used to have mass at Yatina once every three months or so. But the story goes that on Sunday mornings after mass all the fellers would go into the pub for a drink. Now drinking on a Sunday was highly illegal in those days.

Now this drinking after mass had been going on for a good while. It was sort of a tradition. But when the police caught wind of it they decided to have a raid on the hotel. Well of course, these fellers, they always posted a lookout on the outside, just in case. Anyhow on this particular occasion the lookout just happened to be my Uncle Hillary. He was only eighteen at the time, maybe even younger, and he didn't understand the importance of looking out for the police because he didn't drink or anything.

So Uncle Hillary was sent up on the second-storey balcony and he soon got tired of just standing there, looking out at nothing, and at one point he happened to wander off to the toilet. Now this occurred at quite an inappropriate moment because that's when the police arrived and raided the hotel. Fortunately for Hillary he was stuck away in the toilet, up on the second storey, and the constabulary didn't venture that far. So thirty locals, minus Uncle Hillary, were rounded up and taken back to Jamestown where they were duly charged, leaving Hillary back at the hotel walking around, wondering where the heck everyone had disappeared to.

So that was my Uncle Hillary, and he died two or three years later. But it was William, or Bill Travers, as he was known, who was the drover. Bill used to drove down the Birdsville Track, and he got involved on a cattle station way up north, and on this particular occasion he took charge of 1600 head of cattle. Now normally these droves only took about five or six hundred, so this was an absolutely huge number of cattle, and all he had was three young Aboriginal lads to help him out. No cooks, nothing, just these three Aboriginal fellows and himself.

So he got about 200 or 300 miles down the track and, one night, the Aborigines got scared, spooked, and they took flight. Now Bill decided that it was useless taking the cattle back to the station. That'd achieve nothing, so the only thing he could do was to keep going. Well it's one thing to be droving by yourself during the day but, at night-time when you camped, the cattle still had to be watched. So Bill had to drove during the day and he also had to keep the mob together at night—twenty-four hours.

To do this he had about seven horses which he kept rotating, one after the other, to give them a rest. So he kept the cattle moving during the day then, when it came to night, he had to, virtually, rely on his horse to keep circling the cattle while he tried to snatch some sleep in the saddle. And he kept this up, night and day, while he drove these cattle all the way down to Kapunda, which is approximately 50 mile north-east of Adelaide. And it took him three weeks to do the trip—that's after the Aboriginal lads had fled.

So he eventually got the cattle down to Kapunda without having hardly any sleep at all. Then he left the cattle in the Kapunda saleyards and he caught a train down to Adelaide; down to Goodwood, where my grandparents lived. And when he arrived, he got into bed and he slept for twenty-four hours straight. My father said he'd never come across anyone, not anyone, who'd slept for a full twenty-four hours. But Uncle Bill did.

Then later on he decided to join the army and he went over to Guadalcanal. At that time the Japanese were on one side of the island and the Americans were on the other and it was Bill's job to report on Japanese movements. He was the only white person there, with two locals who knew the mountainous terrain like the back of their hands. And they had to too, because Bill could only broadcast for two or three minutes before the Japanese were able to pinpoint where his camp was and, if he didn't move from his position pretty quick, they'd knock him out. And he kept this up, reporting the Japanese positions, for fully six months and over that time he had to fight in many skirmishes, and on his own.

So when Uncle Bill came back he was in a very unfit state of condition, and he was dead scared at night. The only time he could sleep was during the day. So things became difficult at home and he decided to continue droving cattle from the Gulf down to Adelaide.

On one occasion he told the story about the time the cattle king, Sir Sidney Kidman, announced that he was droving 1000 or so head of cattle down from Queensland to be sold in the Kapunda saleyards. It was to be an all-important event. But then, the butchers from around the place decided to take this young Kidman to task. Their line of thinking was that they'd hold back on buying any beef until Kidman arrived and then they'd group together and offer him a very low rate of payment and he'd have to sell because he had no capacity to feed the cattle and it'd be too costly to take them back to the Gulf.

Well, when these cattle arrived, the auctioneer asked for bids and only one butcher made an offer. But instead of offering the usual twelve quid a cow, this chap offered only about two quid a cow. So then there was silence as no one bid against this two quid offer. And that's how these butchers had organised it, for there to be no competition. But Kidman was a pretty smart fellow and he realised what these butchers were trying to do, so he jumped down into the ring and called to the auctioneer, 'Stop the auction. I want

Sir Sidney Kidman and employees at the saleyards.

these cattle taken out. Haul them out. You're not having them at that price. I don't care if they all die!'

Now that suddenly left the butchers without any meat. Like I said, they hadn't bothered to buy any beef for the past two or three months because they thought they'd get it all from Kidman at this low rate. So by this stage, there was precious little remaining in their shops. Now with that in mind, two butchers then jumped down into the yard and they refused to let Kidman open the gate and take his bullocks away.

'All right then,' Kidman said to the butchers, 'have it your own way but I'll make the call.'

'Okay,' they said. 'You make the call.'

Then Kidman announced, 'My offer's twelve quid a cow, take it or leave it.'

So they bought the cattle, and some of it went above the twelve quid, too. And that was another of my Uncle Bill's stories, one that I have no doubt believing because I've heard a few stories about Kidman which were along the same lines. He was a hard man; hard but fair.

The Tucker for Me

I was born in April 1915, when my mother and father were living at a place called Bellevue, just outside of Perth. My father had a butcher shop. Then when my mother died in about 1922, we went out to Kalgoorlie where I went to school until I left when I was thirteen. Then in about 1930 I moved up to the central west, to Wiluna, and I sort of worked around there at various jobs.

I was tailing cattle at the slaughter yards and I met up with an old bloke called William Snell. He owned a butcher shop there as well as a property called Bridle Face, out of Wiluna, and he'd just come back from reconditioning some of the wells on the Canning Stock Route. I think he done up to about Well 29 or Well 30, but then all his men bailed up on him. Then Alfred Canning, the bloke who first surveyed the stock route, well, he come back again to finish the job, the poor bugger.

So I worked for old Snell for about six or seven years. Then in 1937, when I was in my early twenties, I got a brainwave to take off to the Kimberleys. Now I didn't go up the Canning route because I'd been warned about the bush blacks so, me and another young feller, we went by boat up around the coast to Derby, which is in the north-west of Western Australia. From there we went down south a bit to Yeeda.

Back then, Kidman owned Yeeda. In fact, he owned a lot of area around there. But while I was working at Yeeda, a bloke called Sam Cousins come out from over Camooweal, in north-western Queensland, to take a mob of 1500 male cattle down to Oodnadatta, which is in the north-west of South Australia. So I hooked in with him and I went along and I done the job as horsetailer. There was only five of us on that trip and we had about twenty or so packs.

We started in early April, I think. I'm not quite sure now, but I do know we were still going in November. We only done about

8 mile a day, so it was a long way. And we basically lived on corned beef and damper because, over through them places, it was two or three weeks before you got to a place where you could top up your rations. And even then it was only a bit of fresh fruit and vegetables, that's if they had any to spare.

So we took the cattle across to Fitzroy River, where we got rations. Then the next place we had to rely on was one of Vesteys' places, at Ord River, over near the Northern Territory border. A bloke called Joe Egan was there then. So we topped up there and we went into the Territory, through Inverway, where we got a bit of rations off the Farquar brothers. The Farquars were either there or they may've been at Wave Hill. I'm not sure now. But from Wave Hill we went through the Murranji Stock Route to Newcastle Waters.

At that time, Kidman also had some sort of share in Newcastle Waters. So they cut the tail off there and they built the mob up again with fresh cattle. Then we topped up with rations again and we walked them down to Alice Springs, where they cut the tail again, before we went on, down the Oodnadatta Track, to Oodnadatta.

'We basically lived on corned beef and damper.'

But that was all new country for me. And especially through that early part, it was like a drover's heaven in some ways. The only time it got really rough was through the ranges, with the jump-ups and gorges and that. But I don't think there was a dry stage from Fitzroy through to the Ord, with all the rivers and creeks and surface water. And over there you just follow the stock route tracks that'd been picked out years ago by the real old-timers. That's all lost today, but they're the ones that should be getting all the credit. We only followed along what they'd done.

But the thing I was going to tell you: remember how I said we lived mainly on corned beef and damper, well, through that barramundi country we also did some fishing. But we didn't need any fishing line or bait. You don't need that sort of stuff. All you needed was fifteen hundred head of cattle to put through the water, belly deep, so they'll stir up the mud. Then the next thing, the fish were up on top gasping for air, so we'd ride in and, it was like at a fish shop or a market, you just picked out what you wanted, you know. And then once the water settled back down, the fish were okay again.

But corned beef and damper, that was the tucker for me. I liked that. And even after all those years of droving, you'd reckon I'd be sick of eating the stuff. But I still like me beef, and even though there's plenty of bread around these days, I still don't mind a bit of damper now and then, either. But there's nothing wrong with a good lump of corned beef. A lot might reckon that it's too greasy and that, but I still enjoy it. Actually, if I was offered some right now, I wouldn't knock it back.

They Rushed at Well 40

If you followed the real plan of the old Canning Stock Route, from Wiluna up to Halls Creek, it's about 1000 miles. So yes, I think that the Canning's reputation comes from it being such a lonely place.

After you leave Well 9, you don't see anybody. You're isolated. There's no roads, no tracks, no aeroplanes, nothing, until you get to Billiluna, up in north-eastern Western Australia. So you're on your own, not like the other stock routes. They talk about the Murranji, over in the Northern Territory, and a few of the others, but the Canning's completely cut off. When you get to the middle, the nearest place of any size would probably be Port Hedland, which is a good 500 or 600 miles away.

My first droving trip along the Canning was in 1946 when I was back working at Wongawol Station, near Lake Carnegie, in central Western Australia. Ben Taylor, a well-known and well-respected drover along the Canning Stock Route, asked me if I'd like to go up there with some brumbies and come back with some bullocks and I said, 'Yes.'

By that stage Ben had already mustered quite a few of the brumbies, so we put a bit of work on getting some more. Then in the February, Ben and myself and two Aboriginal stock boys started off with sixty-six of these brumbies. We went from Wongawol, up to Carnegie Station, then across to No. 9 Well and from there up to Billiluna, which is the first station you strike at the top end of the Canning. On that trip it took us about ten weeks to get to Lamboo Station.

Ben's idea of going up was twofold as he also wanted to have a look at the condition of both the stock route and also the wells. You see, it could've been drought out in the middle and nobody would've known. That's what I mean about it being such an isolated place. So along the way, we done a bit of work on the wells. Some were starting to fall in and some of the whip-poles were a bit loose. See, there are no wind-driven mills along the Canning. They're called 'windless' because you have to actually pull the water out with a bucket and rope that's attached to a leaning timber pole—the whip-pole—which is positioned over the centre of the well. Then from there, the rope is attached to a wheel and is then tied to either a camel or a horse to pull the water out of the well.

Then when we were going up the stock route with these brumbies we got a real scare. We already knew that other drovers had had problems at Well 40. The rumour was that it was haunted because of the nearby graves of Michael Tobin and a bush native. They'd fatally wounded each other during a surprise encounter around what had once been a soak but was now the well. We got to Well 40 at about midday and the place had an uneasy mood about it. Then we'd just pulled off all the packs when without reason the saddle horses, the plant, and the brumbies rushed, and they galloped flat-strap over the nearest sandhill.

I was told to stop at the well and to fill the water trough and to hobble and water any horses that may return, while Ben and the boys grabbed a couple of spare bridles and halters and ran after the mob on foot. But I'd been riding a grey horse and I'd knotted the reins before hooking him to a light branch and, as it turned out, he caught his back hoof in the loop of the reins and Ben caught him several miles away. Ben was then able to block a couple of saddle horses for the boys and although the brumbies had split from the plant, they caught the lead and returned before sunset.

It was too risky to remain at the well as some of the missing brumbies could possibly have rushed at the troughs overnight. So we had a bite to eat then packed up and camped at least six miles further on, where we hobbled the horses that we'd caught. The next morning we took off on them and caught up with most of those that had rushed the previous day. In all we only lost ten or so, in among the sandhills. Then the following day we packed up and we went on to the next well.

With Billiluna being something like 215 miles away, if we hadn't caught the horses we would've been walking. And without having any bullocks to kill we were virtually living on top-notch (crested) pigeons, as it was. They were quite easy to get because they'd line up on the top rail of the drinking trough, where you could shoot two or three at a time. They provided a decent feed as they were plump and, when cooked, also kept quite well in a wet bag for the next meal. So although each day we only had one small johnnycake, plus a little tea, sugar, macaroni and black sauce, we still managed to make a small stew each evening. In fact, we ate quite well. With initiative and care, and providing you had sufficient water, it is possible to live out there on nature's own resources, which was something admirably demonstrated by the stock boys.

Then once we got to the edge of Billiluna country, we tracked and shot a loner-bull and we butchered him. Though apart from the tongue and the brains, compared to the sweet breast of the birds, the meat and offal was rank, having been impregnated with the terrible, gummy flavour that beef cattle get when they live for long periods on spinifex and they drink salty water.

Then in the May, Ben and I took delivery of 596 bullocks from Billiluna to drove down the Canning, along with three stock boys. Because of the dry conditions we lost a small number of older bullocks at the start of the trip. These were mainly the ones who had lived on surface water, and when they came to the wells, finding it unfamiliar, they refused to drink from a trough. Some of these cattle finally adapted, but only after we encouraged them by throwing buckets of water on the ground next to the trough. Though, because the water didn't smell right, the others rejected drinking above the ground and before long they became aggressive and started charging the horses and so forth, so they had to be shot or they'd perish.

Although the stock route was in drought at the beginning of the trip, the bullocks maintained their condition after the first four or five weeks, which was an example of how well they adapted to the desert foliage.

Another thing that affected the bullocks was a plant known as Narrow Leaf Poison. The drover had to know where patches of it grew so that he could walk his cattle around it. Still, at times, isolated plants are eaten. When that happens, the ones that have eaten too much, they die quickly or later on, at the trough after a drink. But if the beast only eats a little and gets sick he usually recovers when he's left to follow the herd at his own pace. On night watch I've heard the sick ones calling for their mates. Then as they follow the scent, the calling gets louder, causing the herd to become restless. But once they are reunited, it is an event; just wonderful.

At No. 9 Well we turned east to Carnegie Station where we left the tail and picked up fats before heading west again through Wongawol Station, past Yelma Station and into the sheep country, then to Wiluna.

During the eighteen-week trip it was estimated that, for the bullocks plus our horses and the camels, we would have pulled something like 672 gallons of water from the wells.

But in the end, what became important was that I really enjoyed droving up and down the Canning Stock Route, and I had the good sense to keep a diary. The work made a cattleman out of me. And no other man, at the time, could have been a better teacher than the legendary Ben Taylor.

Camels were used as pack animals down the Canning Stock Route.

Three Dead in the Morning

I'm of half-Aboriginal background. My dad was European—white—and my mother was full-blood Aboriginal. My dad and Uncle George left Adelaide in 1900 and they went to Bunbury, in the south-west of Western Australian, hauling logs with bullock teams.

Then in 1902 they went up in the north of Western Australia, driving bullock teams out of Mt Anderson, at Liveringa. Liveringa's out of Derby. Dad got a trucking business after that, then later on, in 1933, I was born at a little place called Calwynyardah. By that time Dad owned a little sheep station there between Fitzroy Crossing and Derby.

Then in about 1935 they sent me to Moola Bulla. I was one of the stolen generation kids. Moola Bulla was a big native settlement out of Halls Creek, where they used to take all of the half-caste and full-blood kids. So that's where I was brought up. It was run by the government, and not a mission or a church thing. They had a superintendent there who was in charge of about four or five hundred people. There was the teachers and the staff and all us boys and girls, and all that.

So I did some schooling for probably about three years and when the war came along they finished Moola Bulla up as a teaching school and they turned it into a working school, where we learnt to do stock work. So you could say that I started working on a station when I was around the age of nine or ten, yeah.

My first job was to walk 5 mile to the windmill with a gallon tin of petrol and a lunch-dinner bag. Then when I got there I'd turn the windmill off, then I'd tie the mill up and take the rods off and connect them to the engine on the pump, then I'd put the old pump on. It was an old farm pump, a Southern Cross farm pump. They used to call those engines the 'miss-and-hit-engine'. So I just hoped that it 'hit'.

Then after I got the pump going I played around, and when it run
out of petrol I ran back and filled her up again and then I went back
to playing around again. It wasn't hard work but when it finally ran
out of petrol you'd have to disconnect the rods from the pump again
and put them back onto the windmill so that the windmill would
work all night. So yeah, after I did all that I'd pack up and I'd head
home, then come back tomorrow and do the same thing, you know.
So that was my first job and I'd walk about 5 mile, one-way.

But in them days, going back then, us kids, we just stayed out
on the flat or anywhere. We slept out on the ground. They had
dormitories and that, but the dormitories never had any beds or
nothing, you know, so we was just running around wild, more
or less.

So all us kids, we had to learn stock work and work with the
mustering and that, you know. And then in the wet season I used
to do a lot of boundary riding, looking after the bullock paddocks.
Then when I was about thirteen or fourteen I went into the saddlery
shop. And I done three years in the saddlery shop, making saddles
and mending and all that, repairing harnesses and everything to do
with leather. The saddlery used to be the wet-time job and you went
back out in the mustering camp again when the season opened.
That was in the dry season.

But my first droving trip came about when a bloke called Bluey
O'Malley came and he wanted some helpers. Bluey owned Elgie
Cliff Station, in the Kimberleys, and he came there and he got
three of us to go on this droving trip with him. There was me and
two full-bloods—Ned and Jerry were their names. Ned and Jerry
were a lot older than me. They were full grown men and I was only
about seventeen at this time.

So that was in 1950, and that was my first droving trip. But
before we took over the cattle, we had to go to Alice Downs Station
to pick up about twenty horses that this Bluey O'Malley had
bought off a drover. Then we walked the horses across from Alice
Downs, down to Elgie Cliff Station, then we went to Lansdowne.

Lansdowne was one of the stations that was owned by the Quilty
family. Tom Quilty was the father and Rod Quilty was the eldest

Aborigines were excellent stockmen.

son of Tom. Then while we waited for them to muster the bullocks up, so we could take them on this droving trip, we built the kitchen and modified the houses for Rod because he was ready to get married. Up until then it was just a big open shed. So we modified that into a bedroom. But there was no cement floors. They were all ant-bed floors. So we broke all the ant bed up and hardened it to make it like a cement, and then they put cyprus bark paper over it. You know the one with the tar. Tar paper, they called it. We put that over the ground and that was the floor, you know.

Then when they finished mustering we took over and we drove the bullocks over to Glenroy Air Beef, at Glenroy. Glenroy Air Beef was the abattoirs. It was built in the middle of nowhere and they used to only kill seventy bullocks at a time. See, they never had a big freezing space at Glenroy, just a small amount, and that's why they could only take seventy head. Then they'd fly out about two trips a day, sometimes three or four a day, and they'd fly the meat over to Wyndham Meatworks.

But that Glenroy mob, the ones we took from Lansdowne to Glenroy, that was all packhorse droving. There was no vehicles in them days. And I remember, we were camped one night and something frightened the mob and they rushed, and the next morning there was three dead bullocks in the camp. See they were too slow in getting up and the others just trampled them to death. Oh yeah, I've been in quite a few of them rushes. Anything gets them started off. And they just go all in one big mob. Five hundred of them, just up and gone. So if there's anything too slow in getting up, it gets trampled to death.

So that was my first droving experience. And that was just a short trip because it only took us about a week and a half to get from Lansdowne to Glenroy. But when I drove cattle, I was only one of the party. Like, I wasn't the head drover or anything like that. That was more a white man's job.

Then later on, I used to do a lot of droving with station plants. I drove cattle from Napier into Derby, from Kimberley down into Derby, from Napier to Glenroy, from Tableland to Wyndham, from Halls Creek to Derby, all over the place. And oh, just out of Halls Creek there's a place called Mount Amhurst and I drove cattle from there. That was the longest droving trip I done. That took six weeks.

But with Western Australia, also a lot of cattle started out from the Broome sector and they took them down what they called the Meekatharra Stock Route, right down to Meekatharra, and then they put them on the train and took them to Perth. And with the

Canning Stock Route, that used to go down to Wiluna and they'd put them on the train from there.

That was the hardest track, the Canning. I knew all those drovers. They were still around when I was a kid. I think they're all dead now. But I knew old Wally Dowling pretty well. And Len Brown and his brother, Mal Brown. They took a lot of cattle down the Canning.

Then there was one old chap, Dave Bickley. Dave took a lot of cattle down the Canning Stock Route. George Lannagan came as a party of Dave Bickley. Mrs Lannagan was the cook for Dave Bickley, but it's never ever been mentioned.

Nobody ever mentioned Dave Bickley and he did a lot of droving there before Wally Dowling started. Dave had his contract plant and Wally Dowling had the station plant. Dave used to tell me a lot about the Canning. Gee, it must've been hard. A lot of cattle died going down there as well.

Too Slow

My name's Merv Buckley and I'm seventy years old. I left school at fourteen and, in Moama, on the Victorian–New South Wales border, near Echuca, there were about five drovers and nearly every young feller in town done a stint with a drover. And that's also what I did.

The first drover I went with was a feller named Jim Hickey, and I was paid three pound ten a week plus tucker. Jim worked for a sheep dealer. Now this dealer owned no property at all—none at all—but one year he shore 18,000 sheep off one little reserve.

See back then, you could buy a mob of sheep off the agent and they'd stand them for three months, meaning that you didn't have to pay until the three months was up. So that's what these sheep dealers done. They bought the buggers on the down market, which was usually during the dry, and they'd sell them on the up market, usually after it rained. So these dealers gambled on it raining within those three months. And most times it did, and that's how they made their money.

Anyway, this sheep dealer bought these 18,000 sheep and he split them into three mobs and we walked our 6000 along the stock routes from Moama, up through the central west of New South Wales, through Cobar to Bourke and almost up to Barringun, on the Queensland–New South Wales border. The other drovers did the same with their mobs. So in effect, this dealer was really buying grass.

We done that trip in a wagonette. We had about eight dogs, a cook, me and the boss and twenty horses, and we walked them up there on what's called a single permit, which meant you could change your numbers around a bit or you could put them on agistment for a week. But then, to turn them around and go back home again you had to get a triple permit and that cost three times as much.

But in those days you might go a whole week and you may only see the mailman go up and come back or the stock inspector might come along once a week to check that you were doing your mileage. It was 6 mile a day with sheep though, even if you done 4 mile he'd leave you alone, just as long as you kept moving and there was plenty of feed. See, they wouldn't let you flog the stock route out, which was fair enough, because there'd always be another mob coming along behind.

And a lot of the time, down that Lane Country, you could let them go at night. By about half-past four the prevailing wind was always west. So you'd get your stock full, then, just on dark, you'd turn them into the wind and they'd feed through until they hit the fence, and that's where they'd camp. Then the next morning you'd get up and you'd ride half a mile further on from the lead, just to make sure none had wandered, and you'd track them back. Then when you got going again you just let them open up and feed along.

See on those trips, after three or four weeks they'd be broke in and they'd travel like bullocks, so you got to know your sheep. Like, some always travelled on the outside, some were always up the lead and then there'd always be some cunning bugger on the tail. They even had their mates.

And you could bet on some of the wethers, you really could. You'd be holding the lead and there'd be a milk thistle in the distance and, just for company, you'd say to yourself, 'I bet that old nobby wether over there'll be the first one to get to that thistle.' And sure as hell, he'd find it. He was always up the front. Though the thing was, if he'd spent more time standing feeding he'd have done a lot better. But in his own mind, he was always after that something a little bit better. There's a lot of people like that as well, too, you know— always after that something a little bit better.

Then with the dogs; Jim Hickey only had eight dogs, but they were good dogs, and he worked them turn about. One dog'd work today while the other one rode in the dog carrier, under the wagon-ette. Next day they'd change about. Then when you got to the burr country, around Wilcannia and them places, well, you had a long saddlecloth and when the burr got bad you'd pick your dog up and

Droving sheep with a wagonette.

put him on that. So there you'd be with the dog sitting up on the back of the horse, to keep him off the burrs. And Jim wouldn't let you push the sheep through that country, neither. He'd open them up and poke them through nice and easy so they wouldn't get too much burr in their wool. And he also kept them off the road, as much as possible, so they wouldn't get too much dust in their wool.

But Jim was a good stockman. He really looked after his stock. And he didn't like you dogging too much, neither. If the sheep were getting too spread out, you'd send the dog up the side and you'd go, 'Hey-ee!' and you'd call him back, just like that. Then when they started to spread out again you wouldn't even have to send the dog. You'd just go, 'Hey-ee!' and the sheep'd turn back in on their own because they knew that sound.

So there was never much trouble. Actual fact, it was fairly tedious. Sheep aren't that sensitive. They don't know too much. If there's plenty of feed it's a very easy job. And back then there was always good watering points, usually a bore and a trough and a few acres of ground that went with it. And sometimes there might be a bloke camped there who'd charge you a ha'penny per head to water your stock, and he got that money plus the use of the ground so he could run a cow or something.

And another thing, back then, you'd hear a quietness that you'll never hear again. You could lay in your swag and watch those Sputnik things go overhead, every so often, and you could hold your breath and there wouldn't be a sound, not a sound. Nothing. So life was good. But now droving's buggered. Trucks are here. Life moves on. Life is faster. I'm too slow, and that's about all I can tell you.

Training Cattle

We live on the east coast of Tasmania, at a place called Cranbrook. Cranbrook's just north of Swansea, which is on the shores of Great Oyster Bay. I mention that because Swansea may be better known. I'd say that very few people would know where Cranbrook is.

So there we were; it was during a drought time in the 1970s, and we had about a hundred Angus breeding cows. And because it was so dry, we soon ran out of feed and pasture. Anyhow, there was a few thousand acres of bush up the back of our property where things were a little better, so we decided to turn them out there. Then once a week we'd go out with a big load of hay on the flat tray of the ute and we'd throw the hay along the track for these cattle to eat.

Now to make the cattle aware that we'd arrived with the hay, we got into the habit of blowing the horn of the ute as we went along the track. In effect, you could say that we were training the cattle to come for a feed when we gave a few blasts on the car horn. Anyhow, it didn't take long before they got into the habit, and as soon as they heard the car horn blowing they'd come from all directions to get the hay.

But then, as the drought wore on, we started to run short of hay on our property, and to make matters worse there wasn't too much feed left in the bush, either. So we realised that we'd have to send these cattle away to where the feed was better, and as luck would have it we found agistment up on the eastern tiers, near a place called Ringarooma. Ringarooma's in north-eastern Tasmania, about 100 or 120 kilometres north-west of Cranbrook. So anyway, we drove all these cattle up there and we put them on this block that we'd been offered for agistment.

Now this particular block did have better feed on it, there's no doubting that, but it had a pretty ordinary fence around it. But we weren't too worried about the poor state of the fence because we

A few blasts of the car horn and the cattle would come from all directions to get the hay.

thought that they'd be pretty keen to stay on the block anyway, as they'd be getting decent feed for the first time in a good while. But then, within the week the local constable was on the phone to us saying how the cattle had been getting out and that he'd already had to go out there a couple of times, along with a few of his mates, and put them back on the agistment block.

'Okay, we'll do something about it,' I said.

Anyhow, we were just about to sort it out when he called us again. 'You'd better come and do something about these cattle pretty quick because they're roaming around everywhere,' he said.

So I got a few of the blokes that worked for me—the station hands—to head up to this agistment block at Ringarooma. Well we loaded up the ute with hay and we got there at about daylight and we started to call the cattle together by blowing the horn of the ute, like we'd trained them to do. But they didn't come, and there was no sign of them. That's strange, I thought. So I kept blowing the car horn but, no, nothing.

Then from over in the distance we heard the 'toot . . . toot' of the local coal train as it came down through the run; down what the locals called the Snake Track, which was a winding railway track that run right down across this property where the cattle were agisted.

Anyhow, I noticed that this train driver seemed to be tooting more than you'd expect him to do. 'Toot, toot . . . toot, toot,' he was going all the way down the Snake Track.

So we went over to see what was going on and that's when we saw all these cows. Our cows. They were in front of the train. They were beside the train. They were behind the train. They were all around the train, and the train driver was blowing his whistle in an attempt to get them off the line. But the problem was, the more he blew his whistle, the more excited the cattle got because they thought they were going to be thrown some hay.

Anyway, there was nothing we could do. The cattle were far too excited about following the train so we just tagged along behind.

Now it was a good few kilometres to the town but then, as we got nearer, we noticed the fences started to become few and far between because the farmers down there just grew crops. They didn't have stock so there was no real need for fences. So by that stage we'd run out of road so we were all out on foot, running around, trying to get the cattle out of the crops and back onto the railway line.

Then when the train eventually went into town, things went from bad to worse. The cows followed it, of course, and by the time we arrived there these cows were: they were in the streets, they were in the front yards, in the gardens. They were everywhere, everywhere you wouldn't want cattle to be. And there were the townspeople, housewives, kids and all, running around with brooms and anything else they could lay their hands on, shooing these cows out of their gardens and chasing them up the street.

Anyhow, we all eventually drove these cattle into the cattleyards, which was right next to where the train had pulled up at the station. And when we counted them, they were all there. We hadn't lost one. So you might be able to say that we trained those cows well, aye.

With the Kids

Well I met Clarry when I was sixteen. At that time he was tank-sinking with his sister and her husband. So we stayed out there for a while and then we got married when I was seventeen.

Clarry owned some horses and he had about five dogs and he also owned a Land Rover, so we first started out droving in that. This was in about '55. And the first trip we done was with about 7000 sheep, and we went from . . . I can't think of the place . . . it was in south-western Queensland, anyway. It might've been from Wellshot Station. That's right, it was, and we took these sheep on the road for grass, for feed, because it was so dry on Wellshot. So we took them down towards Isisford, then we cut back through Barcaldine, down through Blackall, Tambo, and through Augathella. Then when we got out past Charleville they had rain up around Wellshot so they trucked the sheep back, then.

On that trip we took our three daughters. Joyce would've been four, Jenny was three, and Judy was eighteen months old. And when we camped at night we used to put up a tarp like a tent and we'd all sleep on the ground under that, in our swags. By all, I mean, other than me and Clarry and the three girls, we also had three young fellers working with us. I drove the Land Rover and I did the cooking, and we had a trailer and that carried all the necessities, like the food and the water and the sheep break and that.

I suppose it could've been difficult, really, having the three young girls with us, but it wasn't so bad. I don't say it was a bed of roses or nothing, because it wasn't. But the children and I would bathe every afternoon because I brung along one of them big, enormous washtubs. And we got the water from wherever we could, like the turkey nests or the bores, or we went into properties, or we got water going through a town.

Droving with the kids at Aramac Lakes.

Then as the girls got up a bit in age and started riding the horses, they started going around the sheep with their father and that. They were good like that. They loved it. And it was fine by me. The only thing I didn't allow them to do was to go out with the cattle because, well, I always thought that it was a bit dangerous with cattle, you know, especially if something frightened them and they all rushed.

Then when they got to school age, I took a governess out with us to help the children do their correspondence course. She was a half-caste girl and she had a little boy. Her parents were drovers too, so it was a real family affair. And it suited her fine because she had a job with us and she wasn't neglecting her child. So the governess come along and she taught the kids their primary schooling for, oh gawd, about four years, I think.

But how we used to work in the teaching with the droving was that the kids'd go out with the sheep until morning tea. Then after morning tea they'd ride on to where we were going to camp and the governess'd be waiting for them. So she'd put them through their times tables and their spelling and that. Then by the time they done all their work in their books and things, well, the stock was usually coming up so they'd get on their horses and help bring the sheep up to camp.

And another thing I remember: just how much my girls loved cakes made with emu's eggs. If they seen an emu's nest they'd go over and they'd pick out two eggs. They'd only ever take two, no more, and I'd do them scrambled eggs in the morning and I'd also cook the cakes with them. But with the emu's eggs, they tasted like . . . I don't exactly know. I mean, they're very rich. And when there's a mob of youse, you had to put in a enough milk and stuff to break it down. And by doing it like that, it's amazing just how much one egg scrambles up.

So that first trip was in about '55. Then June wasn't born until two years later, then Patricia was two years later after that and the two boys weren't born until '64 and '65. We were still droving then. Young Bob was the last one. Garry was the second last. But with our last droving trip, young Bob was just a baby in the cot.

By that stage I was driving a 10-tonne truck which carried fourteen horses plus all the gear. So we'd built up a bit. And we made a thing off the crate that come out over the hood of the truck and that's where we put all the gear. Then behind the truck I pulled a 21-foot caravan. So there you go. We started out with that short wheeled-based Land Rover. Then we got an Austin truck, then a Tims truck. The Tims truck was shaped something like an Austin but with a shorter-based front on it. I can't even tell you who built it. Then that last one—the big one—was the Ford.

But then, when the children got to high school age and they needed to be taught high grades, me and Clarry, well, we went managing properties then. So in all, we were droving for about ten or eleven years, and we always had our kids with us, and they just loved it.

A Drover's Wife: A Song

There's a light on the hill that's flickering still
A light that's burning my eyes
But out on the track there's no looking back
No matter how strong the ties.

Day after day, while you're away
You just keep them toeing the line
There's no time for tears. There's no time for fears
Yet her voice, it's etched in your mind.

Chorus: A drover's wife, it's no kind of life
           For a woman, keen on settling down
           She needs a man, who's always at hand
           Who takes her out on the town.

The camp fire at night, Lord what a sight
You can't help but wishing her there
A few rums and Coke and you watch them strands of smoke
Curling just like her hair.

Chorus

The tailer calls and it's from your swag you crawl
Back in the saddle once more
By break of day, you're well on your way
Leaving them ashes still warm.

Chorus: Oh, a drover's wife, it's no kind of life
           For a woman, keen on settling down
           She needs a man, who's always at hand
           Who takes her out on the town
           Yes, who takes her out on the town.

The author, just after his stint on the Great Australian Cattle Drive.

Photographic Credits

The author would like to thank the following for generously providing photographs and for permission to include them in this book. He would most particularly like to thank the Australian Stockman's Hall of Fame at Longreach, Queensland, for the many images reproduced in *Great Australian Droving Stories*, and its staff for their help and generosity.

Australian Stockman's Hall of Fame iii, 7, 11, 15, 28, 34, 42, 44, 63, 66, 68, 70, 78, 80, 82, 87, 95, 108, 113, 120, 126, 137, 140, 144, 150, 155, 159, 165, 171, 174, 178, 186, 189, 198, 224, 237, 248, 250, 255, 258, 266
Gordon Beetham 74
Chris Carter i, 90
Judy Dowling 234
Betty Forster 227, 269
Les French 105, 218
Nola and Mick Gallagher 47, 54
Bill Marsh x, 100
Tess and Bruce Smith 182, 212, 243
State Library of South Australia 19, 25, 203